WHITE HOUSE WITNESS
1942–1945

By Jonathan Daniels

White House Witness

Witness

1942–1945

Jonathan Daniels

1975

Doubleday & Company, Inc., Garden City, New York

Library of Congress Cataloging in Publication Data

Daniels, Jonathan, 1902–
White House witness, 1942–1945.

Includes index.
1. United States—Politics and government—1933–1945.
2. Daniels, Jonathan, 1902–   I. Title.
E806.D34   320.9′73′0917
ISBN 0-385-00762-0
Library of Congress Catalog Card Number 74–9482

Contents

List of Illustrations

Introduction

---

by Frank Freidel

The White House was an awe-inspiring sight during World War II, a remote power center amid the bustle of Washington, easy to view, but, except for a select few, impossible to enter. The broad sidewalk in front was blocked off; one had to cross over Pennsylvania Avenue in order to gaze at the cars pulling up to the front entrance and the mysterious visitors moving into the lighted interior. It was a sharp change from the accessible White House of the early New Deal years, from which the benign President, Franklin D. Roosevelt, so often was seen setting forth on countless trips. Now the President too had become remote, a figure seldom seen except in newsreels. The White House had not become a beleaguered fortress, but rather the key power center of the world, the rallying point for the United Nations, and around it there had to be the tightest security. As for Roosevelt, he was the commander in chief of the United States armed forces and the leader of the coalition struggling against the Axis.

There was power in the White House which in its global dimensions surpassed that in any earlier administration, even those of Abraham Lincoln and Woodrow Wilson. And because the effective use of that power required secrecy to protect great projects, it was power for which the President did not need immediately to account to either Congress or the public. The safety of the American people and of all peoples arrayed against the Axis seemed to depend upon that power and its effective use.

The wartime crisis brought an increment of power not only to the President but to his assistants. The range and complexity of the problems confronting Roosevelt were far too large for any one person to manage. Increasingly, as he focused upon the conduct of diplomacy and military operations, he shifted much of the burden of domestic problems to these assistants. In 1939, Roosevelt had obtained from Congress legislation establishing the Executive Office of the President, and providing for a group of administrative assistants, responsible to him, who were to be men with "a passion for anonymity." In retrospect the power they exercised collectively seems potentially dangerous. Wartime secrecy screened them from Congress to some extent and from public attention almost completely. That not a single shadow of pecuniary scandal fell upon them is an indication of their strong sense of responsibility to the nation.

One of these anonymous men of power was Jonathan Daniels. In this diary he not only chronicles what it was like to work in the hidden corridors of the Executive Office of the President, but has caught brilliantly the noble aspirations, herculean labors, and malicious intrigue of wartime Washington. There have been a number of wartime diaries published, from the perspective of the Senate, the vice-presidency, the Cabinet, and even (in the case of William Hassett's) of President Roosevelt himself. None previously has been from the viewpoint of the White House assistants—and none surpasses that of Daniels in its limning of wartime Washington, its vivid portraits, in a few words or lines, of a fascinating array of characters. Like Daumier, he celebrates the humane and deflates the pompous.

Daniels was the sort of young man that Roosevelt both trusted and enjoyed. Roosevelt had known him in the Washington of the Wilson administration, the teen-age son of Roosevelt's "chief," Secretary of the Navy Josephus Daniels.

He had kept in touch with Daniels in the years that followed, as Daniels embarked upon a newspaper career in Kentucky, worked for several years for *Fortune,* then during the New Deal edited the family newspaper, the distinguished Raleigh *News and Observer.*

Nationally, Daniels was renowned as the author of *A Southerner Discovers the South,* which appeared in 1938, a realistic panorama of a region clinging to old traditions as the New Deal rapidly made it over. Daniels was in the forefront of a generation of young Southerners who welcomed and sought to speed these changes. In the opening pages of his book, Daniels celebrated the black heritage as well as the white in the South, and with poignant realism reported the inspirational speech of a black valedictorian at Abraham Lincoln High School:

"He sought so solemnly through his blackness. He grabbed so confidently at the old familiar rungs on the ladder of success. He clung to the old promise and answered with the old pledge. But he was already beyond thirty. And all his learning merely led back to the broom and the shovel, the plow and the hoe. He was too late or too soon. The shining promises were rusty and dull."

It was one of the responsibilities of Daniels in the White House to try to increase the opportunities for blacks through the new wartime Fair Employment Practices program. He worked at the difficult task with a will. The passages in his diary in which he describes his social encounters with blacks would seem commonplace today—an indication of how very far the nation has come. They appear more bold and daring when measured against the fact that Daniels' father, one of the most dedicated Southern liberals of his day, forty years earlier had castigated President Theodore Roosevelt for dining at the White House with Booker T. Washington.

During World War II and ever since, Daniels has been unflagging in his fight against outworn tradition. In 1955, he prodded Adlai Stevenson to take a stronger stand against the right-wing Democrats of the South. Stevenson, in commending Daniels for his editorial criticism of Dixie politicians who wanted a more conservative candidate, granted that he himself had no aggressive notions. Daniels retorted, "This is a time for 'aggressive notions' by those of us who are not willing that Ku Kluxers in pleated bosomed robes run the party down here or anywhere else." There was never a time when Daniels was not firm in his opposition to prejudice whether because of race or religion.

Probity was something he took for granted, and so, it seems, did those around him. In a matter-of-fact way he describes in this diary his several encounters with a lobbyist interested in one of Daniels' responsibilities, the assignment of postwar air routes. One wartime Christmas when meats were scarce, a huge box containing a mouth-watering assortment arrived, the gift of the lobbyist. The Daniels family gazed, but only gazed; Daniels ordered the box immediately closed and returned.

Daniels served his President and his country well. He was one of the countless number who worked in the spirit that President John Adams had expressed in a letter he wrote on his second night in the new Executive Mansion. It was Franklin D. Roosevelt who had the words of Adams carved in the mantel of the State Dining Room:

> I Pray Heaven to Bestow
> The Best of Blessings on
>   THIS HOUSE
> and on All that shall hereafter
> Inhabit it. May none but Honest
> and Wise Men ever rule under This Roof.

Proximity to Power

Franklin Roosevelt in World War II had people writing the history of all U.S. government operations except those in his own White House. America had become involved in a new war without information as to what problems had arisen and how they had been met in the earlier war over a score of years before. Much of that knowledge existed only in the memories of such elders as Bernard Baruch, the great Jewish speculator and benign manipulator, and my father, Josephus Daniels, who as Secretary of the Navy had been Roosevelt's chief in World War I. There were very few younger men like Roosevelt himself whose life span permitted eminence in both wars. So, missing the guidance of what happened before, except in after-the-fact memoirs, the idea grew that this situation must not happen again. Therefore, during World War II historians were mobilized, almost like the industrial executives, investment bankers, and merchant princes of the War Production Board, to make a record which officials in a possible World War III might pull from the file cabinets as a sort of old guide for new tasks in the tremors of global conflict.

It was a beautiful idea. Perhaps it has served in the almost continuous war since, which has never been quite labeled

World War III. It still may be true, as the ancient saying goes, that man learns nothing from history except that man learns nothing from history. Also history of what happened before the atomic age may be irrelevant to what is happening on this side of the detonation at Hiroshima. Some things do not change, however. Man, who may be destroyed by the bomb, has not been much altered by it. Procedures may change but man is constant in his confusion, his courage and his cowardice, his contentiousness, his ambition, his animosities, his devotions, his frailties, and his gossip, which is always close to his perorations. Both majesty and mischief are eternal and often in earlier and recent times it has not been easy to keep them separate. All are the materials of history, but I doubt that recognition of such qualities went into the idea of preparing, in one war, guidebooks for another. Understanding may be better served by glimpses of men in power in war than by academic records of the procedures of the past.

Certainly the diary notes I kept at the Roosevelt White House during World War II, on which this memoir is based, provided no record such as the professional historians were deployed to produce. They would hardly have regarded me, sans Ph.D., as qualified for their company. As a member of what the press called the Palace Guard, I was, however, ready to be one of them. By 1945, after serving President Roosevelt in various capacities for the three years covered in this book, I tried to hitchhike my way to Yalta as his historian. If I had succeeded I might have clarified the story of what happened there—or I might have only muddled it more. In his Oval Office I boldly suggested to the President that as a writer I might put the story of that conference together better than had been done in the bare-bones records of other such conferences.

"No," he said. "I have something better for you."

He wanted me to take over the job of press secretary, which Stephen Early was relinquishing at last; he had often before proposed to leave the White House for more lucrative private employment. So I took that job and missed Yalta, but I saw it, too, when it became my duty to select for release to the press and the public pictures sent back by the Signal Corps, whose photographers were the only American ones allowed on the scene. I was perhaps guilty, as I have since been charged of deluding the American people by releasing only the least tragic pictures of the face of Franklin Roosevelt taken there. Those were sad enough. As historian I might possibly have been similarly selective.

My diary notes escaped that danger. I wrote them first merely as jottings on my engagement lists, without any feeling of the need to protect a President or a people. Since I was my only audience, I wrote of what amused, instructed, or amazed me, some of which may now amuse, instruct, or amaze other people. These notes were not prepared for release to the public, in whole or in part. They remained in a sealed file. So much so that when I wrote a book about Washington in the war years, a friendly critic commented that the book contained too much old lace and too little arsenic. Now a quarter of a century later, in these old entries, no such imbalance exists. Some entries are, indeed, possibly poisonous, some ludicrous, a few revealing about events overlooked or forgotten. Certainly there is gossip here of which so much history is made, but which official history unfortunately misses. Possibly this diary helps to provide a realistic picture of Roosevelt and the compact company about him—many of them unconsciously the valets of his official household—a picture sometimes as startling as the pictures from Yalta which were quickly destroyed.

Roosevelt was much "off the record" in those days. He was seldom off guard. Generally he sat for his portraits majestically draped in the blue naval cape he so much liked as Commander in Chief. Often he showed himself scarcely less dramatically—if more conventionally—clad for varied depiction by the White House press corps. Multitudes saw and heard him. But no historian could have written in coherence the day-by-day story of the man, his moves, and his moods in his wartime operations in his house of world power.

For a man who often seemed indiscreet in his volubleness he could be amazingly reticent, even to those beside him, about great matters and small. Certainly he could not have spared the time to help in the preparation of the detailed and footnoted story of the activities in his White House as told here. These old notes were never made for any such purpose. Roosevelt does not steadily appear in them. They constitute rather a spasmodically drawn miscellany about the Roosevelt circle in World War II. They constitute nothing so formal and dated as a real diary. Sometimes gaps occur at times of the most important events. On such occasions there was little time for dictating or even scribbling.

With some regret I had given up writing at that time for the duration of the war, even if I kept an old reporter's habit of notation. Looking back, I have sometimes wondered if I made a mistake in not accepting a flattering offer from Alfred Knopf, the publisher, to go to Britain and write about the ordinary people there in their courage and anguish after Dunkirk. I had done much similar writing about Americans in the defense boom in the United States. In so many suddenly crowded places from coast to coast the scene seemed more like gold rush than Armageddon. Defense appeared more as the end of depression than the beginning of war. "Thank God for Hitler!" one black man cried when he got his paycheck in a cantonment rising in the Louisiana woods. His sentiments were widely shared even if his cry was not echoed.

Covering that story brought me an invitation to address the National Conference of Social Work, which was eager to focus attention on social alterations or eruptions in the still neutral "arsenal of democracy," as Roosevelt called it. Sometimes it seemed the madhouse of democracy, too. In a great klieg-lit hall in Atlantic City, I talked about defense congregation and confusion as a free observer with no responsibility for haste and hullabaloo. I shared the podium with earnest but quietly humorous Charles P. Taft, son of the former President. I spoke of the defense effort as an outside, often critical Democrat, and Taft talked as the good Republican enlisted in the Rooseveltian defense program to help solve the accumulation of crises. I certainly then had the more comfortable role. When Charlie and I drove afterwards to

New York in the night, it did not occur to me as we talked that I would soon be in the government with difficulties greater than his.

I should have been warned. In July 1941 President Roosevelt asked me to be a member of the Voluntary Participation Committee of the Office of Civilian Defense. This branch of OCD was headed then by Mrs. Roosevelt, with her close friend Elinor Morgenthau, wife of the Secretary of the Treasury, as her chief aide. At the first meeting of this committee Mrs. Roosevelt seemed almost effusively interested in my reports on the people of the whole country in this prologue to war. I had known her since childhood. Also, as a young man I went with my father in the early 1920s on visits to his crippled onetime assistant. Mrs. Roosevelt then was anxious to bring her stricken husband into more and more contacts, particularly with young people. She asked me to bring two young men with whom I was living to Sunday-night supper. One could not go and the other, Henry Cole, later a successful man of the stock market, declined. He was on his way, he told me, and could not spare time with "a has-been." I went.

Now I came. I was aware of confusion in OCD under both Mrs. Roosevelt and her putative boss, Fiorello La Guardia, director of the agency. He was trying to serve New York as mayor and run the Office of Civilian Defense at the same time. Mrs. Roosevelt as First Lady was also a first target for those who opposed the President and the war into which they feared he was leading them much against their will. Many of them were oilonood but not placated when the bombs fell on Pearl Harbor. Soon afterwards La Guardia was pushed out and Mrs. Roosevelt left her office like a woman in disarray, with Republican newspapers and congressmen snapping at her heels. James M. Landis, brilliant dean of the Harvard Law School, who had served earlier on the Securities and Exchange Commission, succeeded La Guardia. I took the office Mrs. Roosevelt had held.

Jim Landis was small like La Guardia but as a Protestant of missionary parents he lacked any Latin quality of release. He talked and wrote with legal precision. As chief of air-raid precautions, he wrote of the nighttime necessity of blackout that "such obscuration may be obtained by the termination of the illumination." This, Roosevelt explained to a press conference, meant "turn off the lights." Order was essential to Landis. I remember his straightening pictures hanging slightly awry in the anteroom of the Secretary of the Treasury. He could be charming but from exceptionally wide smiling his mouth would chop shut into a tight line. He had a small man's Napoleonic ambition. He liked to have military men under and around him. My later, perhaps unjust, judgment of him was that he was a man with foxes in his vitals.

Maybe I was, too. After thirty years I suspect that our differences then came not from a clash of personalities or philosophies but from an already fixed pattern of frustration we took from our almost pyrotechnic predecessors. The word "charisma" was not a regular part of the American vocabulary in those days. Indeed, it is not even listed in the worn 1953 version of *Webster's New Collegiate Dictionary* which I have used for many years. But both Eleanor and Fiorello were loaded with it in a fashion which different people found fascinating or repulsive. The First Lady and the Little Flower loosed the skyrocket. Landis and I rode the stick coming down.

My surroundings in the office quarters first set aside for a First Lady were definitely plush. As a part of defense expansion, OCD had taken over an apartment building on Connecticut Avenue at the south side of Dupont Circle. My office, overlooking the green park, had been the large living room of an apartment. There were rugs on the floor, carefully chosen pictures on the walls. It was a room in which a man might happily contemplate an America as serene as the well-ordered circle below.

No serenity was destined for that office. There had been, of course, no air attack on San Francisco as Mrs. Roosevelt and La Guardia had apprehended in the first aftermath of Pearl Harbor. No air attacks were to follow—a fact which gradually made OCD seem, to many, a useless appendage to

6

the war effort. The attacks on Mrs. Roosevelt were real and intense—and some not without basis.

Part of my heritage from Mrs. Roosevelt was a young woman who was made the mirror of what then seemed to many the First Lady's warmhearted aberrations. I had never seen or heard of Mayris Chaney then. I have never seen her since. Mrs. Roosevelt had made this young dancer an assistant in the physical-fitness program of OCD at a salary of $4,600 a year—pretty good pay at that time. The discovery of her presence on the payroll erupted in an explosion of ridicule and indignation about a "fan dancer" in civilian defense. Mrs. Roosevelt had retreated to the bomb shelter of the White House when I arrived as Miss Chaney's surprised employer, and so far as possible Mrs. Roosevelt's defender.

Miss Chaney's days in OCD, as a sort of dancer in the dugouts, as the press pictured her, were limited. She still remains a mysterious figure. Joseph Lash, in his *Eleanor and Franklin,* noted that the young blonde's first public appearance with Mrs. Roosevelt was as a friend riding on the presidential campaign train in 1936. Her presence in that political caravan seemed strange. Lash quoted columnist Marquis Childs to explain it. Childs wrote that young Miss Chaney and Mrs. Roosevelt "had promised themselves a holiday together and when Mrs. Roosevelt discovered she would not be on the West Coast that fall she wired for her friend, Mayris, to tour with the presidential party. It was as simple as that." That did not seem so simple to everybody, then or later. The press apparently missed Miss Chaney's presence when, under the cover of wartime security, she was one of the few, carefully chosen guests at a dinner for Winston Churchill on his swift visit to Washington soon after Pearl Harbor.

Miss Chaney was only one item in the hullabaloo about OCD. Some others on the staff were wildly charged as being reds. In Congress, Landis was described as "very 'pink.'" The celebrated actor Melvyn Douglas, who had volunteered to head an arts division, was attacked as another radical. Mrs. Roosevelt's dear friend Lash, who has written that he was only an unpaid "adviser," had been for some time suspect as at least a fellow traveler in the red movement. Soon after I arrived at OCD, I was sternly questioned by a government interrogator about criticisms I had made of the red-hunting Dies Committee. (Edgar Hoover told me later that this man was not one of his agents. Such investigators were all over town. Mine looked like a person who might have been inquiring as to whether my credit was good for a piano.)

I survived scrutiny. OCD's plan to do the recruitment of volunteers for all purposes from air-raid wardens to defense-bond salesmen met quick competition from other agencies, the Red Cross, and a variety of spontaneous local and national organizations. Charlie Taft grinned at me and recalled an old story of his father's about a colonel in Texas who had a thousand men who had never seen a horse and a thousand horses which had never seen a man. All he had to do was make a cavalry regiment.

Both Taft and I were fortunate in having the friendship and association of Mark McCloskey, Taft's assistant in the Office of Defense Health and Welfare Services. An indestructibly exuberant Irishman, Mark sometimes made too much, I thought, of his birth on Tenth Avenue as the son of a truck driver. If he drove the big horses, the elder McCloskey had the handwriting of a scholar. Still it served Mark's high sense of the dramatic that he had gone from Tenth Avenue to Princeton, where his classmates were en route from the best schools to corporate careers. Mark went back to Manhattan in settlement-house work. As a teacher at the Ethical Culture School, he filled young Jews with his love of Celtic poetry and the Greek classics. Harry Hopkins and Aubrey Williams had made him head of the National Youth Administration in New York, a post similar to one that Lyndon Johnson had held in Texas. At this time Mark was troubled not only by the confusions of the war but by the problem of educating his three beautiful daughters. He mentioned that to Taft.

"You might as well face it, Mark," said Taft. "You've got to take it out of capital."

Mark's grin at that was part of the spirit that sustained him among bureaucrats not all of whom had to depend upon their government pay. And Mark helped sustain me even when I was most tempted to flee from frustration.

Suddenly opportunity for my escape appeared. Undersecretary of State Sumner Welles called me to the State Department to ask me to join a presidential mission to India, which was then wavering in the Allied cause. Welles and the President were disturbed about the situation there in the wake of great Japanese successes in Southeast Asia and the propaganda about color and colonialism which the Japs pressed. Later Welles wrote that the solution of this situation would "not be made easier by intemperate outpourings from Downing Street, nor by equally intemperate insistence by pundits in the United States that the way to solve the problem is for British authority to remove itself from India between dawn and night." Though I had written much about problems of color and discrimination in the United States, I am not sure that I could have contributed much to that situation. It was, however, an exciting prospect. But when I informed Landis of the proposed appointment, he explosively intervened with both the President and Mrs. Roosevelt. I must not leave a job I had just begun. I was persuaded to stay. And not long afterwards when we were going to one of the interminable interagency meetings, this time in Secretary Morgenthau's private elevator, Landis said, grinning as if he had saved me, "Look what happened to Johnson." Louis Johnson, recently Assistant Secretary of War, had taken the assignment to India but had been invalided home with a serious nasal infection caused by dust. Soon I might have envied his delirium.

Still there were no air raids on American cities. So, bereft of his position as protector of people from assault in the skies, Landis found frustration also on the ground in the civilian mobilization aspects of his agency. Certainly there were a lot of fuzzy lines about that program. Do-gooders, some of them with mildly leftist tendencies, and aspiring socialites eager for attention did cluster about home-front mobilization efforts. Mrs. Gifford Pinchot, noted among other things for hair that grew redder as she aged, while not in the government had a government-paid secretary assigned to her by Mrs. Roosevelt to report to the Pinchot mansion on Scott Circle and serve that lady's enthusiasm for public forums.

The purpose of the program I inherited was not only to enlist civilians in the various home chores of war but to free them, by this participation, from prejudices and discriminations, so that a total people might be engaged in "total war." The image that I tried to give to the concept of total war was not the pattern pressed upon the world by Hitler. To put it into American tradition, I tried to present total war as the current equivalent of pioneers in the Indian-encircled frontier stockade. However good that mobilizing metaphor may have been, it was often regarded as archiac or irrelevant. Restive blacks, reluctant whites, exploited Mexican-border laborers, Jews, Catholics, the threatened and the denied, all had their own wars to win within the war we fought. Momentarily the Japanese folly of Pearl Harbor had created a stunned unity. It did not wholly dispel sometimes angry divisions. Also while OCD undertook to design methods and build morale, other agencies wanted to do their own mobilization of patriots. And there was competition and contention among these patriots at what the organization-chart designers called "the local level." That was the administrative jargon name for the teeming country and its far from docile people.

"Poor Jonathan Daniels," wrote Mrs. Roosevelt, who watched like a mother hen but now at a safe distance from her scattering chicks, "he's up against an impossible situation, I fear."

Though I did not hear of her comment until later, that was not quite the case. My escape route was still available. My literary agents, Carl Brandt and Bernice Baumgarten, had been reluctant to see me enter the government. Bernice had written as I prepared to go to Washington, "Will you promise me one thing. If you find you're sidetracked and not able to get anywhere, will you give it up and go back to writing?" Now she brought another publisher to Washington with a very attractive writing proposal. Carl wrote of a large advance Macmillan was prepared to make for a book about the war and of a possible tie-in with the *Reader's Digest*. I was, however, enlisted for the duration. I was excited about the possibility of organizing millions of volunteers behind the war programs.

In the early summer I spoke again, with more confidence than I was beginning to feel, in a great hall in New Orleans to the National Conference of Social Work. But already what Mrs. Roosevelt had envisaged as a "people's movement" was slipping into limbo under the distaste of Landis and the distrust of Congress for the civilian mobilization aspects of his agency. Of the often more enthusiastic than disciplined volunteers he later said, "Perhaps the best thing for them was to baby-sit for women working in munitions plants." As no bombs fell, he seemed to withdraw deeper into frustration. In a long, frustrated letter of my own to him I noted that there had not been a staff meeting of OCD for three months. I felt somewhat like a harassed baby-sitter myself.

However, soon after my arrival in Washington I was working with Marvin McIntyre, an old friend and one of the three secretaries to the President, about methods of strengthening the bonds between the war President and the people at war. Certainly the declaration of war had not brought about the suspension of politics. The President, however, seemed loftily unconcerned about his political defense. When asked in the summer about politics in his own crucial state of New York, he responded almost petulantly that he did not know anything about it—or care anything either. And he added, "I am too damn busy being President," as in that perilous period he certainly was. But with a congressional election in the offing, McIntyre wanted to be sure there would be no losses to the loudly critical opposition. So did I.

McIntyre seemed a wisp of a man in that cause. Born sixty-four years before in a Kentucky village, he had briefly attended Vanderbilt University. He was twenty-seven years old, however, before he began newspaper work in Louisville. After that by way of Asheville, he came to Washington, where from 1909 to 1917 he was city editor of the *Washington Times,* then owned by Frank A. Munsey, arch Republican, who regarded his several newspapers only as properties to be

11

bought and sold. Munsey sold the *Times* to William Randolph Hearst in 1917 and McIntyre in that year was employed as special information assistant to the Secretary of the Navy.

As such he became the aide and friend of the Assistant Secretary of the Navy, and when that young man, Roosevelt, ran for Vice-President in 1920, he made McIntyre the publicity director of his campaign. In the Roosevelt hiatus in the Twenties the Kentuckian wrote articles on national defense and worked in the production of newsreel films. Again on the Roosevelt staff, he rode to victory in 1932. He was named assistant secretary to the President and in 1937, after the death of Roosevelt's mentor No. 1, Louis McHenry Howe, McIntyre was made one of the three secretaries deemed necessary to take Howe's place.

A couple of years later he had to give up his duties because of desperate illness. His colleague, press secretary Early, had been sure then that he would never come back. Suffering from tuberculosis, Mac should not be allowed to be near the President, Early thought. But McIntyre was back in his big office with windows opening upon the almost grotesque old State, War and Navy Building across the narrow street. Tall, cadaverous, but with eyes as bright as a bird's, he sat in his chair with his thin knees pulled against his chest like a cowboy squatting by a corral.

Early, another village-born Southerner, after high school went to work at the age of nineteen for the United Press in Washington. Then in 1917 he transferred to the Associated Press and was assigned to cover the Navy Department. There he met Roosevelt, Howe, and McIntyre and in 1920 served as the advance man for Roosevelt in the 1920 campaign. In what seemed then the "has-been" period Early, also like McIntyre, worked with newsreels until he joined the Roosevelt staff again in the 1932 campaign. Also like McIntyre, he rose from assistant secretary to secretary after Howe's death. Both he and McIntyre were addicted to race tracks and bridge tables. Some later thought Dwight D. Eisenhower's advancement may in some part have been related to Early's observation of skill at the card game.

Steve was efficient in handling the press. Its members found him trustworthy but all recognized his explosive irascibility. As a man with a low boiling point, he indulged in almost poetic profanity. It began with such phrases as "Jesus Christ on a mountaintop" and ascended from that elevation. Sometimes the temper behind that profanity reached serious proportions as when in the 1940 presidential campaign he drove his knee into the groin of a black policeman in New York. The officer, not knowing who he was, had undertaken to bar him from boarding the presidential train. For a moment the vote of Harlem seemed to hang in the balance.

The more courtly or ceremonial of the President's three secretaries at this time was Brigadier General Edwin M. Watson. In a secret sense he looked upon both Early and McIntyre almost as Southern "red-necks." He came originally from Eufaula, Alabama, on the Chattahoochee River, described as "a quiet city of old mansions and tree-shaded streets." As an officer and a gentleman, he had graduated from West Point. His wife, Frances Nash of Omaha, had wealth and a voice of operatic quality. His wife's Catholicism appealed to the General but he postponed conversion pending the possibility that he might run for the Senate from Virginia, where they maintained a beautiful house on a hill near Charlottesville. Roosevelt sometimes visited them there. Florid, handsome, and jovial, General Watson was sometimes minimized by the unperceptive as a Colonel Bumble. Actually, under his drawling suavity, he was steely shrewd. "Pa," as he was called by all who knew him, amused FDR but kept his affection and respect. Sometimes he appeared crusty in order that Roosevelt might seem only charming next to the Watson bluster.

The General's hesitation between religion and politics amused the quietly devout William D. Hassett, then assistant to Early, whose unique literacy in the small Executive Office Building much pleased the President. In his then obscure position, Hassett was notable for both scholarship and a ready snicker at pretentiousness. Like McIntyre and Early, he came through journalism to the White House but from tart Yankee Vermont beginnings. Most of Roosevelt's eloquent letters

13

were written by him. Later FDR surprised and pleased the staff by making Hassett one of his secretaries. Sometimes he shared his snickers as well as his scholarship with Roosevelt. Certainly he often shared them with Rudolph Forster, career executive clerk of the White House offices, who kept presidential papers moving from administration to administration regardless of the party in power. The extent of Forster's nonpartisanship delighted Hassett, who quoted the career clerk as saying, "They would be terrified if they knew how little I care."

These men constituted the inner circle around the President when I began to go to the White House. Harry Hopkins, whom I described at the time as looking like Death on the way to a frolic, was closer to the President than any of them. He lived in the White House but has his offices, as welfare worker and relief almoner who had become war expediter, elsewhere. That paragon of politicians, James F. Byrnes, only left the U. S. Supreme Court to move his economic stabilization staff into the new East Wing offices of the White House in October 1942. Salty Admiral William D. Leahy, who was to become chief of staff to the Commander in Chief, was at this time serving as ambassador to the puppet French government at Vichy. Squat, smart Samuel I. Rosenman, early FDR aide, did not come permanently to the White House as presidential counsel until 1943.

Though now guarded by soldiers with bristling bayonets, the Roosevelt White House then still maintained an air of informal intimacy. Generals and industrialists-in-arms poured into its doors. But sometimes it seemed more remote from the people and the politicians, who in war as in peace constitute the base of presidential power. In the White House McIntyre seemed almost the only person concerned about that. He wanted me to meet another man as concerned as we were about the situation. He made an engagement for us and I scribbled on my engagement list: "Commander Linton Johnson" (*sic!*).

This commander-congressman was only one of those with whom I worked as I phased out of the disintegrating Office of

Civilian Defense. I had no notion that in serving one President I was working with one of his successors. Energetic, ubiquitous Johnson sometimes seemed as impatient as I was. And that was pretty impatient. Yet as the time approached for the very polite parting of Landis and myself, the President sent me word that under no circumstances was I to leave the government. He had important work for me to do. So while waiting for that important assignment I was transferred with my secretary from my beautiful office above the park to a drab room in the basement of the State, War and Navy Building across the street from the White House. Mice sometimes appeared in the corridors. Around a corner was a room in which as a boy I had been shown the bullet which had killed Lincoln.

I was given jobs to do for the President. With the aid of J. Edgar Hoover, I was instructed by the President to find out if rich and well-connected young men, in and out of uniform, were using jobs in Washington to avoid front-line service. He was much interested in this matter. There had been some such, he remembered, in World War I. He did not mention the fact, but his relative Theodore Roosevelt had been critical of him for not getting into uniform during World War I, even though he seemed essential as Assistant Secretary of the Navy to my father. At forty, TR in the Spanish War had resigned from the same post to lead troops in Cuba, though he was five years older then than FDR was in World War I.

Another matter into which he put me prying was the report that in the Army's school at Charlottesville, to train men to govern enemy territories we hoped to occupy, no friends of the New Deal were wanted. I made my reports. He received them with satisfaction. Then in October he offered me a place on the Civil Aeronautics Board. I looked into this offer. The board was involved in conflicts with the Army and Navy. It was almost bereft of power while the military controlled the skies. Its work seemed a long way from the war effort. Respectfully I declined though later I worked with the board on postwar foreign aviation plans. I waited. Certainly I must have seemed choosy to power above me even if I was impatient down below it. Then the President proposed to nominate me as Minister to New Zealand to succeed there the swashbuckling soldier-politician Patrick Jay Hurley, who had been Secretary of War under President Hoover.

I was ready to be on my way to the Pacific post when the ultraconservative Senator Josiah Bailey of North Carolina checked that off. In a book I had written about our state I had said that he was a demagogue who "struts even when he sits down." I still think the characterization was apt but I can also understand why Bailey now announced that he would oppose my confirmation under the old rule of the Senate club that I was "personally obnoxious" to him. FDR sent a memo through McIntyre, "Will you tell Jonathan Daniels that lots of my friends have said much worse things about me than what he said about Bailey."

It has been my odd fortune in life that those who wanted to hurt me most have been those who helped me best. As the tide turned in the Pacific war, New Zealand, to which Bailey would not let me go, was left more and more in the background. And the week after the Senator stopped me from going to the South Pacific, Roosevelt gave me a front-seat place as spectator and participant in the grand and sometimes minuscule spectacle of the nation at war. He appointed me Administrative Assistant to the President, one of a group of six presidential aides chosen, as the government-management designers of the positions proclaimed, for "high competence, great physical vigor and a passion for anonymity."

The creation of these posts as a possible Palace Guard may have been a crucial step in the expansion of the personal staffs of Presidents. Though, of course, all Presidents have had secretaries, the office of secretary to the President (tripled to include three offices in 1937) had only been created in 1900. The White House residence provided all the office space required until the first Roosevelt arrived. Until the beginning of FDR's third term there were only 130 phones on the presidential switchboard. Indeed, Hoover was the first President to have a phone on his desk. There were fewer lines to snarl in something less than a maze of men, certainly less of electronics.

The assistants I joined were William H. McReynolds, sixty-two-year-old veteran government personnel man; Laughlin Currie, Canadian-born Ph.D. product of Harvard and the London School of Economics; Lowell Mellett, operating then outside the White House orbit; David K. Niles, former aide to Harry Hopkins; and James M. Barnes, amiable ex-congressman from Illinois. Quartered near this group but not part of it was Eugene Casey, a Maryland farmer and housing developer who was listed as "Special Executive Assistant." His status was vague even to the President and his tenure was precarious. Left in limbo, his operations were often eccentric. While great decisions were made in wartime, Casey was an irritation nobody wanted to scratch.

Later Roosevelt himself, at a glad crowded press conference after the Normandy invasion, spoke of the administrative assistants arrayed behind him as "the anonymous and silent people." That was generally true, certainly more accurate than another playful description of us he gave a little later when he told us that "I have arranged for you to have special seats in the 'bleachers' right back of the 'catcher,' but I've got a wire screen between wild pitches, so it's all right, you're perfectly protected." That did not always seem so. At any rate, in safety or peril, I was still a reporter, never assured of absolute safety, even if now I was expected to eschew any audience. Still I was closer to the picture of power than I could possibly have been in New Zealand or even on Dupont Circle.

So from the basement I moved into offices upstairs with other administrative assistants who had dubbed their line of quarters Death Row. The name derived from the fact that an occupant might be worked to death or left there in suspended animation by the President. I found it lively enough as I assumed tasks in connection with racial problems, overseas aviation, selective service, bureaucratic collisions in the Department of Agriculture, the Tennessee Valley Authority, discrimination in employment, forgery on White House stationery, newsprint rationing, platform writing, baseball in wartime, and a variety of other tasks involving holding the hands of many impatient and unhappy people. That included protecting friends and watching enemies. There were plenty of both.

Making the notes on which this book depends was not part of my duties. But they piled up, the result probably of still obsessive, spasmodic reportage. Nearly thirty years ago I deposited them with other papers in the Southern Historical Collection at Chapel Hill, closed except to research scholars with special permission until my death. I had almost forgotten them when in 1971 I examined my papers again. I had forgotten how wide-eyed and big-eared I had been. They re-created for me a dramatic period and scene in American life, portrayed close to the most amazing figure of our century. Other significant characters crowded on that scene.

Some of the entries of the younger man I was, amused this older one I am. One note I scribbled on an engagement list was about Joseph Hergesheimer, the novelist, whose work I had much admired. He came as so many did seeking a job or a "post" in the war effort. I wrote of him: "a pathetic old gentleman with a special nasty way of smoking his cigarette, holding it always in his mouth with one end long wet and the other end long ash. Says he wants to get out in the country and talk one syllable words to people. He and Henry Mencken agreed last weekend that there are enough good men to run this country and that they ought to do it." Apparently there was no place for Mr. Hergesheimer. He was then sixty-two years old. Ten years beyond that age now, I hope for more charity than I sometimes gave back then.

2

My move to the White House was marked by little notes I made on the way. The engagement lists on which I scribbled only begin to appear in my collected papers with the date of April 1, 1942, two months after I came to Washington. Formal and, as first typed, impeccable, on them time was neatly allotted. Hours appeared never packed or distended. Only the rough notes I made upon them seem rushed and ragged, beside the neatly spaced names which are now like a pile of calling cards left long ago by visitors, many of whom are forgotten. To the first surviving sheet I added nothing except one line after lunching with Lessing Rosenwald, recently retired chairman of Sears, Roebuck and a man still active with his family's Rosenwald Fund, which had been so generous in aid to Southern blacks. I scrawled: "He is blind in one eye." Some others in Washington then, often including myself, felt at least as blind in a war effort only astigmatically seen. And second sight leaves much in obscurity still.

Some of the people I saw were described only in a penciled phrase. Of William Green, then head of the American Federation of Labor, still in battle with the CIO, I noted: "an aging, dumpy, unimpressive man—dirty collar." He was sixty-nine. To Miss Winn (first name unrecorded), who came as a reporter from the enemy country of the *Chicago Tribune,* I gave a holograph accolade, "attractive, hard-boiled, out to kill but pleasant and maybe regretting her lethal duty a little." I quoted Alan Cranston, not then U.S. senator but a fellow bureaucrat for war, after a frustrating interdepartmental meeting in the office of an Assistant Secretary of State who was, said Alan, "the most intellectual jackass in the District of Columbia." That was covering a lot of ground.

Apparently I found few heroes on the scene or felt few deserved any doodling description on an engagement list. After the name of John W. Studebaker, U. S. Commissioner of Education, I noted his remarkably short fingers and added: "the soliloquies of Studebaker." I was impressed, perhaps unduly, by Lawrence W. Cramer, a former governor of the Virgin Islands, then trying to end American discrimination on account of race as executive secretary of the Fair Employment Practices Committee. I wrote: "handsome Cramer with one finger lacking on left hand—talked good, liberal sense." He was to need more than that in his job. I was less complimentary about Walter White, who, as head of the NAACP, was pushing Cramer and others. Before the war I had corresponded and counseled at length with him on the improvement of the condition of Southern blacks. Now by his name I scribbled: "very vain—says Willkie gives him credit for peace aims speech." Obviously I was skeptical but possibly painfully aware that he had been charmed away from the Roosevelt camp.

One man who had my admiration earlier and has it still was David Lilienthal, then chairman of the Tennessee Valley Authority and, as such, an authority on Willkie and many other persons and things. At thirty-four Lilienthal had been appointed a member of the Tennessee Valley Authority, the same year in which Wendell Willkie, also an Indiana small-town boy, had become president of the Commonwealth and Southern Corporation. In the same neighborhood the utility and the public-power aspects of TVA's design were natural antagonists. The personalities of both Lilienthal and Willkie had been much fashioned in the debate or duel which ensued and both had mounted in prestige from it. The interests of both spread far from the valley. At this time Willkie after his defeat for the presidency had traveled the world as a sort of evangel for the Allies. Lilienthal's interests also were spreading to distant places, so many of which later he would guide in development along TVA lines.

We had become companions in concern for the South and plans for democracy for people where they lived. He came bearing news about a great crisis involving color which might have concerned me if I had gone to India: "Story that when Henry Grady of U.S. commission saw Gandhi he was squatting in corner of marble palace of Indian textile magnate—L wonders if he is naive—if Indian freedom is a business not of people but of familiar plutocrats seeking power for selves and using Gandhi." In his own diary Lilienthal tells of hearing that story earlier from Dr. Hu Shih, the Chinese ambassador. It puzzled him.

It was not easy to be sure about a lot of things even in domestic affairs. Even the most eminent sometimes seemed most frustrated. After a conference on interdepartmental cooperation I briefly quoted Secretary of the Treasury Henry

Morgenthau, Jr., as saying almost in despair: "We haven't got a friend in town." That was hyperbole even from a super-sensitive cabinet officer. Still I felt a sense of guilt when he told me that, in the absence of any helpful civilian defense organization, his son with other recruits "left Beacon in the cold, neglected dawn." And Beacon was in the Dutchess County of both Mrs. Roosevelt and her first assistant, Mrs. Morgenthau, who headed such civilian organization before I arrived. I accepted, however, the lapse as my own. Such organization not only in Dutchess but in all the other three thousand counties was our job.

My notes thickened as the days passed. Also there was an increase in the diversity of those with whom I visited. Gardner ("Pat") Jackson, a man with a continuity of concern for the underdog from the Sacco-Vanzetti case onward, came to see me in his efforts to free Chicanos and new Mexican migrants in the Southwest from discrimination and the peon wages big farmers wanted to pay them. He was brought by my old friend Roy Stryker, both of them then precariously placed in the Department of Agriculture. That had seemed a safe place for such men when so much of the ferment of the New Deal had centered on personages like Henry Wallace (now Vice-President and chairman of the Board of Economic Warfare), Rex Tugwell (now governor of Puerto Rico), and Paul Appleby (now working in Lend-Lease and the State Department). In the drive for food in war and the mood of "devil take the hindmost" of the little farmers and tenants, not only were Roy and Pat not secure. Also C. B. ("Beanie") Baldwin was fighting for his official life and that of his Farm Security agency. Particularly doomed seemed Farm Security's "Historical Section," which was the name or the mask for the magnificent photographic operations of Roy Stryker.

Roy was then a man capable of both hilarity and high indignation. His photographers had made remarkable and revealing photographs of Americans in the rural and small-town lower depths, particularly in the South. The people re-alistically pictured in their poverty became the prototypes of the characters in John Steinbeck's *The Grapes of Wrath.* A former economics teacher at Columbia who had earlier been a cowboy, Roy looked at the world through thick lenses (thicker than any I ever saw except those Harry Truman wore). He had produced the great documentary films *The River* and *The Plow That Broke the Plains.* But the pictures were now all too clear for many in the country and the Congress who wanted portrayed all the strengths and none of the weakness of the nation. As Farm Security was threatened by the reactionary war mood, Stryker feared even for the preservation of his pictures. Later I was to help get Archibald MacLeish (never blinded by his war concerns as director of the Office of Facts and Figures) to take them into the safekeeping of the Library of Congress. But that was after this time. Now I wrote that Stryker "wished to God Wickard would make up his mind on Farm Security—he's a big honest guy but he's still a farmer with manure on his feet." Actually then Claude R. Wickard, who did sometimes move as if he were bogged in a barn lot, was himself much beset by the congressional friends of big agribusiness men closer to the commodity market than the family farm.

Wickard's position was not unique. Some other officials felt beset even in closer proximity to the President. I scribbled a few notes after lunching with Lowell Mellett. This gentle Hoosier newspaperman had ended a successful career with the Scripps-Howard newspapers in 1937 to become the director of the National Emergency Council when the emergency was one of domestic concern, not foreign war. I had known him when much of his efforts were directed at Southern economic problems. I remember that then he had unimpressive offices in an obscure building for the rooms in which there was not much demand. Then as war approached he became both administrative assistant to the President and director of the defense information agency euphemistically called the Office of Government Reports. He had quickly erected an emergency building of his own where a small green park had been at the intersection of Pennsylvania Avenue and Fifteenth Street. He was not happy in it. I put down, almost like a string of expletives, my immediate memory of his conversation: "talk of newspaper evils—the *Post*'s attack on his information building—*Chicago Sun*—the President's luck in timing of criticism."

Most of that cryptic notation is clear. Unprotected by any "anonymity" but set up as a target close to the President, his talk of "the evils of the press" reflected the wounds he was receiving from his own old craft. Turning out information and "coordinating" movies in connection with the war, he was made to seem almost a calliope of war propaganda. Even more, the anti-administration press made his agency seem politically rather than patriotically oriented—and in all things frenzied. The *Washington Post* had not been alone in describing his building as "Mellett's Madhouse."

In the face of such raps and ridicule, Mellett was evidently taking the consolation he could from the pro-administration *Chicago Sun,* which Marshall Field had established the year before to counter, along with his *PM,* the politically muscular, if, as some thought, also politically malignant *Chicago Tribune.* Evidently Mellett saw hope for himself in the timing of the crests of criticism. The 1942 congressional elections were still six months away. That seemed pretty close to some.

Criticism was by no means restricted to Republicans. After the neatly typed note "Lunch, George Creel, Carlton Hotel," I wrote: "defends Jesse Jones—critical of FDR—seems sympathetic with Byrd 'a gentleman who is horrified by waste'—World War I story about putting Roger Babson off on Secretary of Labor W. L. Wilson and Wilson saying who are we to put him off on now—'Washington place where people should take their fig leaves off in front and put them on behind.'"

As a boy in Washington I had known Creel as the World War I information chief, a position which Mellett already knew he would not attain. (Neither would Archibald MacLeish, now head of the Office of Facts and Figures.) In his day Creel had toughed it out against equally sharp criticism. A man of sensitiveness and humor, he was of rougher quality than either Mellett or MacLeish. He looked it. Under a mass of black hair, he had a head like a gargoyle but in it eyes that flashed and teeth that gleamed and seemed ready to bite. He had come through the violent journalism of Denver but with a political philosophy which appealed to Woodrow Wilson. Now while maintaining his dramatic flair he had grown gray and more conservative than he had been as Wilson's man.

Jesse Jones, vastly rich Texan, stood tall under a mass of white hair but he always wore the expression of a man whose feet hurt him. Herbert Hoover had chosen him, in the last beset year of his term, as a Democrat to head the Reconstruction Finance Corporation, which it was hoped would bail business out of the Depression. He turned out to be the sort of conservative Democrat Hoover would have chosen but with a power Roosevelt could not disregard. Some critics said that regardless of what the RFC did for American business, for Jones's native Houston it provided an explosive power hardly exceeded when the Manned Spacecraft Center was established there. Senator Harry Byrd, endless advocate of economy in government, was for more than a quarter of a century the boss of the Byrd machine in Virginia, which under a surface of gentility was as ruthless as any political organization in America. Jones and Byrd were Democratic twins of dissent from many New Deal programs.

Creel's Babson story indicated that there could be comedy as well as conflict in mobilization for war. In World War I he had happily welcomed Roger Babson's services because of his great reputation as a popular economist. Soon, however, he found Babson to be the sort of fuddy-duddy who always brings the wrong papers to a conference. With a show of reluctance he had let Babson go to Secretary Wilson. When Wilson made the same discovery, he quietly asked Creel to help him find somebody else to palm Babson off on. The Babson pattern persists from war to war. Creel's line about the fig leaves was a sort of surrealistic comment on the confusion and infighting which accompanies all wars, too.

A sense of humor was not always easily maintained by those who felt a sense of personal and political peril. An old friend John Carson came to see me. Now with the Cooperative League of the United States, he had been when I first knew him secretary to Ford-stock-rich and very liberal Republican Senator James Couzens, of Michigan. Carson brought with him Congressman Jerry Voorhis, of California. Strong supporter of the President, Voorhis—a rich, religious young man serving his third term—was much concerned about election to the next one. First elected in 1936 with less than a 10,000 majority, he had run it up to a 45,000-vote victory in 1940, but now he was disturbed. By Voorhis' name on the engagement sheet, I wrote: "Says White House gives Congressmen the run-around—Can only speak to a woman clerk if he lacked Presidential help." Voorhis' fears were not justified this year; he was re-elected but by a majority reduced to 13,000. He was not defeated until 1946, when a young man named Richard Milhous Nixon came home as both a Quaker and a commander from the war. Nixon then won by 15,592 votes.

My concerns in California that year were not political. On the margins of my neatly prepared itinerary I noted such details as "barrage balloons over Mare Island Navy Yard, about 50 of them, silver little stubby things like small blimps—high over aviation towers." I also jotted items about people, most of them connected in one way or another with civilian defense. I quoted a Dr. Hardin as saying: "I've been called a communist by the cossacks and a cossack by the communists." I wrote: "Beautiful bar of the Bohemian Club, brown woods, bright colors of picture-hung walls—carpet on barroom floor." In the club I lunched again with George Creel, who "speaking of the difficulty of getting club help, says fortunately most of our waiters are so old that we have to help them with the heavy trays." As a man looking at a younger generation running a war, he was critical still but this time about a matter which gave me much concern, too. We talked about the roundup of thousands of Japanese-American families who had been taken from their homes and farms and shops and packed into concentration camps in the interior with no charges against them except their ancestry. General John L. DeWitt, who had handled this uprooting of the innocents as they proved to be, Creel said, was "an advanced case of constipation." He approved another's comment that the General was "Coolidge in armor." Woodrow Wilson once told him, Creel said, that "war is too serious a business to be trusted to soldiers." Unfortunately in this case, as I knew sadly then, Soldier DeWitt had only acted on the authority of the chief civilian in Washington.

There are notes about that other most romantic of American cities, New Orleans. Troop trains slowed my journey there, where for the second year—this time from the inside looking out—I made one of the two chief speeches at the National Conference of Social Work. The other address was made by Malcolm MacDonald, British High Commissioner in Canada, who talked of the British social-service equivalents of our operations in America. I don't remember much about our speaking. I made no marginal comments about that. I was concerned with a party after the program at the house of Roark and Mary Rose Bradford. I had been in the writer's house before. After going to see the Bradfords there when I was working on *A Southerner Discovers the South,* I later described it: "The dirty front and the old blinds chained together gave it an abandoned look. But within the court between the house and the old slave quarters was another world, old, private, quiet and green."

War outside in 1942 had not changed it. The people in it seemed far from any Armageddon. Those sharing Bradford's libations made a merry group and a gossipy one. Lyle Saxon, the Louisiana writer, told strange tales about the city around us. As certainly one of the gayest of the do-gooders, Fred Hoehler, executive director of the American Public Welfare Association, showed no such solemnity as might have been expected of the man who would soon assume duties as chief of the operations of the Office of Foreign Relief and Rehabilitation in North Africa, then in the European area. Loula Dunn, who would succeed Hoehler as director of the national welfare association, was then an adviser to the Army in the formation of the WAACs but this evening she showed herself as the liveliest spinster ever to come out of Grove Hill, Alabama. Howard Hunter, formerly one of the chief aides of Harry Hopkins in Depression relief and now deputy administrator of the War Food Administration, spiced the conversation with tart comments on some personages in the nation at war. Bradford added to such comment the blurted remark that one under discussion "hasn't got sense enough to pour piss out of a boot." Others added to conviviality. Decibels rose and smoke thickened. It was still clear that the group which had assembled after exhortation would get back to the war's concerns through the dark streets of the Vieux Carré, possibly restored in spirit even if aware of hangover. War has its moments of both.

Also a party could be an explosion. "That Dance!" I wrote beside a meeting with Landis in his office. Evidently this was about one of the personnel parties Mrs. Roosevelt had urged to make people in government happy. This brought about a collision between deeply prejudiced white personnel and a handsome dark young woman employed in OCD to help bring Negroes into the war effort. Pauline Redmond was quiet but strong. She brought to her aid Frank Reeves, assistant then in the NAACP to Thurgood Marshall. I told Landis that Miss Redmond seemed in her position "rather admirable."

It is difficult to understand the situation today. So many things which seemed bold and innovative in race relations then are commonplace now. It is an almost incredible recollection that shortly before this time Senator Ellison D. ("Cotton Ed") Smith, of South Carolina, had swaggered in anger out of a session of a Democratic National Convention merely because a black minister had been put on the program to pray. What cannot be forgotten now is that Senator Smith was the top man in seniority in the Senate at that time. In Washington then, Negroes were permitted to eat in no "white" public restaurant except the one in the Union Station. Some interpretation of discrimination in interstate commerce ruled there but not in the national capital all around it. There were no beds for blacks at any leading hotel. Restive as they must have been, even the most distinguished blacks seemed to take the situation for granted. Oddly enough, visitors from India with the darkest skins went under their turbans to any place they desired.

That evening Landis, my wife Lucy and myself, Melvyn Douglas, Justine Polier (daughter of Rabbi Stephen Wise and herself a distinguished liberal lawyer of New York), and Agnes Inglis dined at the White House with Mrs. Roosevelt. It was obviously a command performance. I noted: "Mrs. R. offered to get President to do something about OCD budget —Landis declined." I have no memory that the dance was mentioned at the dinner.

Saturday came and at ten I went to Landis' office. Then I put down the exclamation "That Dance!" In the afternoon I spoke in the river-front garden of the house of Hugo and Josephine Black in Alexandria. I have no memory of what the occasion was or what I said but I remember the feeling of the pleasantness of the company and the charm of the place by the river of the Supreme Court justice who had been a member of the Ku Klux Klan but now was a leading racial liberal on the Court.

So far as my notes show, no repercussions followed the office party. On Monday morning Landis came down to my office concerned about other things: "feels that Mrs. R.'s friends determined that her program must be justified—he thinks it not necessary for me to go with him to Budget hearing at Capitol." I put no exclamation point after that though I was beginning to feel that the Director was opposed to all but the paramilitary aspects of civilian defense. And they seemed atrophying in the absence of any air raids.

There seemed plenty of action at hand, however. My engagement list in the late spring was thick with scribblings:

5:00 p.m. Met Lt. Commander Lyndon Johnson, Carlton, for cocktail—an energetic and intelligent Texas Congressman disturbed about public relations of U.S. government—wants for sake of political future to get into danger zone though realizes talents best suited for handling speakers and public relations.

Immaculate in blue uniform with the two and a half gold stripes on his sleeves, he seemed still the rangy Texan. No premonition of his destiny stirred in me then. He came striding into the Carlton bar, then subsided into a relaxation apparently complete. He talked slowly with a tone that gave the impression that he was confiding completely to one whose attention he greatly desired. But there was no rest in his dark bright eyes. His mood altered easily. Slim and curly-haired, joking and laughing, he looked less like the conventional portrait of a congressman than the equally conventional picture of a movie actor in seagoing costume. I left him to go to realism in the White House:

5:30 White House. McIntyre said President wanted me to make some suggestions for deputy to Nelson to handle small businessmen using $100,000,000 revolving fund being provided in Murray bill—said President planned to get to information consolidation next week—thinks Speakers Bureau should be there perhaps under Joe Davies—drove home with him in White House car—McI looks very old and frail—says Wayne Coy always suggests himself for any job that comes up—but McI recognizes ability.
Tired went to bed at nine o'clock.

I have no memory about the appointment of a man to aid small business in the war effort. I hope now that I recommended Maury Maverick, impetuous Texan impatient with the "gobbledygook" he found and described in government language and procedures. Joseph E. Davies, who had been Ambassador to Russia and at this time presided over the vast establishment of his wife, Marjorie Merriweather Post, did not seem to me likely to accept a subordinate position in war propaganda. Wayne Coy, not quite thirty-nine then, was one of the ablest young executives in the government. He was much trusted by the President in the Office for Emergency Management and the Bureau of the Budget. He had moved up fast from job to job since he had entered politics under Governor Paul V. McNutt in Indiana. Nine years before this time he was running a newspaper in Delphi, Indiana, a town of less than 2,500 people chiefly notable for the fact that James Whitcomb Riley had composed bucolic verses while fishing in a nearby creek.

I was obviously too tired to make such notes in elaboration then. But underneath that entry I wrote: "Trees are all green in Dupont Circle—lovely wisteria on east wall of house at 2929 Massachusetts Avenue."

No wartime security steeled the spring. Beyond the black iron fences the grass before the White House was as green, the flowers as bright in those first uncertain months of war as in any days of peace. The President's front yard was plush and pleasant. But sometimes under its mistress social purpose and social party seemed remarkably intertwined. Lucy and I were invited to what would certainly have seemed a ceremonial occasion, a dinner in honor of Princess Juliana of the Netherlands and her consort. Her mother, Queen Wilhelmina, maintained her government in exile in England. If Juliana came to America asking for aid, as most such representatives of ghostly governments did, there was little sign of it in the company assembled around her. I described the occasion.

Strange dinner party for the Princess Juliana of Holland and her consort—not a single high government official except Harry Hopkins present—good many young people in International Student Service there—Dr. Will Alexander told Hopkins that best Lincoln story he knew was in 1940 when Hopkins in room in which Lincoln signed the Emancipation Proclamation was phoning and cussing about how to keep the Negro vote in line for FDR— The President looked very old. Realized for the first time that Mrs. Roosevelt is growing pretty deaf.

Hopkins may have come to dinner only as a long-time house guest in the Executive Mansion, but as actual head of the Lend-Lease program he was the almoner who might help the Dutch government in exile. Dr. Will W. Alexander, wise and genial veteran worker for better race relations, had been head of the Farm Security Administration and now was a chief figure in the Rosenwald Fund. Mrs. Roosevelt often consulted him. The odd-seeming guests were the young people of the International Student Service. Juliana, at thirty-three then, was no youth. Evidently they were invited as the friends of Mrs. Eliot D. (Trude) Pratt, who like Hopkins was often a guest in the White House. Mrs. Roosevelt's biographer, Joseph P. Lash, described her as one of a trio of Mrs. Roosevelt's closest friends, along with Mrs. Morgenthau and Mrs. Roosevelt's secretary and friend, Malvina ("Tommy") Thompson. Trude, née Gertrude von Adam Wenzel, had come to the United States from Germany in 1931. Soon afterwards she had married Eliot D. Pratt, son of the socially redoubtable George DuPont Pratt. Now she was about to marry Lash, who wrote later that Mrs. Roosevelt lent them her Hyde Park cottage "as a hideaway before they were married." He added that "her gift of empathy enabled her to enjoy vicariously the love affairs of her friends; for her 'there was no love, save borrowed love.' "

At the time of the dinner for Juliana, Lash at thirty-three had just been inducted into the Army after much hullabaloo about his draft status involving pressure by the red-hunting Dies Committee. After his induction *The New York Times* reported that Mrs. Roosevelt was using his car. Certainly she was concerned about him at the time of the dinner for Juliana. Soon Trude would succeed Joe as general secretary of the International Student Service.

Lucy and I went to a more informal dinner at the White House on May 19. My rough notes about it read:

7:30 Dinner at White House—called and asked to come at 7:15. Lucy and I spent first quarter hour alone with the President who with shaking hands fixing old fashioneds—he had one—I had two—Army tells him not to trust Russian war reports—Naval Hospital has his appendix, tonsils, a tooth—Story of the *New York Times* and tcht; tcht, tcht—Hopkins brought back scarf from London to Mrs. R designed with ————. Lucy pointed out to me later it was Liberty silk, silk being rationed here—young Franklin a little tight when came in—recently had operation for appendix—Pharmacy mate told him he had never taken one out but thought he could do it—John (Roosevelt) and Mrs. R fearful that limiting incomes to $25,000 would injure private charities—

The President's desk in round sitting room cluttered with gadgets—dinner for six in end of upstairs hall—
Young Franklin ate a prodigious, greedy dinner.
Strange that with FDR I feel like a man and equal—Mrs. R makes me feel like inferior with a great, good but a little intellectually gusty Lady.

So far as I recall there was no particular occasion for this dinner. I do not remember that the President's hands had begun to shake at so early a time. His story about *The New York Times* was a much dramatized one he often told to the effect that that great journal in taking a positive position editorially could only make a sound like the clicking of its tongue against its teeth. Franklin, a lieutenant in the Navy, had been operated on in February but he had been back at sea and in Britain since that time. John, also in the Navy, was soon to see duty as a lieutenant in the Pacific.

There seemed something conspiratorial about some of Mrs. Roosevelt's social operations. She called people to prod them. Some used her as a great prod to others, sometimes their superiors. One afternoon in May I met Conrad Van Hyning, then welfare director of the District of Columbia, in Lafayette Square. The park, of course, was the great anteroom of the White House. Baruch maintained his bench and held court there. Some citizens merely looked from it to the guarded center of the war effort. I noted that Van Hyning and myself met there at 4:15 and talked about "what DC needs in CM." Evidently Van Hyning, maybe me, perhaps Mrs. Roosevelt, was unsatisfied with the civilian mobilization activities in the capital under its commission government headed by John Russell Young. Van Hyning and I had time to talk before we crossed the street at five o'clock. I made only a baffling record of the talk over the tea Mrs. Roosevelt served us:

5:00 Tea, Mrs. Roosevelt, White House. Van Hyning—Commissioner Young a soft good fellow—obviously a man of no fire who is good natured & good liver—also probably good company—Mrs. R makes all feel like small boys subjects of great lady—

As went up in elevator to Mrs. R's tea table usher operating elevator told Young story of husband who called his wife from Australia that he had met a girl. Wife: "What's she got that I haven't got?" Husband: "Nothing but she's got it here." We laughed and went into the first lady's sitting room—young Mrs. Pratt there but she left as we came in.

Commissioner Young was much as I described him then but I did not do him justice. He knew his way around the White House, having been correspondent there for the *Washington Star* since 1920. Twice he had been president of the White House Correspondents Association. He was also a member of the more prestigious Gridiron Club. Something of an antiquarian, he belonged to societies of Natives and of the "Oldest Inhabitants" of Washington. Devoted to oratory and histrionics, he noted in his *Who's Who* biography that he was the "founder of the J. Russell Young School of Expression." He also listed himself as Republican but he had pleased the first Democrat by serving as chairman of the anti-polio fund-raising President's Birthday Celebrations for four years. He had shown no genius as a reporter. Now possibly he needed a prod as District commissioner. But he combined humor, a love of tradition and dramatics, courtliness and conviviality. Those qualities did not add up to greatness but in Washington often they served survival, which is not always easy in war or peace—and perhaps especially in the great white building opposite Lafayette Square.

I was not sure at this tea-table time that I wanted to survive on the scene. Bernice Baumgarten, my agent, came to town again, this time with her husband, the quietly-desperate-seeming author James Gould Cozzens. He made no secret of his feeling of awkwardness in his new naval officer's uniform. Bernice held out another book to me as bait to go back to my typewriter. But though sometimes I felt as ill-cast in bureaucracy as Jim Cozzens did in his blue uniform, I was as much enlisted as he was. I recognize my condition now as a case of Potomac fever, to which later I became completely immune. Lyndon Johnson came back from his politically essential plunge into the Pacific. While he was gone Lady Bird, on energetic duty in the House Office Building, called me about a job for a Johnson constituent. Johnson and I went together to see the frail, sardonic McIntyre. I went more often alone to McIntyre's office close to the President's. And one day, sitting high in his chair with his knees clasped against his chest, McIntyre said, "With my access and your brains, we ought to see each other more often."

I am as susceptible to flattery as any other man but at that time I was certainly not sure I was wise. As I remember it, my reply to him was one short dirty word. I can look back now on that period of impatience with more humor than pain, perhaps with more clarity for having been caught in confusion before I was named as one of those supposed to help the President confront the complexities with which he is always surrounded. That makes it possible also to understand how sometimes those named to guard the palace might confound—even corrupt—it. Certainly I am glad that beyond confusion, impatience, sometimes comic bureaucratic captivity, I stayed to see a war in proximity to power—power which can never be shared, with absolute safety, at any moment in the story of the Republic.

Diary

1942

[In September I began to dictate sometimes long and often brief passages of observations and impressions to my secretaries, Elizabeth Brite and Anne Blakistone. They kept them filed in a locked case. The first long report I made related largely to a meeting with J. Edgar Hoover, then at forty-seven already the veteran head of the FBI. He agreed to help me gather information for the President about young men in bombproof jobs in Washington. He secured lists of people who maintained quarters in plush hotels and clubs. About the same time I talked on the same subject with General Lewis B. Hershey, director of the Selective Service System, who was destined to be almost as durable in office as Hoover.]

Tuesday, September 22. J.E.H. has wonderful layout as office, not one room, but a long room and then his office is beyond it through a double door. Fat, talkative, but pleasant and more impressive than I expected.

Says feeling against playboy officers in bombproof jobs is greatest in Hollywood, New York, and Washington. The greatest concentration in D.C. seems to be in the Office of Naval Intelligence and Army Intelligence.

People do not like Army and Navy football teams which are going around playing but never play on home grounds.

[Of facts I wanted, he said], "We can get all this information except from the Shoreham—that's the only bad one."

Says two men came from Hollywood after such an avalanche of wires announcing them that he suspected a racket. Even Drew Pearson called up day they arrived. Wanted jobs as special agents to escape draft, but investigation showed bad records, traffic, drunken-driving arrests, etc. Hoover met Dorothy Lamour, who urged him to hire them.

J.E.H. told me that his greatest trouble is the stupidity of the Coast Guard. The Guardsman who found the saboteurs on Long Island [near Amagansett on June 12, 1942] was unarmed. Accepted $300 bribe and then went back and reported to headquarters, which was only a short distance away. But instead of notifying FBI or starting search in neighborhood went to place on beach where saboteurs had been, dug up their material, and destroyed all fingerprints on them. Saboteurs meanwhile had gone to a little railroad station nearby and sat on benches and waited several hours for stationmaster to come and sell them tickets to New York.

With proper warning that part of Long Island could have been blocked and watched so that men could have been caught right away. Instead FBI was not even notified for twelve hours. Guardsmen went back to spot landing, saw the submarine still hanging around, but did not even notify Navy for two hours. As a result, men were only caught through informants of FBI in German group. After FBI was notified and demanded supplies, etc., Coast Guard still held back couple of shovels, hat, vest, and only gave them up after FBI discovered they had them.

Hoover expects a token bombing or bombings. Says he himself walked all over California coast before airplane plants near Los Angeles and San Diego without ever seeing a Coast Guard watcher. Says one of his agents in Maine walked the coast for twenty miles without ever seeing a guard.

[Hoover] says German intelligence is terrible—seized and ran one of their radio stations in United States for months without arousing their suspicions. That so far there has not been a single act of sabotage committed by Axis agents. Jap plane from submarine did recently drop an incendiary bomb on Oregon forests—no doubt that fragments found were of a Japanese bomb.

*　*　*

General Hershey says you can defer people without popular protest in direct proportion to popular awe for them:
Any preachers
Doctors
Chemists, physicists, men who use symbols. But lawyers, newspapermen, administrators, public doesn't believe they have anything they haven't got—not in awe of them. Draft 'em quick.

*　*　*

[Meeting in McIntyre's office], David Niles talked of a decorative blonde in the administration who he said was an agent for the Republicans. As his employee in WPA she furnished Senator Henry Cabot Lodge questions to Hopkins which it was immediately apparent could only have come from inside. Lodge knew her when both were reporters on the *New York Herald Tribune*. Lodge, who is a friend of Niles, told him about it later. Lodge wouldn't see her then. Niles says that when she was in WPA she made staff stay at night to copy confidential lists helpful to her husband's private business. She also served as spy in government for Republican National Committee.

Wayne Coy disgusted with Leon Henderson's folly in letting Frank Bane lead him into turning OPA patronage over to governors and leaving senators entirely out. David Niles even more disgusted. [As administrator of the Office of Price Administration, Henderson seemed politically naive. Bane, though performing a number of jobs in the federal government, including at this time director of the field operations of OPA, was executive director of the Council of State Governments and as such primarily beholden to the governors.

Political manipulation as well as minorities concerned Niles as former Hopkins man now administrative assistant to the President.]

Coy has a low-grade kidney infection which makes it necessary for him to take sulphur pills. Had kidney stone in Philippines [where he was administrative assistant to High Commissioner Paul V. McNutt from 1937 to 1939] and, in effort to remove it with instruments, infection introduced. Spent months in hospital but says he weighs more now than ever.

McIntyre, after talking on phone with Anna Rosenberg (to whose smartness he and Coy both testify), says, "Of course, she's a chiseling bitch, but she's our bitch."

[Anna Rosenberg was a hardheaded charmer in public relations. Her perky hats were a conspicuous part of Washington's wartime foliage. FDR purred at her gay flattery. At this time she was said to be employing her talents to make smooth the way of Nelson Rockefeller as Coordinator of Inter-American Affairs. She was also New York regional director of the Social Security Board. She had her pretty and precise finger in many pies. Later Truman made her an Assistant Secretary in the Department of Defense.]

Niles says that when Landis doing Securities and Exchange Commission job he spent much time with Felix Frankfurter but that when *Fortune* in an article alluded to Frankfurter's help Landis and wife resented it and clearly showed it to Frankfurter. [In a real sense Landis had been the protégé of Frankfurter. The latter, born in Vienna in 1882, was already a luminary on the Harvard Law School faculty when Landis came there from Princeton in the early Twenties. The professor undoubtedly had much to do with the choice of Landis as law clerk to Supreme Court Justice Louis Brandeis in 1925. Also, in 1928, when Frankfurter was forty-six and Landis was twenty-nine, they collaborated on a book about the business of the Supreme Court, to which Frankfurter was appointed a decade later.]

Tuesday, October 6. [Notes made in passage from OCD to the basement of the old State, War and Navy Building, now the Executive Office Building.] The old houses across the street from OCD and a girl in a little room under the roof fixing up in late afternoon for a date. Another little girl in blue satin pajamas framed by window brushing her yellow hair. Miss Redmond's apartment and friends. "You know we can't go places for cocktails." Crowded apartment of Molly Flynn, lovely and hardheaded liberal Catholic. Frances Knight, the faded blonde with a thirst for domination and a badly concealed sense of insecurity. Arthur Harlow, eager, able Jewish boy out of the jewelry business, restive and full of ideas in the midst of idleness and futility. Garden of Jim Schramm [Iowa department-store owner in OCD war service], where the owner had made the air-raid warden insignia in the pavement of the terrace.

Dave Niles moving from office to office with hands that taper like those of an Assyrian rug peddler, the same combination of sensitivity and indecency in his fingers.

Aubrey Williams [dark, abrupt, humorous egalitarian direc tor of the National Youth Administration] talking like a man about his ex-wife about Harry Hopkins, who has accepted the feeding and the weekends of the rich, married a society wife, and turned his mind to military matters and away from New Dealing. The most important news item that of his White House marriage, to which General George Marshall and Admiral Ernest King were invited and the old New Deal comrades were not. They were invited to a party a night or two before the wedding. [Hopkins, who had been living in the White House since May 10, 1940, was married to Mrs. Louise Macy on July 30, 1942.]

The millionaires in their new Navy uniforms on Kalorama Road. Frances Alexander [whose one-eyed husband, Bob, had finally gotten himself accepted in the paratroop engineers] left terribly alone by his departure to parts unknown, buying a little house in Georgetown.

Louis Weiss and his description of Marshall Field torn between his honest feeling as to his responsibility for wealth he did not earn and his loyalty to his class of the fellow rich and well-born. Weiss proud of his son-in-law, young physicist who is the Navy expert on degaussing ships, that is, making them immune to magnetic mines. [Weiss was an attractive, very able New York lawyer who served as a sort of almoner and conscience for Field. Too important to scorn, backed in his good purposes by one of America's greatest fortunes, Weiss attracted some of the same high-level prejudice Louis Brandeis met in his confirmation as a Supreme Court justice. Later when I joined in sponsoring Weiss for membership in the Century Association in New York, he was blackballed.]

The very sad-looking Benjamin Cohen. "You can go back in the front door now, Ben," says Leon Henderson. [Benjamin Victor Cohen was, with Thomas Gardiner Corcoran, one of FDR's famous legislative team in shaping much New Deal legislation, including the regulation of stock exchanges and utility holding companies. As twin operators the Jew and the Irishman were both admired and reviled. Opponents of the New Deal saw them as manipulators. Actually both held the advanced law degree of Doctor of Juridical Science from Harvard. The older, quieter Cohen looked like a rabbinical scholar and had early in his career served as counsel for American Zionists at the Versailles Conference following World War I. In 1932 he had joined the New Deal working on power matters under Secretary of the Interior Harold Ickes. Corcoran, who looked and moved like an Irish actor, after Harvard had been one of the distinguished company of men who served as legal secretaries to Justice Oliver Wendell Holmes. Strangely he had come into the government in 1932 in the Reconstruction Finance Corporation headed by Jesse Jones. None of Jones's conservatism rubbed off on him. He moved his operations with the arrival of Roosevelt in power to the Department of Justice. But as frequent emissary from the White House some felt that he played the Congress as well as he played the accordion, to the delight of FDR.

[Neither Cohen nor Corcoran was ever officially connected with the White House but nobody doubted their ties with the Boss there. Then, perhaps because their visibility became too great, perhaps undercut by jealousies of others around the President, their favor faded. Corcoran retired to restlessness in private practice. Cohen was briefly an adviser to Ambassador Winant in London. Now he was back in the White House as assistant to James F. Byrnes, director of the Office of Economic Stabilization.]

*   *   *

Hugh R. Jackson, back from the West Coast to OCD uncertainty, but still Hughie Ha Ha. [Jackson, able young New York welfare executive, had, along with his talents, brought a frequent nervous laugh into government.]

Barney Baruch on the bench in Lafayette Square basking in both the sun and his career of elder statesman—wears his fancy of himself as a sort of behind-the-scenes Disraeli as another, lower-level Jew might wear big diamonds, but then Gandhi may wear his nakedness as a dandy wears new clothes.

The President is cut off from learning not only by the few and the picked he can hear, but by his desire to do the talking even when he is with them.

Mrs. Hopkins very prettily playing mother to little solemn, sallow Diana at a White House luncheon. [Diana was the child of Hopkins by his second wife, who died in 1937.]

The women in the Mayflower smell just as they did when there wasn't a war.

The rats and the mice in the State Department Building.

Thursday, October 8. Lunch, Cosmos Club.

[Periodically off Lafayette Square, in the pleasant old Cosmos Club, composed of men in and out of government distinguished in science, art, and literature, there met a group largely composed of New Dealers. I do not remember who called this group together or fixed the subjects for discussion. The whole business was definitely informal though sometimes marked by irritations, even indignations, in the changed wartime Washington. More often the meetings served as occasions for the release of amusement, sometimes wry, about the most serious subjects. As often beset men, they were comfortable together in the stresses of war.

[Those present on this occasion were: Leon Henderson, Ben Cohen, Beanie Baldwin, Isador Lubin, Harry Dexter White, Mordecai Ezekiel, Paul Porter, Edward F. Pritchard, Jr., and as a guest, Undersecretary of War Robert P. Patterson, a Republican who had resigned from the U. S. Circuit Court of Appeals to join the war effort. Lubin at the time was on leave from his post as Commissioner of Labor Statistics to do special studies for FDR. White, director of monetary research in the Treasury and engaged in postwar monetary planning, was a man of testy nonconformist views which later made him a quarry of the red hunters. Ezekiel, an old hand in the Department of Agriculture, who had helped draft the New Deal's farm-relief legislation, was now working with the War Production Board. Paul Porter, Kentucky raconteur extraordinary, was deputy administrator of the Office of Price Administration with special authority to keep the lid on rising rents. Pritchard, who along with Cohen was aiding James F. Byrnes, was the youngest man present. He was also one of the most articulate. A Falstaff figure of a man, he had recently been a brilliant student in the Harvard Law School. When he was later drafted he commented, "They have scraped the bottom of the barrel and now they have taken the barrel." His military career lasted only about two weeks. On a six-mile conditioning hike, a truck had to be sent to pick him up as an utterly exhausted fat man. His remark on this occasion is preserved. "They didn't ask Christ to go the second mile." Recognized in Washington for his precocity, his knowledge, his acumen, and his wit, after the war, in Kentucky, he became involved in a ridiculous election-fraud case. His friends regarded it as a sort of Halloween prank but it brought him a term in federal prison. Truman paroled him. Rehabilitated, he became a successful lawyer in Kentucky.]

Judge Patterson expressed very strong sentiment indicating his feeling that the colleges have become centers in which the well-to-do can escape military service by means of education. He said he had heard it said that in the Civil War a man could avoid military duty by paying $300. In this war he pays a tuition fee. He said he felt that colleges would, in effect, have to close up for the war.

Harry White of the Treasury brought out the fact that there is a great stockpile of educated men and we would have to live on our capital in this regard, without training more men. Mordecai Ezekiel asked the Undersecretary, who advocated lowering the draft age to eighteen years, what that meant; he said that available statistics with regard to shipping indicate that it will be impossible for us to ship an army of any more than 3,000,000 men overseas in 1943. If this is so, how to explain the need to lower the draft age.

Judge Patterson said that Secretary Morgenthau had followed a regiment of men from induction center to transport and that he was much impressed with their appearance. But that he was shocked by a group of inductees he had seen, in terms of their age and physical condition. Judge Patterson said that the Army was surprised that the draft boards took so seriously the law raising the age to 45, that many of the men inducted were too old for any use in combat and that what the Army needed was not so much a bigger Army, but a physically better one. Contrary to General Hershey's statements of an Army running up to 13,000,000 men, he gave, I believe, the top figure as 7,500,000; pointed out that the average age of the Army is about 26 while the average age of the Navy is around 22 (my memory may not be exact as to these figures).

In connection with the colleges, the Judge said that they had been able to secure from the colleges usually only the less perfect physical specimens by enlistment, as the perfect speci mens had been taken into the reserve corps and deferred from service on account of education. He spoke with amusement of a report from a Middle Western draft board which satirically declared that they would go down the line, that they would take men from their homes and snatch workers from farms, but they would never, never touch the college boys. He was opposed to holding the Army-Navy game this year, but indicated that Secretary of the Navy Frank Knox, acting for the Navy, rather insisted upon it "on the grounds of service morale and a lot of other foolishness."

Judge Patterson, in a discussion of manpower, said that he felt the Manpower Commission had been going into details with regard to manpower and missing its over-all policy-making function. He expressed the view that there should be a commission composed of the Secretaries of War and Navy and Donald Nelson [chairman of the War Production Board], with an administrative officer to administer policies made by the board. Fat young Pritchard thought Agriculture should be represented but Patterson felt Nelson could represent all production.

Sunday, October 11. Cocktail party at Lyndon Johnson's apartment. Speaker Sam Rayburn said to Elmer Davis [director of the Office of War Information], "I certainly hope that the President won't feel he has to kick Congress between now and the election. Also, I hope he won't bring up the extension of the Selective Service to nineteen- and eighteen-year-olds. We can't enact any such legislation between now and the election and it will only serve to raise a new question and have a lot of crying mothers."

Davis said, "You must remember, Mr. Speaker, that there are just as many wives and children whose husbands and fathers are going as there are mothers of younger men." Also Davis said, in a tone which Lowell Mellett later described as "righteous," and which Rayburn later called "a tone of cool authority," that he thought the people wanted the President to make the impression that he was intent on winning the war and not merely the election.

The difference between the two men did not reach the stage of argument. I remember that I moved over with Rayburn in the shift of the company and found him pretty deeply disturbed by his relationship with the President. He only sees him on Monday morning in the company of the Vice-President and the Vice-President is always agreeing with everything the President says, trying to assure himself of the succession to the presidency. "And he won't make it." He said he felt he could be much more useful if he could see the President by himself. I asked him if he could not do this and he said of course he could—but—and he gave the impression of feeling that his advice was not wanted. There was not, he said, a single man close to the President who had any interest or knowledge of politics apart from that devoted to the advance of a single man, rather than party government. "You know Hopkins is no Democrat, he is just a New Dealer and doesn't care anything about the party."

Later, in conversation with Davis and Lowell Mellett, I spoke again about the dangers to the war of the loss of the election. Rayburn had already emphasized this, pointing out that people in the other countries do not understand our system and would feel that the President had fallen as a Prime Minister would if he lost control of the House. Also, he pointed out that Ham Fish, in the event of Republican control, would be chairman of the Foreign Affairs Committee or the Rules Committee or both. [Fish was anathema to Roosevelt not only because of his voluble isolationism but also because in antagonism the two men were so similar. Both came from aristocratic lineage in the same Hudson Valley area and lived in the same congressional district. Both were Harvard men, though in their separate times at the old college Fish excelled as both a football great and as a *cum laude* graduate. Reactionary as he later seemed in many matters, Fish as a combat officer in World War I served as the commander of Negro troops.]

I wondered aloud to Davis and Mellett as to whether Lincoln had control of the House throughout the Civil War. Mellett said yes, but by the damnedest finagling you ever heard of; certain troops were allowed to come home and vote, while others were not.

Also met Tommy Corcoran and heard a recording, on Johnson's radio-phonograph, of Corcoran singing to his own accordion accompaniment the song "I Hate the Constitution." I must get the words to this. [Actually I discovered later the song was "The Good Old Rebel," a defiant ex-Confederate poetic outcry by Innes Randolph.]

Talked about the *Chicago Sun* with Bascom Timmons

[friend and biographer of Jesse Jones] and kidded a little about the *Sun* being a New Deal paper and employing Timmons as its Washington correspondent. He was ready to defend his Democracy. On the walls of his office he has the pictures of Robert E. Lee, John L. Sullivan, and Grover Cleveland. In the picture from the *Police Gazette,* Sullivan very modestly has his hands across his breast in order to hide the nipples.

Senator Tom Connally with his wife, the former Mrs. Morris Sheppard (widow of the late senator from Texas). In her fifties she is still a rather warm-looking blonde, and it is hard to imagine her ever having been the wife of the leading prohibitionist in the Senate. [Lucille Sanderson Sheppard Connally was at this point just a bride of six months. Senator Connally was sixty-five. She had been widowed just a year when she remarried.]

Monday, October 12. Winning the war. Went out to lunch with McIntyre. Played bridge at the Press Club from a quarter of two 'til four. Lost $2.25.

Tuesday, October 13. I had written, at Lyndon Johnson's request, in the office of Speaker Rayburn, a statement to be made this morning by Chairman Andrew J. May, of the Military Affairs Committee, stressing the fact that Congress is able to act with dispatch. Johnson and I went down to a little sort of hideout office, which Rayburn has down below his own office in the Capitol. There, for some reason, Johnson decided to tell me some background stuff and talked particularly about Tommy Corcoran, for whom he expressed great admiration.

He undertook to tell me what had happened to Corcoran. There was no doubt, he thought, about Corcoran's ability. Corcoran was not, he thought, merely a salesman for Cohen, but had a way of pushing people around. If he called up somebody and asked for some information or action and was told he could have it tomorrow, he said, "To hell with that, I want it at two o'clock this afternoon." That cost him some friends, Johnson thought. Rayburn, he said, was devoted to him.

Not long ago Wayne Coy came into this little office of

Rayburn's and said, "Mr. Rayburn, I am going to have to ask you for a lot of things for the White House, but I am not going to be Tommy Corcoran." Rayburn got up pretty sore, pointed to the door, and said, "I guess Tommy Corcoran has come in that door a thousand times and he never came in once when he wasn't welcome. He never lied to me in his life."

Corcoran's difficulties began, Johnson thought, when he began to get too much coverage in the newspapers. He and Hopkins didn't get along too well and Corcoran, after doing a great part of the pre-convention work in '40, stayed away from the convention because, he said, "Jim Farley is going to mess us up and Hopkins will put the blame on me." After the convention Corcoran resigned and went to New York to set up a sort of Democratic committee to collect funds to further Roosevelt's cause. There he began his enmity for David Niles, whom he now bitterly hates.

After the election the President planned to make Corcoran Assistant Secretary of the Navy in charge of air, "and he would have made the thing go," Johnson said. Knox agreed, but there was some delay in the appropriation and in the meantime somebody got to Knox and said, "He'll take your department away from you and he will move so fast it will be a month before you know it." So when the time came Knox declined to name him. Then Corcoran was scheduled to be made Solicitor General of the United States. Six members of the Supreme Court, Rayburn, and Majority Leader McCormack went down to the White House to urge his appointment. Johnson went too and the President said to him, "Lyndon, stop this pressure, I am not going to appoint Tommy."

But the President wanted him to have a place in the Administration and told Wallace to find him one. Corcoran wrote a letter to Wallace saying that for sixty days he was open for any appointment regardless of salary in the federal government. He had, however, gotten married in the meantime to a nice little Irish girl (Peggy Dowd, his former secretary and daughter of a postman) of no particular background, Johnson said, but she began to think of babies and a house and things and for the first time Corcoran had to think of money.

Wallace went to see every member of the Cabinet and each one of them was afraid to have Corcoran for fear he would try to take over his show.

Corcoran has since been very bitter about it, particularly since he has been criticized for making large sums of money as a sort of "fixer." Cohen, until his recent appointment as Byrnes chief counsel, had an office in the Interior Department, but received no pay. Johnson said he thought that though Hopkins and Corcoran did not like each other, Hopkins had generously stated that he thought Corcoran was so useful a man that he ought to have a place in the Administration. Johnson also said that he felt that Corcoran had gotten the opinion that the Administration couldn't get along without him and he said, "You know, anybody can get along without anybody."

In Rayburn's office I was surprised again to see Rayburn's rather petulant pride aroused over the fact that he had called the President about his plans to push the 18–19-year-old-draft bill, but was told that the President was at lunch and would call him when he came back. However, at half past three the President had not called. Johnson called up the President's private secretary at the White House, Grace Tully, and told her of the situation; the President called Rayburn. Like other congressmen, Johnson, though close to the President, feels that the White House does not have as easy and pleasant a contact with leaders in Congress as it ought to have.

* * *

Johnson is a smart young politician, very vigorous and also very young. There is something of the campus politician about him and a willingness to run in and do things which an older man might hesitate to do and which might not be accepted from an older man. He has a very low opinion of Jesse Jones as a participant in the destiny of the Democracy of Texas. "He is really a Republican," he said, "and just by the accident of birth a Texan and a Democrat, but he has great power in Texas." Also Jones devised a system for dealing with the President. If the President asks him to do anything, he says he will and puts it in his drawer and forgets about it. If the President asks him about it a second time, he says he is having it investigated. If he asks him about it a third time he says he will have a report on it. If he asks him a fourth time he gives him part of what he asks for. Usually the President does not remember so many times. In fact, in some of these cases Mrs. Roosevelt was the active person and it was a contest between her insistence and Jones's forgetting, with the forgetting usually winning out. Johnson says that James Forrestal in the Navy Department has learned to operate on the same basis. Incidentally, David Niles told Johnson and myself that in the President's own district, workers on the defense projects, during the congressional elections, had had to go to Ham Fish's office to get jobs and that this was stopped only after about three demands on the Navy.

*　　*　　*

Wednesday, October 14. The President spoke of Clare Boothe Luce, saying she had at last acquired a proper name and that he had to hope that there were still enough good solid people in Connecticut who would not elect "a Luce woman." "You know she was Barney Baruch's girl," he said. "Yes," he said, "he educated her, gave her a yacht, sent her to finishing school, she was his girl." [Evidently the "good solid people in Connecticut" were believing no such tales. Mrs. Luce, wife of the editor and publisher of *Time* magazine, Henry A. Luce, was elected this year by 5,858 votes over a Democrat who played up his role as a veteran of World War I but had only been elected to a single term in Congress in 1940 by a majority of 953 votes.

[In their bitter political hostility, Roosevelt was ready to believe almost anything about Clare Luce and she was ready to say almost anything about him. In the neutrality period there had been a time when FDR had hoped for the support of the Luces and the Time, Inc., empire. Then the Luces were invited to the White House. Afterwards they said he moved too slowly from isolationism. Clare was quoted as saying, "All famous men have their characteristic gesture. Churchill has his V sign. Hitler his upraised arm, and Roosevelt . . . ?" She wet her index finger and held it up to the wind.

[Such suggestions that he moved too timidly would have angered FDR more than clamor that he was moving too fast.]

The President looked well. He was smoking when I came in. I remember I got out a cigarette to smoke and then thought I had better wait until he asked me if I wanted one, held the cigarette in my hand, but didn't smoke. He was in good spirits and seemed very much interested in the report I had made [on men in bombproof jobs]. When I left he said, "This is grand."

I told him that I expected to see him again tomorrow morning at 10:15 with Lyndon Johnson.

I went out of the President's office and back into McIntyre's office, where I had left McIntyre and Lyndon Johnson talking about the congressional elections. They were still talking and had a bottle of Old Forester on McIntyre's desk. It was empty, but McIntyre gave me a key to a cabinet next to his desk. I got out a quart of Old Taylor and had a good drink.

*   *   *

Met Gene Tunney at the Mayflower at lunch and asked him about the heavyweight championship. He said, of course Joe Louis still held the title and that nobody could take it away from him until after the war. He (Tunney) seems to be a very nice boy and still a boy, though he has grown up to the three stripes on his sleeve.

Cocktail party at Sam Rayburn's bachelor apartment in the Anchorage.

Present, George W. Stimson, Texas newspaperman; Jack Bell, of the Associated Press; Bascom Timmons; Tommy Corcoran; Ben Cohen; David Cohn; Judge Fred Vinson [strong, soft-speaking Kentuckian, chief judge of the U. S. Emergency Court of Appeals, who would succeed Byrnes as director of the Office of Economic Stabilization. Later he became Secretary of the Treasury and Chief Justice of the Supreme Court.]; R. Ewing Thomason, congressman from Texas; Jimmy Byrnes; Lyndon Johnson; and one admiral, name unknown, who was there early drinking tea and left early because he couldn't bear to see others drinking when he was not. Impressed by the diminutiveness of Jimmy Byrnes.

[Not much over five feet tall, James Francis Byrnes packed a lot of personality, charm, and power into his small frame. In his time (the date of the beginning of which he always kept secret) he had been court reporter, editor, district attorney, congressman, senator, Supreme Court justice, and now a sort of Assistant President; he later became Secretary of State and governor of South Carolina.]

Byrnes spoke about being at the party congress of the Nazis in 1937 and being aware at the time that war was inevitable. Somehow Germany seemed a long way from his Catholic boyhood in Charleston. We discussed some Army reports that showed that the selectees in Southern camps were of lower intelligence than those in any other sections. It was a Southern group and there was general agreement that these tests could only show information and education and not intelligence. Byrnes talked about the intelligence of the mountain stocks of the South, intelligence which was often hidden behind a mask of seeming stupidity. He told a story about a Southern mountain congressman who described the people of his district as being so thrifty that if a Jewish peddler passed through when he got out he would have to holler for the B'nai B'rith. Byrnes also mentioned having testified that day or the day before at a congressional hearing at which some congressman had made much of the fact that he had had to pay $14.00 for a hotel room. Byrnes said he started to ask what went along with the room, but he felt that, as a former justice of the Supreme Court, he should not be so flippant. Sam Rayburn lived in one town in Texas where it used to be the custom, when any man rented a hotel room, to ask him "with or without."

Congressman Thomason reported a lot of feeling in Congress against General Hershey.

Wednesday, October 14. To the President's office. In the anteroom was Ambassador Loudon of the Netherlands, come to present a fat Dutch admiral. Also there was Ambassador Dr. Don Francisco Castello Nájera of Mexico, coming to present an earthstone, gift of President Manuel Avila Camacho of Mexico. Nájera talked very pleasantly about my father, who had recently retired as our ambassador there, and asked about my mother's health.

[While persons waited patiently—or impatiently—to see the President, that big sunlit anteroom was the scene of much interesting conversation. I remember particularly a long talk I had there with Lord Halifax of Britain, a thin, tired man. From a distance he had seemed to me when he first came as ambassador too much the epitome of a British past, overbred to delicacy and arrogance. But as we waited to see the President, he talked directly and quietly of those days in England when the chief of the British air forces dropped to his knees when France fell and thanked God for it because his last few planes were saved to fight with a chance, if not much chance. Halifax was matter-of-fact about it. He recalled how Britain, unarmed, waited for discarded American rifles. Britain lived in a strange reversal. Help was in the New World, where so few centuries before the wilderness had been. But Britain seemed, in 1940, a sort of pioneer outpost counting time, waiting for aid in a sudden wilderness of its own. And the savages were not far off. In the quiet room, as Halifax talked, you could see on the charts the ships which they watched coming, full speed but slow in the eyes of those who waited. They could feel the victorious German push across the Channel. Halifax was very simple about it, tired now but patient in the anteroom.]

When I went into the President's office there was no sense of time pressure. I told him what had happened, told him about the proposed plan for letters to the Secretaries of War and Navy. [This conversation was in connection with his concern about the presence in Washington of young men with important connections, some in deferred status and others in bombproof jobs in uniform. I brought him a list of such men which I had compiled with the aid of the FBI. I have omitted here the amusing, sometimes caustic comments of the President on some of the names he found on the list. However suspicious-seeming their status may have been then, some afterwards performed important and hazardous service in war zones. Possibly this presidential interest prodded or pushed them but it would be improper to classify them now on the basis of their presence in Washington in this early part of the war.] He glanced through the letters and approved, but suggested that perhaps he might add a postscript asking that records of deferments be reported once a month to him.

I suggested that it would be a good idea to bring back to Washington for duty men who had been injured at the front who had lost an arm or a leg, but were still entirely capable of desk duty. He spoke of some necessity for rotating reserve officers and mentioned specifically the commander of the destroyer on which Franklin has been on duty. He said the commander had been on duty on a destroyer for three years, almost always at sea, and declared that is a long time for a man of forty-one to be at sea. He seemed very much interested in my suggestion that disabled officers be brought to desk duty here and said he was going to speak to Ross McIntire, the Surgeon General, about it.

Then he told me a long story about a man named Charles Fry, expert in gasoline engines. He had gone to school with the President but had lost an arm cranking a gasoline engine, had gone on to become known around Pennsylvania as the best man on gasoline engines in the world. During the absence of my father, as Secretary, Roosevelt, as Assistant Secretary, had commissioned Fry as an ensign, though he had only one arm. Father called Roosevelt and asked him about it and, when he explained, agreed. Fry went first to Philadelphia, where he was hailed as the boon of the service so far as gasoline engines were concerned. Admiral Wilson asked for him in France; then he had been promoted to lieutenant. When Roosevelt arrived in France he found that Fry had become lieutenant commander and was the principal expert on gasoline engines for England, France, and America. Unfortunately, shortly afterwards Fry died of influenza.

Thursday, October 15. Yesterday McIntyre told Lyndon Johnson and myself that the President wanted to see us at the White House before he came to his office this morning, at 10:15, to talk about Johnson's plan to help in the re-election of Democratic congressmen. We went to the White House and waited a little while in the Red Room, then we were told that the President would see us at the office instead. We went over to the office wing and talked with McIntyre for a time and then went to General Watson's office, which is the anteroom of the President's office.

After a little while Watson came over and said, "You gentlemen will not be in there for long, will you? Make it snappy."

Johnson said, "I have nothing to talk with the President about, he wanted to see us."

Watson said, "The President hasn't anything to say to you, but you go in and speak to him, even if just for a minute," and Watson went back into the President's office.

Johnson was obviously getting his feelings hurt. He said that he had talked to the President a week ago and the President told him to go ahead and do this work but he had been unable to reach any understanding as to how it should be done; that there was only about two weeks left before the election and that he was beginning to feel that he had raised the hopes on the Hill and that the men would be left flat on their faces. In a little while General Watson came back and said the President said maybe it would be better to see us later.

McIntyre had come into the room in the meantime and we told him about the situation, but then Johnson went out, practically striding; it looked for a minute as if he had gone out in a pique. I think that was what it was, but we caught up with him and he said he thought we were right behind him. I stayed after he left for the Capitol, with McIntyre, who was disturbed about what had happened. He said that in his opinion, Watson was not too bright about such things and was so devoted to protecting the President that the result was that he had alienated people who are important to the President. But he described Johnson as "one of these thin-skinned Southern gentlemen," and when I said that Johnson was trying to do a job for the President with people like Rayburn, whose pride is worn thin by their treatment at the White House, McIntyre said that Rayburn, like all other Speakers, had gotten swell-headed. I also brought up with him my own situation, about the job that I had done, and had finished, and asked him to keep me informed as to whether the President signed the proposed letters to the Secretaries of War and Navy and that I would like to be given some sort of definite status.

[When Johnson became President in 1963 I wrote to him recalling this incident. He replied that in his administration I would never have any trouble getting through his door. Strangely, it seems to me now, I never presumed on that promise. By that time I had passed the age when I wanted status or anything else from a President.]

Incidentally, said McIntyre, Mrs. Roosevelt held the President up for a half hour over at the White House this morning. Then he mimicked her: "Franklin, something has got to be done. The Negroes are *not* getting a square deal."

*   *   *

The President asked me yesterday if I knew anything about the Army Administrative Corps. I said I had heard of it, but that I did not investigate it in the study because it was located at Charlottesville, Virginia, but that I understood that no New Dealer could be a member of the Corps. He nodded, with the great wide-eyed significant shake of his head which is characteristic of him, in agreement, saying he understood that and was aware of what was going on. We did not pursue this question further.

* * *

Saturday, October 17. McIntyre said the President is just so bull-headed that Friday he went out in a light suit and wouldn't put on a raincoat or his cape "and insisted that I keep the window open so Fala could see out." To see the flood in the Potomac—caught cold.

* * *

Senator Bob Reynolds told Jesse Cothrell, correspondent of the *Charlotte Observer,* "They can't beat me now, Jesse, I can run on the baby kissing."

Wesley McDonald, Reynold's secretary, says no elaborate delivery room was built in the McLean house preceding the arrival of the new Reynolds baby. They just fixed up a room. Reports of grandeur are incorrect, he insists.

[Robert Rice Reynolds had clowned his way into the U. S. Senate from North Carolina in a campaign in 1932 in which he had made former Governor Cameron Morrison seem like a stuffed shirt who restuffed himself regularly with "fish eggs"—caviar—in the plush Mayflower Hotel. "Our Bob," as he liked to be called, in this depression year ran as a poor man in a jalopy. But on October 9, 1941, at fifty-seven he had taken as his fifth wife young Evalyn Walsh McLean, heiress to the largest Washington fortune. Her mother was the owner of the fabulous and supposedly fated Hope Diamond.]

* * *

Monday, October 19. Difficulties seem to be growing in the domain of Paul McNutt. Mark McCloskey, who a few months ago was expressing his pleasure over the fact that McNutt seemed to have abandoned the type of politics he practiced

56

in Indiana, devoting himself to really statesmanlike effort in good administration, is now disturbed by the apparent widespread return of the political approach in the Federal Security Agency. He mentioned the incident of McNutt, at a meeting of his own staff, making a short introductory speech which he read from a piece of paper instead of speaking without notes.

Apparently Charlie Taft's setup is in trouble with General Philip B. Fleming, of the Public Works Administration and his assistant, Florence Kerr [formally with Hopkins in WPA], in the spending of money for welfare, recreation, etc. Federal Security is given the veto power over projects rather than the planning power which veto, of course, is the most unpopular power of all. McCloskey finds that Florence Kerr is apt to reduce all conferences on this subject to a feminine personality basis. All the details here are not clear to me, but there seems a general feeling of weakness in both Manpower and the Federal Security Agency, which indicates that something may have happened to the triumphant advance of the beautiful Paul.

[Paul Vories McNutt seemed to have everything a politician pointing toward the presidency could hope to possess. A citizen of the crucial state of Indiana, he had graduated with Phi Beta Kappa marks from the university of that state, then gone on to take his law degree at Harvard. His war record, as an officer in the field artillery in World War I, led to his election as national commander of the American Legion in 1928 while he was dean of the University of Indiana Law School. Almost as a matter of course he was elected governor of Indiana in the year in which the Democrats swept Hoover out of the White House. At the end of his term in 1937 Roosevelt made him High Commissioner to the Philippines in recognition of his party position and possibly to get him as a potential rival in the future as far away as he could. He still appeared to be a comer in 1939, when Roosevelt made him administrator of the Federal Security Agency. His year of presidential possibility was 1940, when he was a glamorous forty-nine: but Roosevelt ended McNutt's chances when he overturned the two-term tradition in the presidency. Now he was a man in anticlimax, though in addition to his Social Security post, he was the director of the Office of Defense Health and Welfare Services and chairman of the War Manpower Commission.]

*　　*　　*

McIntyre, speaking of the manner in which even experts are often impressed by FDR's knowledge of their subjects: "But, boys, between ourselves," said McIntyre, grinning, "sometimes he can make a mighty little knowledge go a long way."

The President wears on all his coat sleeves the wide mourning band for his mother.

[Sara Delano Roosevelt had died more than a year before this entry on September 6, 1941, at a time when the President was aroused by the attack of a German submarine on an American destroyer en route to Iceland. He had infuriated both Hitler and some American isolationists when he told the American people that this country sought no "shooting war with Hitler. But . . . when you see a rattlesnake poised to strike, you do not wait until he has struck before you crush him . . ."]

Lyndon Johnson's wife is the sharp-eyed type who looks at every piece of furniture in the house, knows its period and design—though sometimes she is wrong. She is confident that her husband is going places and in her head she is furnishing the mansions of his future.

Story of Wilbur Schramm coming in to see men taking up his rug. When he protested, somebody made a speech, to shame him, about this being war and what did he care about a rug in his office. "But it made me a little mad," Wilbur said, "that whoever was getting it could not do without a rug in time of war." [Schramm was a charming expert in communications in OWI whose own communication was attended by stuttering. He later became one of the leading figures in his field.]

*   *   *

John Cathcart came with brother Jim [Lucy's cousins] to call—John has just been commissioned a lieutenant in airborne infantry at Camp Benning—a neat unremarkable-looking kid of twenty-two. Spoke of parachute jumping as a man about a technical trade. Discussed TNT which they carry in their belts—no danger at all. Take no prisoners—kill enemy so they can make no sound—equipped with a leather strap for strangling a man to death. Went off to Bolling Field, hoping to bum a ride to Columbia, S.C. Army has ordered a stop to such hitchhiking by air—has instructed that rides be requested "through channels," but that takes two weeks. John hoped to talk himself into a ride.

Tuesday, October 20. Met Mrs. John B. Martin on the street at noon today. She was very cordial in her greeting and said, "Things at OCD are in just as much of a hell-of-a-mess as ever. I don't think my husband could stay there if he didn't have such a strong nervous system." [John B. Martin was assistant to Landis.]

*   *   *

I met Leon Keyserling on the street today and asked him how they were getting along in the remodeling program, providing more housing. He said, "It is going fine, we are taking over the old houses and making some fine slums." [Keyserling was then general counsel of the National Housing Agency.]

*   *   *

Cocktails with Melvin Jones, one of the founders in 1917 of the International Association of Lions Clubs and its secretary general ever since, and his aide and bodyguard, Henry Kruger.

Old man Jones is a round man with practically white hair,

59

with something of the look of the retired evangelist about him. Young Kruger is a handsome, tough young American, who seems to me in hope of falling heir to Jones's kingdom. In a discussion of the difficulty in getting government expense accounts, young Kruger reported that in his former days with the FBI he was in the Middle West, playing around with some local police, one of whom was an expert at shooting a pistol with cardboard over the sights—I take it, the same as the old Western "shooting from the hip" technique. They got a call from a filling station that a car had just been by with guns, including a machine gun on the back seat. They found the car at a restaurant. Kruger stood at one side by some store windows while the two policemen engaged the driver in talk. The driver began to resist and one of the cops knocked him down. He grabbed for his gun, but Kruger, from where he stood, shot him. "Did you hit him?" somebody asked. "I blew half his head off," Kruger said casually. "He lived a little while, calling for his girl, and we got one of the nurses to pretend she was his girl." He was somebody named Green, related to the Dillinger group. Kruger told the whole story to point out the fact that when he drove the gangster's car to a nearby town, he couldn't collect $2.40 for the gasoline he put in it because he had forgotten to secure a signed receipt.

Jones was in Washington to formally invest the President as an honorary member of the Lions Clubs. He said that the Rotary Clubs represented the fascist element in small-town life and the Lions Clubs represented democracy. He gave the impression that the President, in effect, shared this view.

Thursday, October 22. Newspaper friend telephoned me tonight and told the story Gardner Cowles related after he returned from his trip to the Middle East. Story of the Russians saying there are two ways to get a second front, a natural way and a supernatural way. The natural way would be for all the angels in heaven to come down and attack Hitler in the rear. The supernatural way would be to get Winston Churchill to keep his word. [Gardner (Mike) Cowles, Jr., of the well-known publishing family, had returned to the directorship of the Domestic Branch of OWI after accompanying Wendell Willkie on his world-wide tour in the early fall of 1942.]

Friday, October 23. McIntyre talked about a conference he had with Foster May, who is running on the Democratic ticket against Senator George Norris of Nebraska. The White House is very anxious that May withdraw from the race.

[Senator George Norris, then eighty-one, had been in the Congress, House and Senate, since 1903. On his re-election to his fifth term in the Senate he had added "Independent" before "Republican" in his party designation. Republicans counted him as an apostate and New Dealers regarded him as sage and darling. His greatest monument is the Tennessee Valley Authority, which he greatly helped to create. One of his chief disciples in the Senate was Lister Hill, of Alabama and the TVA country.]

McIntyre told me that May suggested that the President appoint Norris to the Supreme Court and that Norris withdraw. McIntyre did not think much of this suggestion. Norris is not going to withdraw. He also said that talking with May he could not be sure whether he was a big man or a heel. That May talked a great deal about having burned his bridges behind him and having a wife and a couple of children to support. "Maybe I was wrong," Mac said, "but I got the impression that he would be glad if someone would offer him ten or fifteen thousand dollars to get out of the race, or would make him a definite proposition if he would get out. I told him we would do no such thing, of course, but he would make friends here by withdrawing and that he would amount to something politically in Nebraska if he made the sacrifice in this race."

[May did not withdraw. In a three-way race Kenneth S. Wherry defeated Norris though with less than a majority vote. May received more than a hundred thousand votes. The story as told in Washington seemed to be that of an ambitious young man putting an end to the great career of a sage. Actually the political tragedy might better be told in reverse terms. When Norris at eighty-one indicated he would not seek re-election,

May, a popular radio broadcaster of thirty-six, sought and won the Democratic nomination. Then belatedly, under White House pressure, Norris changed his mind and ran as an independent. That ended the political careers of both Norris and May. May went to Europe as a war correspondent for NBC. In 1950, he underwent surgery for throat cancer. But he ran unsuccessfully as a voiceless candidate for secretary of state of Nebraska. In that year he was hospitalized for an overdose of sleeping pills. He moved to California in search of a cancer cure. He found none. When, at age forty-six, he was buried in Omaha in April 1952 only forty people attended the funeral.]

I asked McIntyre about the matter on which I reported to the President. He said, "Hell, you see the President as much as I do." I must have shown my surprise because he said, "Of course, I see him seven or eight times a day, but I never get a chance to talk to him any more and am hardly ever with him without somebody else. That is the reason I have to do a lot of these things that I do here without consulting him." I asked him how often the President's administrative assistants saw him and he said, "Only once in a great while. Of course, they are supposed to see him after the press conferences and they go up and whisper to him a minute or a minute and a half, but that is all they see him." When I told him that I had nothing to do and I was glad to do anything I could to help, he said, "We are going to get around to you as soon as we get a breathing spell."

He has very little hope that the Democrats will win in New York. The Jewish vote in the crucial race for governor there seems to be badly split because Dewey is attacking mobs of hoodlums that have been harassing Jews and the report is out that John J. Bennett, Jr., the Democratic candidate, attended a meeting of the Jew-baiting Christian Front. The President gave to the press this morning his telegram reiterating his strong support of Bennett. Some of Bennett's friends wanted the President to stop in New York at a big meeting to be addressed by Al Smith and Senator Robert Wagner, or to make a short radio address to the meeting. McIntyre, talking on the phone to Ed Flynn and others around Bennett's candidacy, thought that would look much like desperation.

Young Major Frank McCarthy was putting a dollar bill in his brief case. McIntyre asked him what it was for. He said he got a dollar every week and the Army had to arrange to get a dozen lemons to Biddle in London. [McCarthy, as military secretary to General Marshall, ran a regular schedule from the office of the Chief of Staff to the White House. A graduate, like General Marshall, of V.M.I., before the war McCarthy had been a reporter, a teacher, and a theatrical press agent. Later he was to be an Assistant Secretary of State and a prominent figure in movie production. His lemons were probably going to Eric Biddle, then head of a special Budget Bureau mission to Great Britain.] McIntyre said Mrs. Roosevelt is having trouble deciding what she ought to take to London, that when Hopkins went over he took all the wrong things, cabbages and potatoes when all they have to eat over there now is cabbages and potatoes.

McIntyre spoke of his good friend Ben Smith, who lives near Farley's home town, Grassy Point, New York, and the Christmas present he gave him just before the first inauguration. [Bernard Smith, wealthy New York stock-market operator.]

Lunch with Clarence Pickett of American Friends Service, who pointed out his feeling that postwar planning may take the form of Army administrators and technical commissions becoming the agents for an American capitalism under the name of the century of the common man. They would be the foreign emissaries of an American capitalism with plants which the big boys had picked up at bargain prices built by the government during the war, coupled with some continuance of manpower controls granted during the war.

Sunday, October 25. Lilienthal telephoned and then came out for a drink. He has been under quite a tugging and pulling strain with the War Production Board. [The WPB was established in January 1942, the month after Pearl Harbor, to exercise general direction over the war procurement and production program. Headed by Donald Nelson, former top executive of Sears, Roebuck, sometimes its operations not only baffled Lilienthal but also antagonized more powerful forces in the Pentagon. Lilienthal's complaint, whether or not he knew it then, related to the most significant and secret wartime operation—the development of the atomic bomb.]

Dealing with WPB takes forever, Lilienthal said, but the crowning situation of all is that which brought him to Washington. One branch of WPB has insisted that TVA produce power in new plants equal to the total present consumption of the city of Cleveland. The plants are already going up. One strange one he mentioned has been receiving the attention of the leading physicists of the country. It is a queer building, which I remember as something like a mile long and two or three hundred feet wide in which the pure science of atom smashing is going to be reduced to the applied science of war. However, another branch of WPB has recently sent them an order stopping the construction of power projects necessary to supply these plants which are being erected.

So far Lilienthal has not been able to get the two parts of WPB together. I mentioned this matter briefly to McIntyre, who said that Lilienthal's situation was simple, that he ought to say to Donald Nelson—here, we have two branches telling me different things. Mac added: "Lilienthal is a fine fellow but he hurts mighty easily. I have worked with him a lot. Also James Pope has done pretty well down there and I am crazy about old man Harcourt Morgan." I said I rather think that Pope has done well because he has had sense enough to let Lilienthal run the show. McIntyre agreed. When I later told Lilienthal about McIntyre's suggestion, he was glad to hear it but he indicated that for him to see Nelson was not a very easy matter. Today he said, "They have got a new committee to hear us, fully equipped with a mining engineer!"

It is interesting to watch Lilienthal's continuing emotional feeling about Willkie. Out of their experience Lilienthal finds Willkie a continually interesting man but one who is utterly a showman for himself. I remember his remark about how simple the second front looked to Willkie. Lilienthal spoke of John B. Blandford, Jr., formerly general manager of TVA, now with the National Housing Agency, in such a way as to indicate no feeling that Blandford is a miracle worker. He said he didn't know, but that whatever the cause, Housing did not seem to be working out.

He told the story about the meeting of directors of a great New York banking house at which one director who had been given a property to resuscitate reported the property to be even more in the red than when he took it, but eloquently and logically cited reasons why this was so. All the directors were gentlemen from the greater colleges and schools, sons of directors and the like, except one little director who had come up from the streets of Brooklyn. Comment on the report of the director went around the table with each one saying that he expected the situation could not have been bettered, until they came to the Brooklynite, who said, "As I get it, we won a moral victory."

"Maybe Housing is a moral victory," Lilienthal suggested, "but it doesn't seem to be a housing victory." I mentioned Keyserling's remark about the remodeling program to the effect that it would leave a lot of slums, and Lilienthal said, "I know Housing is full of doctrinaires."

*   *   *

Sunday-night supper at the residence on 36th Place of Donald Hall, first secretary of the British Embassy.

Donald Hall, bald, lanky, not stuffy, and his wife, prettyish, curly dark hair nice at the back of neck, but with the bird look so many English women have, coming, I think, from wide-apart deep-set eyes.

The Halls live in a modest white house, looking more like the home of an insurance man than that of a British diplomat. Small room, fire of logs which looked as if they had literally been acquired by "sticking" in the nearby suburban woods, small portrait of Mrs. Hall painted on wood above mantel. Only assistant at supper was a suburbanly conventional Negro man in white coat. Liquor set up on a card table. Hall broke the glass container full of red rum cocktail, but I had a weak scotch before supper—red American wine served straight out of half-gallon bottle of cheap Embros—one other scotch just before leaving.

Largely a war information company: Elmer Davis, director of OWI; Milton Eisenhower, assistant director. Other OWI men: Alan Cranston, Bradford Smith, Anthony and H. K. Hyde. Others present included: Good-looking Englishman, name not recalled; T. A. Roman, British journalist lecturing in U.S.; Dr. Liu Chieh, counselor of the Chinese Embassy, who did not open his mouth and kept his eyes shut most of the time. Lucy and some other wives.

Milton Eisenhower said that within last two weeks OWI had finally won right to be in on Navy and Army decisions as to withholding news, said only one piece of bad news now withheld—the loss of an aircraft carrier. Also, I think, three submarines—not putting it out because would soon be followed by an impressive roundup of the sinkings of enemy ships by our submarines and afraid public would feel that roundup after bad news was just something to palliate. I said I hoped they could get to a point where the news could be released as it came from the war just as news comes from a courthouse. He hoped and believed they would reach that point soon. He agreed with the suppression of the news of losses to Japs of men in raid on Tokyo. It was necessary to protect the men, some of whom were grounded in Chinese territory unoccupied by Japs which soon was occupied—and also to protect the missionaries who helped our flyers. Would have been a general massacre of missionaries if this had been known, but disagreed with the impression Army gave that all escaped from the raid.

[Eisenhower was referring here to the air raid on April 18, 1942, in which Lieutenant Colonel James H. Doolittle led sixteen Army Air Force B-25 bombers from the U. S. Navy aircraft carrier *Hornet* on a spectacular low-level attack against Tokyo and other Japanese cities. All of the planes were lost in bad weather over China but most of the crews were saved.]

Cranston told of Ruth Mitchell, sister of General Billy

Mitchell, who had just returned from Germany after imprisonment following her capture as a member of women Chetniks of Yugoslavia—says Germany collapsing—people know it—what is needed now, she is telling everybody, is a second front not to help Russians but to prevent the spread of Russian Bolshevism to the world over a collapsed Germany. Otherwise, victorious Russia will dominate world and impose Communism upon it, says best place for a second front is straight across the Mediterranean and up into Serbia—is telling that General William J. Donovan [Republican lawyer and World War I hero] of OSS has told her that whenever she wishes he will drop her back into Serbia by parachute.

Dr. T. A. Roman, diminutive, dark, former newspaperman in England and Europe and on two Indian newspapers, now an agent of the British Ministry of Information. This last fact was not mentioned, indeed it was rather suggested that he was an independent writer, nor was the fact concealed. Dr. Roman's description of the reason for the British failures in India seemed to pull India out of the air of mystery and the East and pulled the politicians of the Congress party to the stature of a body of Mississippi politicians. He has been close to Gandhi but apparently now regards him as irresponsible and perhaps dangerous. He has a great deal more hope in Pandit Nehru.

More significant was his description of some of the Congress members on the committee which negotiated with Sir Stafford Cripps. These men were elected in 1939 and could not, he thought, be considered as representative of Indian opinion today. Also, many of them are closely related to the small group of Indian industrialists. He indicated that the Cripps mission failed, not for lack of British generosity, but because some of these politicians felt that they had nothing to gain by assuming the responsibility of government in the midst of the war. If they postponed that responsibility and the British won, they would still have as good a chance of securing Indian independence after the war. If the Germans won, they would not have been in the position of having participated in independence against them.

He felt that the hope of settlement lay in the success of the present British administration in India and the failure of the nonviolence campaign against it. He said that enlistments in the Army have risen since the failure of the Cripps mission. United Nations rallies which have been held in towns and villages throughout India since that time give hope that the administration will succeed. It will have a better chance if there is some successful operation by the United Nations, for instance, in North Africa. He quoted, off the record, Nehru as answering a question he put to him—whether if he were given the power in India and Gandhi interfered with the fight for a United Nations victory, he would order his death; Nehru said he would.

"What would be the death of one old man when hundreds and thousands are dying?"

Dr. Roman also said that Gandhi's economic ideas are "of the vaguest" and that sometimes he is used by the rich industrialists who are interested only in making more money. He said that German propaganda had never been successful in India, that the people all regarded the Germans as brutes, but that the Japanese were more successful, particularly since they have made Indians governor of Burma and mayor of Singapore. These men broadcast in Hindustani to India. However, he said there were only 250,000 or so radio sets in India and only 12 per cent of the people are literate.

He made an impressive case, but I know that some of us and particularly young Bradford Smith, of OWI, felt a one-sided pro-British statement of the case. Dr. Roman grew sharp only at one point when he said that to suggest that the thousands of Indians enlisting in the Army are mercenaries for British pay is an insult to India. The men going in the British Army can now make much better livings outside and many of them come from good and well-to-do families and are not stooges of the British Empire.

Bradford Smith argued with Roman and later indicated he felt he was a British stooge, even though a sincere one.

Cranston and Anthony Hyde stopped by my house for beer. Hyde told story of ludicrous efforts of individual Germans to get a record made of individual acts of kindness in occupied countries as anchor to windward in case of defeat. "Here's a sandwich. Now write it down on such and such a date Hermann Kaufmann gave you a sandwich."

Monday, October 26. Dismal, rainy day. Went in the White House and McIntyre said suddenly, "It never pays to get mad." He went on to say that he was mad and for the first time had almost blown up his staff. It seems that he was expecting a phone call from young May in Nebraska with regard to the possibility of his withdrawal from the Senate race. He left word at the White House on Saturday where he was and to let him know. He called in twice on Saturday night to see if any call had come, and asked if there had been a telegram and was told that there was not.

This morning, on his arrival at the office, he was presented with the telegram from May which had arrived on Saturday, saying that an unbiased survey of the state by telephone indicated that Norris could not win and that his withdrawal would only mean the election of Wherry, the Republican candidate. In the telegram May repeated his friendship for the Administration. McIntyre was sore as hell that he did not receive this when it came. He seemed to have a better opinion of May today than last week. He said that Edwin W. Pauley, of the Democratic National Committee, had heard that the Republicans were underwriting his backers, but that May's monetary difficulty was not any desire for money for himself, but that he was caught in the fact that his friends had already spent ten or eleven thousand dollars for him. He rather felt that they were keeping him in the race and I get the feeling from him that he thought the National Committee might relieve May of this feeling of responsibility for his friends. McIntyre also suggested the possibility that rather than go down to defeat, old man Norris might make a gesture of withdrawal for unity.

We spoke about the fact that Norris is eighty-one and probably would not live out his term. McIntyre said it was hard for him to stomach when you had to go up on the Hill to urge him to run and Norris said, "Mac, I am lonely up here, all my friends are dead." McIntyre said, "Yes, but you don't realize how many of these young fellows up here, like Lister Hill, just depend on you."

Also McIntyre went again into another case of friction with General Watson, who got mad because McIntyre arranged through Hopkins for the President to see Representative Melvin J. Maas, a strong Republican on the Naval Affairs Committee who has just returned from service as a Marine colonel in the Pacific. "If the next President of the United States ever asks me for any advice," McIntyre said, "I am going to tell him not have but one secretary." And then he grinned and said, "Boy, I certainly could do that job."

Friday, October 30. McIntyre, speaking of the future of the President, said it was his present personal opinion that the President would not run for a fourth term. He also said that he had an idea for the future of the President, beyond the White House, which he had only mentioned to the President casually once or twice. It was for the creation of a great string of big newspapers, such as for instance *The New York Times,* all to be individually owned and published, but to be edited by the President. He spoke again of Ben Smith with the possibility that he could buy *The New York Times* for ten million dollars [*sic!*] and end up as something more than a Wall Street speculator. He felt that Mr. and Mrs. Joe Davies might buy another paper and that it would be possible to get wealthy friends of the President to put together such a tremendous news organization with some radio tie-up as well. The President could work in it with people he trusts "like Steve and you and me." McIntyre pointed out that at the end of his present term the President would be sixty-three and would have, at the very least, ten more years of active life. Incidentally, in this connection he pointed out that the President was not taking enough exercise—he hardly ever went into his pool any more. I gathered that the big newspaper idea was more McIntyre's baby than the President's.

Also, in discussing my own difficulties, McIntyre uncovered a case of his own hurt pride when he pointed out that in the current issue (fall of 1942) of the *Government Register,* the secretaries of the President are listed in order, Early, Watson, and McIntyre. McIntyre blames this on Mellett, who, he says, is an old woman and a troublemaker and without sense enough to get along with anybody. He indicated that he thinks Watson is a nice old fellow but very dumb. He has much more personal affection for Steve Early, who has been through the whole Roosevelt story with him, but said that once every month he has to go in and tell Early to go to hell and that soon afterwards Early comes in to tell him how much he loves him.

In conversation with Mellett he uncovered the increasing bitterness in Mellett's relationship with MacLeish. Mellett felt that he had been very helpful and kind to MacLeish but that MacLeish had interfered in his moving-picture operations improperly, under the pretense of a poetic innocence about such matters. He recalled that MacLeish had pretended at first that he did not want to be Librarian of Congress and that Mellett had to convince him against MacLeish's statement that he had a great poem brewing. Mellett was particularly bitter against Leo Rosten, the writer, who had been chief of the Motion Picture Division of the Office of Facts and Figures under MacLeish. Mellett felt Rosten wanted to take his job. Rosten had come to him to try to persuade him that he was too big to take a job in a subordinate capacity in OWI. Mellett felt that Rosten was giving him advice so he, Rosten, could get the job. Mellett felt also that MacLeish had tried to impose on the OWI his old system of deputies which he thought was administratively impossible since it prevented branch chiefs from dealing directly with other agencies. Mellett said that Cowles had rejected the whole idea as soon as he came back after Mellett had pointed out its difficulties.

Undated, October. Caught a ride downtown with a labor lawyer from Birmingham who has left CIO to work on the legal staff of United Mine Workers here. Spoke of the death of Mrs. John L. Lewis. "He is still Steel John," he said. "Undertaker did the best job on her I have ever seen. I have seen people fixed up after their heads were crushed in accidents, but she died of cancer of the brain and half her head was cut away." [Myria Edith Bell Lewis died in September while her husband was engaged in bitter intra-labor fighting with Philip Murray of the CIO and William Green of the AFL.]

Aubrey Williams' story of the coordinator: Young man sitting at a big desk in the lobby of a hotel terrifically busy, giving orders to everybody. Very old man with white beard came through the lobby with a big trunk on his back and carried it all the way up a long flight of stairs. Young man hollered at him "Come here." Old man turned around with the trunk and came all the way back downstairs. Young man, "Where are you going?" Old man, "Up those stairs." Young man, "Well, go on then."

Wednesday, November 4. Lyndon Johnson told me of a Mrs. Johnson who has about a thousand feet of floor space which she thought she could remodel into four rooms that could be rented to people in the District. Essential to the remodeling was the installation of bathing and toilet facilities. "She has got a couple of degrees, but I don't say that she is too smart, but I assigned a $3,800-a-year man to her who is supposed to be an expert at bottleneck breaking. They worked on it for a week or so and finally got to the man in charge of plumbing, etc., in WPB and never could get a yes or no answer as to whether they could put it in. But I wouldn't have given a damn which it was—if he had said, 'Hell no, you can't have it, we need it in the war effort.' But nobody could give us an answer one way or the other. The same sort of thing is happening all over the country."

Johnson thinks I made a serious mistake in not taking the Civil Aeronautics job. He says somebody could get in there and make a fight and beat on the table in the President's presence and get the future of aviation worked out. I told him I investigated the situation and presented it to the President; if the President had wanted to back me in a fight he could have given me that indication. Johnson said, "Hell no," that I would have to go in there first and then fight.

He said all the people I talked to in investigating it had some other candidate for the job.

*   *   *

Of yesterday's elections, Johnson said, "Sam (Rayburn) will have ten or twenty majority, I think, but in the majority there will be thirty or forty members who have the Democratic title but vote the Republican ticket. All the boys who went down were Roosevelt men, men who have voted with him come hell or high water. It looks like we lose thirty and could go as high as forty-five. I don't think we will lose the House, but unless Rayburn is awfully careful Joe Martin [Republican minority leader] is going to run the House with the help of some of the Democrats who were re-elected. We will have the chairmanships, but if two or three members of the committees vote with the Republicans, they will run it just the same."

[The importance of the control of Congress by a war leader had been demonstrated before Pearl Harbor when only weeks before the bombs fell the House had agreed to extension of the draft by only one vote—203 to 202. Now before the 1942 election Roosevelt's party support in the Congress and the country seemed seriously threatened. Johnson was not unduly pessimistic. In June 1942, the alignment in the Senate had been 65 Democrats, 29 Republicans, and two others. The division in the House was 262 Democrats, 166 Republicans, five of other designation, and two vacancies. After the 1942 election Democratic strength in the Senate had been reduced to 58 seats. The Republicans held 37. Again there was one Independent. In the House the Democratic strength had been reduced by almost fifty seats from 262 to 215. The Republicans were up from 166 to 210. Fortunately patriotism and partisanship were not identical. On some measures the President could count on more support from Northern Republicans than on such Southern Democrats whose conservatism tended toward the later Dixiecrat label. At the same time these Southerners had been less tainted by the prewar isolationism which in some measure lingered on.]

Johnson told me, "It just means Republicans in '44, that is all. There is not a doubtful state that did not go to town for the Republicans."

Of course, he went on, at a time like this the executive has got to be the central figure in all government but it has got to be able to work with the legislative department. "Can you name me one man in the administrative branch that ever got elected to anything?" I pointed out Secretary of State Cordell Hull, but agreed that the people who had been elected to anything were very few and far between. "This may jar us into something. We ought to find some people with some conceptions of the democratic process," Lyndon said.

I went over to the White House and found McIntyre very chipper, though definitely aware of the seriousness of the defeat. "What did you expect," he said, "with the National Committee we have got?" He had been up there last night, said he started to telephone me. The whole thing, he said, was ridiculous. There was practically nobody up there who knew anything about politics. People still think of Flynn as a ward heeler and Pauley is unpopular and unknown. There wasn't even anybody up there with enough knowledge of politics to be able to figure out the meaning of partial returns. [Edwin W. Pauley, California oil man, was the treasurer of the Democratic National Committee.]

I asked him if Flynn was going to be Ambassador to Mexico, and he said he didn't see how he could be anything. He has enough money, McIntyre said, and he didn't see how they owed him anything. I asked him who was available for chairman of the National Committee and he said, "Almost everybody I know agrees that the best man for the job is Alien Property Custodian, Leo Crowley. I don't think he is anxious for it, but I think he would take it if it was offered to him." [Crowley, a Catholic—as seemed to be required of the national chairman—had come from the paper and utility business into government as chairman of the

Federal Deposit Insurance Corporation. He was at this time Alien Property Custodian.]

McIntyre said that his report from the President in Hyde Park was that the President is not greatly disturbed by the election returns, and he felt that the President would not be much moved by them. He said in terrific confidence that he thought this man was more immune to it than Wilson had been, but that he began to be surrounded by people who only told him what he wanted to hear about himself. He particularly mentioned Anna Rosenberg. Said he went into the President's office when Anna was there and the President mentioned some idea, McIntyre said it was so obvious that he had thought about it himself and Anna Rosenberg immediately began to pat herself on the knees and say how wonderful, what a mark of genius. McIntyre made a face as if he were saying a dirty word. "No wonder he lets her in to see him all the time," he said.

I also got the impression that he felt that the President was unfortunate in seeing only Hopkins so much of the time. He spoke again of his feeling that Leon Henderson's distribution of jobs has been fatal for the party and of the time that he spoke to Hopkins about it and Hopkins said, "For Christ's sake, Mac, lay off of Leon, he has got the hardest job in the war effort." This made McIntyre pretty mad, I gathered.

He said that Hopkins had been trying to run for President in 1940 and that Howard Hunter and others were going around the country trying to build up his stock. McIntyre said he spilled that right before the Boss when, in regard to some matter, he said, "Harry, I don't know whether you know it and I can say it to you because you have done a good job, but you are about the most unpopular man in the country. You make one set of people mad because they think you are giving away their money and you make another set of people mad because you have given them the money and nobody thinks he gets as much as he thinks he ought to have. I don't know whether you think you are going to be President or not, but you ought to call off these boys of yours who are trying to run you."

He said Senator Joe Guffey of Pennsylvania had called him up this morning, mad about the results of the election, and that in his conversation he had said that Hopkins had told him the President wanted him to run Bill Bullitt for governor because the President wanted to build Bullitt up for the presidency in 1944. McIntyre expressed his disgust at the thought that Bullitt could be elected to the presidency, and told the story about Hopkins thinking that he might run as an example of Hopkins' political stupidity.

We went into Steve Early's office to look at the news ticker. The room was empty and McIntyre said, "Here is the trouble around here. As soon as the President goes out of town Steve and Pa just disappear." McIntyre did not seem to be of the opinion that the President would devote himself to building up the party strength between now and the 1944 campaign.

To correct the impression perhaps made earlier, McIntyre said that he went to see Norris to try to persuade him to run a long time ago, but that Norris declined. "If he hadn't dilly-dallied to the last minute," he said, "he could have been elected."

Called up Dave Niles to ask him how bad the election returns looked. "It looks like Texas is all right," he said.

Returns may indicate many things: War has solved the economic problems of most people. No longer feel need of fighting for New Deal. Also FDR in war administration has turned to anti-New Deal leaders in industry and business. As a result, does not seem to have created a new political unity taking strength from the right. At same time political unity of Administration has been weakened. Lack of political coordination among Democrats shown by Rayburn's resentful sense of not being in on things so far as President is concerned, President's slaps at the Congress in which his party had a majority, Leon Henderson's disregard of Democratic congressmen and senators and dependence on governors regardless of politics in OPA patronage. McIntyre at the White House has been talking contemptuously of work of National

Committee. Even leadership in Congress seemed to have low opinion of work of Democratic Congressional Committee under Patrick Henry Drewry, who holds job on seniority basis —sixty-seven years old.

But White House, while following a deliberate general course of "no politics in war," has apparently been ill-advised on every entry into politics: Waited until late to support nomination of Senator James M. Mead against Bennett in New York—lost; waited until late and got charged with halfheartedness in support of Bennett against Tom Dewey. Waited until late (apparently) in getting old man Norris into Senate race. (Norris did the delaying.) Showed only slight interest and cooperation to young Lyndon Johnson, who tried to get things going during last month on congressional elections. General Watson put off and put off his seeing the President. President and his advisers may have been wise in overriding Rayburn's objections to raising 18–19-year-old draft within two weeks of election—maybe not.

Hard to see any good in President's recent attacks on press. Also political fumbling in bringing case against *Chicago Tribune* which could not be sustained. Doubtful wisdom also in suit against Associated Press. [The government's antitrust case against the Associated Press followed the *Tribune*'s veto of the request of the pro-FDR *Chicago Sun* for AP news service. The Supreme Court in 1945 upheld the government's contention that such denial of service to a competitive paper was an illegal monopolistic practice. However, the hostility of the President and the *Tribune* was no secret. Neither was FDR's welcome to the new *Sun*. Many regarded the case against the AP as a punitive action against the *Tribune*. Also, some in the Administration believed that in the publication of a verbatim war message the *Tribune* had provided information which threatened the security of a major secret code. It was said that action could not be taken in this matter without disclosing in court even more vital information. So this case was dropped.]

Main difficulty seems to me to lie in lack of real ability of President to talk plain to his own government. Well understood in White House, if not by President, that many officials are politically antagonistic to the administration in which they work. This coupled with fact that no real mutuality of action exists between the Democratic majority in Congress and the administrative branch of the Roosevelt administration.

The President, though master politician, not interested in party politics now, and seems to be sometimes acting in politics on advice of poor and unrealistic political advisers.

Friday, November 6. McIntyre says he (the President) is finding it awfully hard to be polite to me these days, I am bearing down on him too hard. "By golly, Monday we begin to work. Joe Guffey tells me that neither he nor any of the President's friends have been able to have a real conference with him for a year on political matters."

In his office after the cabinet meeting this afternoon, McIntyre conferred with Postmaster General Frank Walker, Attorney General Francis Biddle, and Jesse Jones. McIntyre outlined his plan in general to be a reorganization of the National Committee and the creation of an over-all policy committee to consider all matters of policy and report to the President with regard to that. He really seems to be pushing the President pretty hard to get his mind on politics and domestic questions.

I asked him if Budget wasn't supposed to do what the over-all committee would do and he said, "No, Budget has nothing to do with policy matters. Besides, I don't quite trust Wayne Coy, he is smart all right, but he is so personally ambitious—there hasn't been an important job suggested since he has been around here that he hasn't recommended himself for."

* * *

In McIntyre's office yesterday morning, after talking to me about his strong feeling that a good deal of reorganization had to be effected both in the Democratic National Committee and the government itself, he said, "I am going to call up

Jimmie Byrnes," and did forthwith. He told Byrnes that they are going to have to get together and talk and also talk with the Boss about the situation. He felt that changes were necessary, extending perhaps to three members of the Cabinet, whom he did not name. He said that he had talked around and Leo Crowley seemed to be the best man for the chairmanship of the Democratic National Committee. "I understand he is well heeled again," McIntyre said, "he lost a lot of money in 1929 but I understand he has made it back. He would be the best man for the post."

After talking to Byrnes he said to me, rather casually, "I think that the place for you is vice-chairman of the Democratic National Committee. In that spot you could receive a nominal salary and have plenty of time to do your own writing and speaking on the side." I did not say definitely that I did not want the job, but definitely did not pursue it. I have no inclination to get directly into politics. I didn't want to make any argument about it. Apparently McIntyre and some people around the President feel more strongly than the President himself does that considerable reorganization is in order. McIntyre said that the President got irritated with him yesterday morning for talking about failures in organization.

Lunch with Herman Kehrli of the Budget, who seemed very much worried about the whole civilian mobilization aspect of OCD. He said they had had Landis for a session the night before and that he thought that at last he was very much worried about the situation. Kehrli tried to find out from me how strongly the President would support Landis, but while I said I thought the President approved the course I had taken, I said he had never made any comment to me about Landis or his feeling of how well he is doing the OCD job. Kehrli had the feeling that while Landis had lost much prestige in Washington, in the country he has not, that there is still a feeling there that he took on a very tough job and that things are going on better than they were. He wanted to know if I felt that OWI ought to, in effect, force OCD to take on the full speaking job. I told him that I doubted the wisdom of making them do the job if they were not enthusiastic about it. He said they were also having trouble in the facilities security program, that at the beginning Landis had felt that he must have an Army officer. Kehrli urged him just to get a good man and now things are not going too well and that Philip Bastedo, assistant to Landis, pops in on occasion to deal with matters in connection with it and then out. In the afternoon after I had left Kehrli, Miss Brubaker, in charge of the Director's files, called Mrs. Brite to ask what had happened to the correspondence with regard to the creation of an interagency committee designed to create order in federal programs in which OCD assisted. The correspondence had been given to Bastedo on September 11, after all the agencies had agreed to appoint members on the committee. Apparently nothing had been done about the matter since that time.

At cocktails with Louis Weiss, he expounded the theory that what had happened in the election was that the old-guard politicians and particularly the Catholics had deliberately sold the New Deal down the river, seeing that the time had come when they could take over again. In effect, he charged a sort of Machiavellian conspiracy to Jim Farley, who, seeing that he was going to be defeated in the Bennett race, undertook to get his fellow Catholics in politics to sabotage the ticket in strategic centers. He spoke of Boston and New York, Boss Frank Hague of Jersey City, and mentioned Butte, Montana. I pointed out that the situation in New York might better be explained by refusal of the Jews to vote for Bennett on account of the Christian Front issue. Weiss showed a certain sensitivity about this and the necessity to justify himself. He said that the Catholic bishop, Thomas E. Molloy of Brooklyn, who is the "Bishop of the Christian Front," was at the Democratic convention in which Bennett was nominated, giving orders to the Brooklyn delegation. He indicated the intensity of feeling between the Jewish and Catholic groups, a feeling which he shares.

[In his "no politics" frame of mind at this time the President seemed to have fumbled badly in this election. His old friend and now his feuding enemy, James A. Farley, played no stand-off game. He had successfully pushed for the Democratic gubernatorial nomination of New York Attorney General John J. Bennett, Jr., whom Roosevelt did not want and Roosevelt's liberal and labor friends could not support. Still Roosevelt gave the nominee what at the time was called "mild and dutiful" endorsement. Actually Bennett's defeat by Thomas E. Dewey could not have been too distasteful to FDR, much as he disliked Dewey. A Bennett victory would have meant Farley control of the New York delegation in the Democratic National Convention of 1944.

[The Christian Front founded by Father C. E. Coughlin was regarded as sharing Nazi anti-Semitic views.]

* * *

After dinner last night my brother, Worth, now colonel in the Army Medical Corps, spoke of the amazing delays due to red tape in the Army. Sometimes when they are checking as to whether the Army owes a man $2.00 or the man owes the Army $1.00, the man will be kept in the hospital before discharge for many days at a cost to the government of approximately $5.00 a day. Other such delays in discharge cause an amazing loss in manpower, he thinks.

Saw at the Carlton bar Dave Cohn with a couple of Englishy-looking gentlemen, Jimmie Byrnes coming in with the fat, bright Pritchard boy, and Dave Niles leaving Agnes Inglis and myself to run speak to Byrnes.

Sunday, November 15. Supper Sunday night at Drew Pearson's house. Went in and found Luvie Pearson and Robert Pell, of the State Department information division, had practically filled the house with smoke in an effort to light a fire in the big fireplace at the back of the Georgetown house. Present at dinner, in addition to Pell, was Captain Horace Fuller, Boston, college mate and friend of Jimmy Roosevelt, who was recently invalided from Guadalcanal because of malaria. Fuller an honest, attractive young man, devoting his fifteen days' leave to trying to stir up newspapermen, members of Congress, and others with regard to his feeling that the Marines on Guadalcanal were disgracefully deserted. At the same time he gave a vivid picture of the situation at Guadalcanal, and the terrific strain the Marines underwent in the jungle under constant Japanese bombardment.

[The Americans had landed on Guadalcanal on August 7 and at this time the fighting was most furious. It was not until February of the following year that the Japanese withdrew after the loss of 24,000 men. American losses in action were much lighter, though many like Fuller were stricken with tropical diseases.]

Fuller is bitter against MacArthur, whom he called "Dougout Doug," representing the Marines' feeling that MacArthur is never nearer fighting than a dugout, and against the older officers of the Navy, who he felt did not know how to fight modern war. He said that the transports which landed the Marines sailed off without landing their equipment, and that although they were promised aerial support the next day, they didn't get any planes for about ten days, but that when the planes came you could hear the shearing through the jungle as they moved up toward the airport.

For both Fuller and Drew Pearson the supper had ulterior purposes; Fuller was anxious to load up Pearson and Pearson was anxious to get copy out of him. I was not going to be a party to any such general criticism of the Administration, though much that Fuller said seemed true. I suggested that it seemed clear now that the job of equipping the African undertaking made it impossible to give all the equipment desired in Guadalcanal. Pell was pretty cagey too. Pearson read a long letter from an unnamed naval reserve officer who had been in the battle of Midway [June 3–5, 1942] and other fighting in the Pacific in which he was highly critical of the Naval Academy officers who are his superiors. Fuller said that he thought Jimmy Roosevelt called his father from the West Coast to tell him the same sort of things that he, Fuller, was telling in Washington.

Later Lucy and I drove Fuller home to the Wardman Park Hotel. As we went into the drive a big car with a New York license was parked across the driveway and an Army officer in uniform was helping a lady shoot her lunch in the shrubbery. Fuller got out and got the car to move over and we went by to drop him at his hotel.

Incidentally, without naming him, I spoke to McIntyre about this young officer the next day. His reaction was that officers coming back and running around to Congress and newspapermen ought not to be encouraged, but really ought to be court-martialed.

Monday, November 16. McIntyre hopes that on the basis of what I told him today, I will recommend in my report to the President that the government of occupied areas be placed under the direction of the State Department, in collaboration with such agencies as Federal Reserve, Treasury, food, justice agencies in the government. There must be a point where the Army is in control, but as soon as possible civilians should take over.

M. S. Szymczak, member Federal Reserve Board, says that the school at Charlottesville, in which he has been offered a commission as lieutenant colonel, seems to be modeled on the schools maintained by the German and Japanese armies. Szymczak is going to make a supplementary report with regard to the financial situation. He pointed out to me that all sorts of difficulties are created when our currency goes into occupied regions. It immediately goes into hoarding while the other currencies are circulated, creating alarming conditions of inflation.

Tuesday, November 17. Sumner Welles feels very strongly against the school at Charlottesville, says the State Department was consulted about the matter only in a very casual way until about three weeks ago. The President told him that there was a sign over the door of the school at Charlottesville that no friend of the Administration can enter here. Says that the State Department does have in its auxiliary staff men who could be used in the government of occupied territories. Also that in part the work is being planned in Relief and Rehabilitation under Dean Acheson. Says that in the occupation of North Africa plans were worked out whereby Robert Murphy, who has been in North Africa, is in effect doing this work. He is under Eisenhower, but the State Department is sending him some five or six well-qualified men to assist in his work; that in the whole North African venture the State Department worked out relationships with other concerned agencies. Abe Fortas, of the Interior Department, recently suggested to him some sort of committee of departments which could do the planning for occupied countries.

The President's word for this occupation is "trusteeship" and Mr. Welles feels that this is a very good time to bring that philosophy to this matter. He definitely feels that the Army has gone ahead with this thing without properly consulting the State Department, though a great part of the question is political. Welles feels that the Army school is based on the planning of German and Japanese schools and represents the same philosophy.

Recommend Lilienthal to head Army Occupation Authority, as the American who has the best possible approach to the administration of large-scale policy in terms of local people involved.

Went to see Szymczak, Federal Reserve Board. He told me about going to the West Coast at the urging of the Treasury to get the San Francisco Federal Reserve Bank to take over the job of handling the property of the Japanese. After he was halfway through the job of browbeating and arguing people into working together and prying information out of General Dewitt as to what he planned to do, it suddenly developed that Leo Crowley as Alien Property Custodian had been given control and Morgenthau had no authority. He would like very much to have the opportunity to do a big job in fiscal matters, but he does not want to be left at a desk in the War Department where he cannot do a job. I think he would like to go to North Africa if he could go with authority and as one of the governors of the Federal Reserve System.

Thursday, November 19. Went to War Department and saw the Provost Marshal General, Major General Allen W. Gullion, pleasant, amusing, youngish-looking man who said that he was the most surprised man in the world at the charge

Portrait of Daniels as newspaper editor by Robert Shoaf, 1941.

Eleanor and Franklin Roosevelt were still unmarked by
war in this picture made for Christmas 1941.

Prewar. Daniels interviewing in the defense boom
at Alexandria, Louisiana. December 1941.

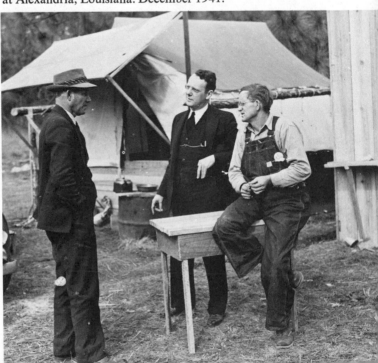

Magazine picture of a wartime family in Washington.
Jonathan and Lucy Daniels with their four daughters.

Roosevelt wore his naval cape as Commander in Chief in this portrait done by Elizabeth Shoumatoff in 1943.

Congressman Lyndon B. Johnson in 1942 seemed still a sort of campus politician in his commander's uniform.

On the day in 1943
that President Roosevelt
began his eleventh year
as Chief Executive, he
is shown in his study at
the White House with his
secretaries.
Left to right, Marvin
McIntyre, Grace Tully,
Stephen Early, Major
General Edwin Watson.

William D. Hassett
— for his literate aid
FDR called him his Bartlett,
Roget, and Buckle.

Clare Boothe Luce, to FDR "a Vanity Fair Huey Long."

David Lilienthal, great shepherd of the Valley of the Promise of Life. At his TVA desk in World War II.

James M. Barnes, genial Illinois ex-congressman, whose polite poker playing made him useful as a presidential aide.

Bernard M. Baruch (right), who basked on his Lafayette Square bench like a behind-the-scenes Disraeli, photographed with Wendell L. Willkie, 1942.

Harry Hopkins looked
like Death on the way
to a frolic.

Jonathan Daniels
appearing before the Senate
Agriculture Subcommittee,
in connection with Harry
Slattery's resignation, 1944.

Life printed as its "Picture of the Week" in December 1944 this photo of Jonathan Daniels as he seemed to be bringing the White House line to *(left to right)* Sidney Hillman, C. B. (Beanie) Baldwin, Philip Murray, Henry Wallace, and James Carey (head of the Electrical Workers Union). Actually Daniels, on his way to Denver, had only dropped in for lunch at the CIO convention then in session.

Jonathan Daniels was threatened with citation for contempt for refusal to testify about the Slattery case when Jim Berryman drew this cartoon for the *Washington Star.*

—STILL HE WONT COME DOWN!

All Good Wishes to Jonathan Daniels
WITH FOND RECOLLECTIONS OF YOUR FINE FATHER

he had been hearing that he was getting ready to be prepared to take over the whole federal government, that he was training a whole body of gauleiters at Charlottesville, and that all the people at Charlottesville were enemies of the Administration. When I went into the room he introduced himself by saying, "I am a Kentucky Democrat and I was New Dealer enough to run the NRA [National Recovery Administration] in Hawaii." He said that the school was established as a result of a staff proposal that such a school was necessary.

Afterwards he introduced me to the school's commandant, General Cornelius W. Wickersham, a nervous man with his gray hair parted in the middle, nicotine-stained fingers. He has a tic in his face which shows itself in a constant nervous blinking of his eyes. He introduced me to Colonel Jesse I. Miller, a diminutive Jew, pertly intelligent, who speaks with a Southern accent. Both of them were defensive as Gullion had been.

Miller said that he had heard it charged that the school was trying to turn out a body of incompetent imperialists. Both of them, however, completely defended the quality of men that they are getting and the type of work the school is training them to do. General Wickersham read me a long passage from the War Department Basic Manual of Military Government, which stressed the fact that emphasis must be placed upon "such just consideration and mild treatment of the governed by the occupying army as will convert enemies into friends." Miller expressed the opinion that, if anything, the school had been teaching too humane a doctrine and said that while he favored it, he sometimes doubted whether it would work with the Japanese.

Neither felt that the lawyer influence at the school was too great. Both thought the school had profited by Army rules putting top limit upon the ages at which men can have combat duty in certain ranks. It also profited, Miller thought, by getting good National Guard and Reserve officers whose commands were taken away from them for the benefit of Regular Army men.

In my preliminary talk with Gullion he mentioned the fact

that Lieutenant Governor Albert Carmichael of Alabama was the only man he had personally selected and he did that at the solicitation of Lister Hill—or, on the nomination of the man who nominated the President. He mentioned that they hoped to have Szymczak soon. General Wickersham indicated he might get Charles Poletti [who had succeeded Herbert Lehman as governor of New York when Lehman, FDR's successor in that post, resigned to become director of foreign relief and rehabilitation operations in the State Department] and one or two other persons of prominence in New York. Wickersham appealed to me most as a well-meaning, ineffectual gentleman. I gathered from Miller's attitude that his subordinates are respectful of him, but a little contemptuous at the same time.

I think Miller and Wickersham are both sincere, but neither impressed me as being big enough to shape the body of men who will administer the world. Apparently only about two or three people in each class have flunked. My feeling after seeing them is that the school is a well-intentioned mediocrity.

[A month before I made this entry the President, on October 29, had written rather sharply to Secretary of War Henry L. Stimson about the school. His memo said, "This whole matter is something which should have been taken up with me in the first instance. The governing of occupied territories may be of many kinds but in most instances it is a civilian task and requires absolutely first-class men and not second-string men."

[As was the case often in FDR's operations, I was not the only man assigned to look into this matter. William C. Bullitt, recently Ambassador to France, evidently made a more favorable report about it to the President in December. On December 30 he wrote Undersecretary of War Patterson that he had assured the President that "accusations against the school were without foundation," and that he should "cease to worry" about it. However, Bullitt suggested that the President might have somebody else take another look during the following February.

[In that month I gave the President another report on a memo he had sent me which he had received from Secretary of Interior Harold Ickes proposing some interdepartmental participation in the school's selection and training of the military governors. I told him that I thought such a plan "might insure the proper democratic attitude in the selection, training, and use of men who, as our representatives, will be responsible for the American impression" in the postwar world.

[Provost Marshal Gullion was not pleased by this presidential nosiness into his plans. He wrote the President's appointments secretary, General Watson, that "our military government plans have been attacked as unprecedented, un-American, imperialistic, grandiose and personally ambitious." The General was overwrought in his reaction. The school survived until 1946, during which time it graduated 2,905 officers for occupation duties. In general they performed well but this presidential inquisitiveness may have served to emphasize his concern about the kind and quality of the government of the conquered that he meant to have. And that may have been the most important lesson taught in the school.]

Wednesday, November 25. Lunch at the Cosmos Club. Present, Isador Lubin, Assistant Secretary of the Interior, Oscar Chapman, Aubrey Williams, Abe Fortas, soon to be Undersecretary of Interior, colonel (named Ed), a dark young man, Mordecai Ezekiel, Paul Porter, a silent man, Harry White, and Pritchard.

White brought up the question as to what could be done to prevent the Republicans from taking over in '44. Two lines of thought were presented. Lubin led in the presentation of the necessity for some real organization of the forces interested in the continuation of the New Deal. Aubrey Williams insisted that organization was less important than the presentation to the people of a real fighting philosophy: What the aftermath of the war would mean to the ordinary man and how the recurrence of such a war could be prevented. It was pointed out that the two positions were not antagonistic. I raised the point that there were no congressmen present, which seemed to be one evidence of the lack of necessary efforts to make the New Deal a team. Committees were appointed to look into both these aspects of the problem and to report at a night meeting with some plans for action (on the evening of Monday, December 14th). We agreed that nothing would be said about this.

Earlier at the luncheon Aubrey Williams said he wanted me to write an article entitled "It is not the time," the substance of which would be to say that with regard to advance of the Negro there never had been a time when the people did not say "it is not the time." He is going to see A. Philip Randolph [President of the Brotherhood of Sleeping Car Porters] and said he would like to talk to me before he goes.

* * *

David Lilienthal phoned from New York on Monday saying he wanted to see me about an important matter on Tuesday. Came to my office this afternoon very much steamed up about the whole idea of making the TVA plan a model for the occupation and development of countries after this war. He feels, as I do, that the emotional meaning of such words as democracy, etc., has grown pretty thin and that only as working democracy is shown in such tangible terms as water and soil can we really catch the enthusiasm and help countries in such a way as to develop a lasting peace.

I showed him my report on the School of Military Government which I had made to the President in which I had suggested very much the same thing, naming Lilienthal as a man with the most knowledge of the TVA brand of democracy. Lilienthal talked of writing articles or a book on methods by which his idea might be put into the public mind. He was very much interested in the work to which Governor Lehman has been appointed as director of the Office of Foreign Relief and Rehabilitation, and was anxious, if possible, to arrange some sort of meeting with him. Also he had an engagement to see Vice-President Wallace, who, in his recent speech on the anniversary of the founding of the Russian republic, spoke of an international TVA as an aspect of the peace after this war. Dave had planned to write a book about TVA itself, but I suggested that if he wishes immediate results for his ideas in terms of planning after the war, it might be a good idea to take Wallace's suggestion as a beginning, briefly and with broad strokes outline certain river systems and regions of the world which might be developed under the TVA plan, then go into the TVA experience and apply that experience to the world. He liked the idea and I expect he plans to undertake it.

As he was leaving he said almost casually that he figured that it was time for him to leave TVA, that he was under no illusions about the work being done there, but it rather irritated him when people, in resigning, suggested that they had done everything. However, he felt that a man can overstay his time on such a job and he believed he ought to be moving to other fields. He said he had no specific ideas. My own feeling was that he was eager to have the chance to put these ideas into being, but he insisted, rather overinsisted, I thought, that he was only interested in the ideas themselves.

In connection with his interest in Lehman's job, I said that I felt it would be impossible to name him to work with Lehman because, while the appointment of one Jew to feed Europe, where the Jew has been so mistreated by Hitler, was a grand gesture, that I did not think two Jews could be named. I had the feeling that Lilienthal is almost overmodest, almost falsely modest, about his insistence that he is not interested in anything for himself. I spoke about this later in the evening to Lucy, who is very fond of him, and she said, "Don't you realize that a part of his strength is that he goes all the way from the extreme of the brassy Jew?"

Lilienthal phoned to say he had had a long and very satisfactory talk with Vice-President Wallace, who seemed entirely sympathetic with his ideas [about overseas occupations as opportunities for the development of the world's resources for the benefit of its people everywhere], and that Wallace said that he felt Lilienthal ought to see the President about them. Lilienthal said of course he would be delighted to see him, but would not like to make the move to ask for an appointment. I gathered that Wallace said he would tend to that. I told Lilienthal that I understood that Paul Appleby would be set up in the State Department to deal with this problem.

"Then count me out," said Lilienthal, indicating that he felt that Appleby represented the Department of Agriculture type of operation in AAA [the Agricultural Adjustment Administration]. Lilienthal spoke about the President's statement at the press conference yesterday with regard to plans for rehabilitating distressed and impoverished countries after the war, which includes more than merely feeding, but a longer-range program for the permanent well-being of less fortunate countries. I wondered when I read this in the morning paper whether my memorandum to the President on military government had entered at all into his thinking. I gave him my report on Friday [November 20], urging such a development as Lilienthal is urging. This statement of the President's came on the 24th.

I told Dave that in view of all the circumstances I hoped he would not plan to do anything precipitate about his suggestion that he might resign. He said no, in any event, he had not thought about resigning until next spring. On the phone at the White House this morning McIntyre suggested to Appleby that he might very well get in touch with me since I had made some investigation of plans with regard to military government. McIntyre also said that General Gullion had said that he had a very interesting talk with me and that also Bill Bullitt had come to see him saying that the President had asked him to look into the matter.

Lilienthal today reiterated the fact that he is not interested in any job in this business, but my own hunch is that he would jump at the chance.

Monday, November 30. Appleby says that the distinction between himself and Lehman is that Lehman's appointment, in effect, is his nomination to be the head of the relief and rehabilitation program of the United Nations. He will, in a sense, be not an American, but a United Nations official, and his present job is the grooming of himself for that work. Presumably he will work under the direction of a United Nations council. On the other hand, Appleby is planning now to create the staff for military government in various occupied countries. He seems to have the job which I outlined in my memorandum to the President and he is under the impression that I was partially responsible for its creation. I don't know whether I am or not. His job is certainly exciting but I don't know what places there are in it. Also he said that he worked best with people that he knew and I gathered that he has considerable staff in mind from his contacts in Agriculture and Lend-Lease.

Appleby is sending on Monday a mission to North Africa. He asked me if I thought there was any use in saving the School of Military Government at Charlottesville and whether the staff they have produced would be any good. He is very anxious to get a staff of New Dealers to organize this whole world occupation effort. Apparently he has full charge of that. He hopes to have Dean Acheson, who has been handling relief and rehabilitation in the State Department. Appleby is attached theoretically to the State Department's Division of European Affairs, but he took the job only on condition that he is responsible only and directly to the Secretary of State himself. All the planning is based on the idea of the creation of a United Nations Authority, which will do the whole job.

Appleby told of a dinner given when the School of Military Government at Charlottesville was first being projected, which Pat Jackson had attended as a substitute for him. Said under the conditions, Jackson was very quiet, but late in the evening he asked one question. He asked General Wickersham what they were doing to see to it that the officers chosen had the proper attitude with regard to democracy, race, etc. General Wickersham blinked and looked confused. "Why, nothing," he said, "we presume that they are correct because these men were chosen by the Army."

*   *   *

McIntyre spoke of General Watson. "He has got sense enough to be a military aide, but he really is almost a half-wit."

Met Henry Kaiser at the White House this morning. Big, impressively vital individual. Spent a good deal of time with McIntyre, who said later, "I know what he wanted to see me about, he wanted me to get the President interested." Kaiser left some beautifully bound books containing designs of radical innovations in warships.

[Kaiser had emerged as a sort of Paul Bunyan of the West in the swift building of desperately required ships. He had emerged from highway construction and the building of great dams to ship construction in clamorous, hard-driven shipyards. In September before this visit to the White House, Kaiser in his yards at Portland had shown Roosevelt a completed ship whose keel had been laid only ten days before. He was becoming a legend and he knew it.]

McIntyre said he talked to the President and Judge Sam Rosenman today, reminding them to remember my name in connection with personnel to be considered in the reorganization moves now planned.

McIntyre also said, when I asked him about Eugene Casey, who has the title of Special Executive Assistant to the President, as to what he did, "I don't know what the son-of-a-bitch does. Here is another expense account from him and I will be damned if I am going to approve it. Steve says I ought to fire him. Some time ago the President said that he worked for me, but I don't think it is up to me to fire him."

Tuesday, December 1. At the White House this morning found McIntyre and Miss Jackson and Rudolph Forster, career director of the White House Office Staff, chatting around McIntyre's desk. McIntyre was grumbling about the President doing things he ought not to do.

"Maybe I am wrong," he said, "Steve and the others think I am, but I was talking to him this morning about a thing I think is liable to raise a stink. They are going to make a picture called *The Travels of Fala*. There is a little woman up at the library at Hyde Park, 'a little wren.' She sits around just adoring the President and he likes to have her around. She can't write, but she has written this scenario and has sold it to the movies. They are going to make a short of Fala at the Atlantic

Charter signing, etc. The President has agreed to have his picture taken in a short piece to go with other pieces collected from the newsreels. It is going to get Harry Hopkins in trouble, too, for Diana is running around in it and everybody is going to think Harry got something out of it. The President did it because he wanted to do something to help this woman—and he is just a good-natured sap. That is all he is. He would do anything for me if I would let him—and he thinks this Fala is the smartest dog that ever lived. Hell, I had a dog that was twice as smart as Fala is. I like dogs—the only thing I like better are cats. My idea of solid comfort is to sit reading with a cat in my lap and just pat her. But the President is just a good-natured sap." [The "little woman" in this case was Margaret Suckley, called "Daisy," a cousin of the President, who had given Fala to him.]

*   *   *

Mrs. Crystal Bird Fauset came in with many umbrellas, galoshes, gloves, etc., to discuss the Negro question, which she brought to McIntyre at the White House this morning. She is very anxious that the President, before the end of the year, see Dr. Mordecai Johnson, president of Howard University, as a representative of the Negro race and hear from him about the Negroes and the war. Mrs. Fauset is speaking frankly as a Democratic politician. She thinks this would be a good beginning of an effort to secure the Negro vote in 1944.

She believes that Johnson would be accepted by all Negroes as a fair representative. She says that the President has seen no Negro political group since 1936 and no Negro group of any sort since the war started. Indeed she said unless he has seen Lester Walton, Minister to Liberia, who is being kept on the shelf in this country, he has seen no Negro officially since the war began. She does not think that Frederick Patterson, of Tuskegee, or Dr. Charles Johnson, of Fisk, would be acceptable substitutes, and if Mordecai Johnson is not the man, she would prefer Channing Tobias, prominent black figure in YMCA and other welfare activities. We discussed the possibility of sending an able, tactful Negro to Liberia in Lester Walton's place.

Mrs. Fauset says that when she wrote a letter to John McCormack with regard to the political situation among the Negroes, somehow the letter got into the hands of Lawrence Cramer, executive secretary of the FEPC [Fair Employment Practices Committee], and that from Cramer the letter, which I gathered was critical of trends into which Philip Randolph and others were leading the Negroes, was distributed and carbon copies sent to Mary McLeod Bethune, director of Negro Affairs in the National Youth Administration, Randolph, Walter White, and others. She feels that Malcolm S. MacLean [chairman of the FEPC and president of Hampton Institute] and Cramer are both anxious to use the Negro as a means of getting closer to the President and to power.

Cramer resisted transfer of his committee to Manpower because, as he told the President, he wanted the President to get all the credit with the Negroes for what was done. When it was transferred, he told McNutt that he wanted him to get all the credit for what was done. Also she says that in order to have full control Cramer began a campaign to take over Dr. Will Alexander and Dr. Robert Weaver, who had been dealing with these questions in Manpower before the Cramer committee was attached to it. In order to do this Cramer sought the support of the Democratic National Committee. Mrs. Fauset said she stopped that. [Weaver, black economist, later became, under President Johnson, Secretary of the Department of Housing and Urban Development.]

Then Cramer began to cry through the Negro press to the effect that the committee was losing its power and Randolph and White, who feel that the committee is their creature, came to its assistance. Just before the election, she said, Fowler Harper, deputy chairman of the War Manpower Commission, had told her so. MacLean went to McNutt and Harper and told them that if they did not transfer Alexander and Weaver to a position under the committee they would lose votes among the Negroes. McNutt resisted, but under this threat Harper says he agreed and secured the agreement of McNutt.

Wednesday, December 2. I told Dr. Alexander, in reference to Mrs. Fauset, as I had mentioned to Lucy the evening before, that that afternoon I had spoken with a cream-colored lady who I imagined must have been a very good-looking girl when she was fifteen years or so younger. Alexander said, "Do you know where Crystal Bird got the money for her education?" I said "No" and he said, "She got it from a breach-of-promise collection from Roland Hayes." He said he had learned that from Dr. Charles Johnson, who told it as an explanation why all the Negro men are scared to death of Mrs. Fauset. [Hayes was the celebrated Negro tenor. Perhaps I should have been as wary of Mrs. Fauset. Despite her concern as a Democratic politician at this time, *The New York Times* reported in September 1944 that she had joined the campaign forces of Governor Dewey.]

*   *   *

This morning McIntyre told me a joke on the President which he said was an old one, but one which I had not heard before: The President died and went to heaven and asked for a great choir, said he wanted 10,000 tenors, and St. Peter said that could be arranged; then he wanted also 10,000 sopranos and St. Peter said that could be arranged, too; he wanted 10,000 contraltos and St. Peter agreed. Then St. Peter said, "What about the bass?" The President said, "I am going to sing bass."

Had lunch at Cosmos Club with Dr. Will Alexander, who feels very strongly that Cramer is doing a very bad job as the executive of the President's Fair Employment Practices Committee. Dr. Alexander and Dr. Weaver have been, in effect, set aside as a part of the demand which the committee made on McNutt prior to the election. He says that Dr. MacLean, chairman of the committee, is in a very precarious position in his job as president of Hampton Institute, that he has had trouble with his faculty and trustees and now the alumni are turning on him. He thinks that MacLean is acting as he is to try to secure the support of Randolph and White. He thinks Cramer is in a pretty strong position because if he should be fired he could say, "See, what happened to one, happens to everybody who tries to help the Negro. I was fired for trying to help them."

Dr. Will told me about the situation at Lockheed in the existing labor market. He spoke about the excellent cooperation that he had had with Lockheed, which has, he said, a very fine and able personnel man. They agreed to hire Negroes and Dr. Weaver and Dr. Alexander were working with them to bring about large employment in the best and easiest way, with the full cooperation of the management.

In the midst of this situation, some Negro who had not been employed wrote to Cramer and complained that he had not been employed because he was a Negro. Without ever consulting Alexander or Weaver, Cramer wrote a letter to Lockheed threatening to hold a public hearing on the grounds that they were discriminating against Negroes in employment. Dr. Alexander is particularly opposed to the publicity policy of the committee, which he says is always telling what they are going to do and not what they have done. He says that the committee has not followed up any of its hearings and that it has become largely a publicity agency for the doctrines of Walter White and Randolph—and incidentally he thinks that White, while pushing the Administration, has become increasingly closer to such Republicans as Willkie, Clare Luce, and Dewey.

I spoke to Dr. Alexander about the possibility of appointing some very able Negro as minister to Liberia, where he might, in the midst of the dramatic quality of Africa today, do a job of which Negroes could be proud. He spoke of the two men who might possibly be able to do the type of job needed to be done there. Channing Tobias, who has come up through the YMCA and whom he likes as a very able man—and a young man whom he regards as one of the ablest young men of America, Albert Dent, president of Dillard University in New Orleans, about thirty-six years old. He was a child abandoned on the streets of Atlanta and picked up and raised by a Negro postman and his wife, who were childless. He was brought to New Orleans by Dr. Alexander to run the large new Negro hospital there. He said that Alvin Howard, executive of the *Times-Picayune,* or one of the big New Orleans papers, had opposed a Negro to head this hospital, but that a year after Dent came he was not only proud of the management of the hospital, which from its beginning was never in the red, but had begun to consult Dent on the problems connected with the management of his newspaper. Incidentally he said Dent, who had got his administrative experience in a Negro insurance company, had never seen anything of the inside of a hospital until Dr. Alexander got him to come to New Orleans to take charge.

Coming out of the Cosmos, Dr. Alexander introduced me to Frederick Paul Keppel, president of the Carnegie Corporation, etc., etc., who told me that he had thought about getting me to do something for him recently but he realized I was too busy to do the job, but that he wanted to get someone familiar with the South and Negroes to read for the possible slips of a foreigner the study of the American Negro being made by Dr. Gunnar Myrdal. [*An American Dilemma: The Negro Problem and Modern Democracy,* 1944.] Incidentally Dr. Keppel said that if I ever wanted to have any money to make a study I was the sort of fellow they were looking for and that they would be delighted to make funds available to me.

Somebody ought to make a study of the part played by foundations set up by rich men in connection with people in Washington. They could start in the suite in the Hay Adams where the University of Chicago's Louis Brownlow et al. entertain on Rockefeller money. Last week I went to the dinner party given by Donald Young, of the Social Science Research Council, working on Negro questions in the War Department, which was paid by foundation funds. As we came down in the elevator in the Cosmos Club I spoke to Dr. Will Alexander about eating on him so often and he said he didn't want me to think he was less hospitable, but not to worry because he had an angel. Agnes Inglis is an expert in this field and it seems to me almost everybody I know is on the payroll of some foundation or other.

* * *

At the White House this morning McIntyre said he wished he knew what the President was going to do about this reported reorganization of government. He said he thought the President was going to sign the order making Ickes the acting over-all petroleum czar, but that he had his doubts as to whether all this general reorganization which has been discussed was going through. That he wouldn't be surprised if all the talk hadn't stirred up the President's Dutch stubbornness. Incidentally, speaking of politics and what could be done, he said that he didn't think it made much difference what was done, that nobody but the President or someone on whom the President put his finger could be elected in 1944. I said I doubted if anybody but the President could be elected in 1944 and mentioned Wallace as the man he had put his finger on. McIntyre indicated that he had put it on and taken it off. As to building somebody else up, he said that just had to happen. Nobody could tell when it would happen. He said again that he hoped the President would not run again in 1944. He said he didn't think it would make much difference in history even if the President were beaten, that his place was already secure.

Friday, December 4. Lyndon Johnson's hideaway office on the top floor of the old House Office Building, room 544: the green burlap and wood screen around the basin where the pretty blonde secretary in red mixed drinks and made coffee; dark-red steel filing cases; green figured carpet; black leather couch with red satin pillow on it; big red desk with congressman's feet on it; statuette of a fighting Irishman, labeled "I'm Dimocrat"; photographs of politicians on the walls; hat stand with light-gray Texas hat on it; green steel wastepaper basket; monk's-cloth curtains; scotch and soda bottles behind monk's-cloth curtains on the bookcases.

Johnson repeated the story about Leon Henderson going to

Texas to settle the row over gasoline rationing, which he only made worse. One instance: the president of the Texas Anti-Saloon League makes a habit of giving Texas sombreros to visiting celebrities. He went up to Henderson's room, where Henderson had already had two or three scotches and sat with his belly bulging while the Texas prohibitionist said, "Mr. Henderson, I would like to present you with this ten-gallon sombrero as a visitor in Texas." Henderson replied, "If you really wanted to be useful, why didn't you give me ten gallons of scotch whiskey?"

Lyndon Johnson says that as a result of Henderson's unpopularity, there is practically not a member of the Texas delegation who wouldn't be defeated if he came up for re-election now. Johnson was engaged in securing all the publicity he could from his speech at the scrapping of the cruiser *Oregon*. As far as I could gather, the speech was a joint product of Johnson, Edward Jamieson of the *Chicago Sun* and a string of Texas papers, Bill Douglas of the Supreme Court, Marshall McNeil of the Scripps-Howard papers, and David Cohn. He said Cohn and McNeil said it was lousy but that the INS correspondent on the Hill said it was the best speech a congressman had made this year. It is a pretty good speech but no world-beater. As I was leaving he gave me a photograph of himself inscribed "with affection and admiration." I would have been more grateful if he hadn't taken it out of a pile of about a hundred prints which I presume will go to others for whom he feels equal affection and admiration.

*   *   *

Lunch with Moyer Sink [my OCD aide], Fred Hoehler, Mark McCloskey, and Melvyn Douglas who had just finished his examinations before his induction as a private at Anniston, Alabama. Lunch was one of the most pleasant dirty-story-telling occasions I have ever attended, with McCloskey and Douglas setting a high standard in the business. Stories to remember: Douglas' story about the imaginary mongoose; the big dog's a ventriloquist; the taxi driver with the fat-lady fare;

the traveling troupe of Shakespearean actors crossing the Mississippi River on a manure scow; the old ladies in the brownstone mansion entertaining the soldiers; London cabby who could claim it at Scotland Yard if it wasn't claimed in three weeks; Mrs. Margot Asquith and Jean Harlow; and Harpo Marx's description of the Army physical examination. [Surely these must have been vintage jokes. I am as frustrated as a reader may be by my failure to recall the stories or their punch lines.]

*   *   *

David Niles called me up to say that Carroll Kilpatrick, correspondent of several Southern papers, wanted to get Mrs. Roosevelt to issue a formal denial of the rumor, or story, about her going to a Negro hotel in the South. I told him that I thought Mrs. Roosevelt would make a mistake if she formally recognized these rumors at all, that the people who wanted to believe the rumors will believe them anyhow and a denial would merely give greater currency to them.

Monday, December 7. Came up on the train from Raleigh with Douglas Poteat, Duke law professor serving with Economic Warfare. He had gone down to Raleigh on the three-o'clock train Saturday, which was due to arrive at ten o'clock at night. The train didn't get in until one. After some difficulty he got a taxi to the bus station. There were three times as many people waiting for the two-o'clock bus to Durham as the bus would accommodate. He went to the Carolina Hotel and couldn't get a room. He was not able to get another bus until seven o'clock in the morning, so he phoned his family in Durham and told them if they had any gasoline at all to come and get him. This, in contrast to the fact that he plans to spend three months after the first of the year traveling by bomber to every South American capital, spending ten days in each.

He also told me the story of the head of the Foreign Division of BEW [Board of Economic Warfare] and Robert D. Murphy. Shortly before our landing in North Africa, the

BEW man on Monday suggested that they have lunch together that day. Murphy had another engagement, so he suggested Tuesday. Murphy said no, he could not do that but he would be able to have lunch with him on Wednesday. On Wednesday they had lunch together and Murphy said that he had seen a certain man the day before who sent his regards. This man was not in this country, so it developed that Murphy had flown to England on Monday and had been back in time for lunch on Wednesday. Poteat also said he understood what he said was the true story about General Mark Clark's visit to North Africa. He said that Murphy and his men had made all the arrangements for greasing the way for the American troops into North Africa but that there was a two weeks' delay in the original plans for the arrival of the troops. The French began to get restive and for a moment it appeared that unless something happened quickly they might shoot Murphy, suspecting some sort of double cross. For this reason it was arranged to give them a token of the arrival of the troops and Clark was sent to Africa. Poteat said there was nothing to the whole story about mysterious and dangerous meetings, that it was all perfectly arranged and that all Clark did was to go after the arrangements were completed to save Murphy from the possibility of getting shot.

*　　*　　*

Wednesday, December 9. Note for Lilienthal biography: Lilienthal says that when he was eleven years old, James H. McGill, of Indianapolis, whom he referred to as his second father, gave him a copy of *Progress and Poverty* and started him in the directions he has followed.

*　　*　　*

Major Morden Murphy, Mark McCloskey's friend, told us about Ned Murray, an American portrait painter who used to get large fees in London and who recently painted a portrait of Princess Martha of Norway. It was arranged through a secretary for the picture to be sent to the White House and the artist was disappointed because he could not get in when it was shown there.

Major Murphy told an amusing story about the manner in which the Catholic campaign against birth control is keeping Catholics away from church. He said that when he was a boy his mother and father hardly ever went to church but when his father began to get along in years he paid $100 to the Life Extension Institute, which provided for physical examinations for all members of the family. In the course of her examination, the doctors reported that his mother had an inverted uterus, which made it impossible for her to have a child. She asked how long it had probably been in that position and the doctor said probably since the birth of her last child, which meant that she couldn't have had a baby for twenty years. As soon as she found that out, she hurried home, threw away her syringe, and ran to the church and ever afterwards was regular at both the church and the confessional.

Friday, December 11. Items in Portrait of the President: His mannerism of puffing out his cheeks on such occasions as the press conference almost amounts to a tic. Other mannerisms, scratching his forehead, throwing his head back. [In this list I should have mentioned his use of his long cigarette holder as a scepter, a magic wand—sometimes almost as a switch.]

* * *

Luncheon in office of Edwin A. Halsey, secretary of the Senate. Present: Joseph C. O'Mahoney, Wyoming; Harry Truman; Alben Barkley; Senator James M. Tunnell from Delaware, who talks through his nose and has slight palsy; Guffey; Charlie Michelson, long-time Democratic publicist; Judge and former Senator Sherman Minton, Indiana; McIntyre and myself. Also Pauley, treasurer of Democratic National Committee. Drinks before lunch in Halsey's office. All the senators violently down on Leon Henderson. All agreeing that the President must be seen. Barkley said he had made arrangements for a committee to see the President, of which he would not be a member. Guffey said that the President tried to get him to run Bill Bullitt for governor of Pennsylvania and he told him he couldn't do it and the President said, "I don't understand that. I got them to run Edison for governor of New Jersey." Guffey told him, "Yes, and you ruined the Democratic party in New Jersey." Said the President didn't like it. [Charles Edison, son of the inventor, had resigned as Secretary of the Navy in 1940 to run for governor of New Jersey. His resignation made it possible for FDR in July 1940 in the midst of the presidential election campaign to name Frank Knox, Republican candidate for Vice-President in 1936, to the Navy post.]

It did not seem to be a very productive or very intelligent meeting. All aware that something must be done, nobody with very clear ideas. McIntyre told them that he thought they were 100 per cent correct that something ought to be done and they ought to see the President to get it done. He also said he thought they would find the President very much more receptive than they expected. Guffey said he wished one thing, that was to get the Supreme Court to declare the Hatch Act unconstitutional. [This law prohibited all federal employees other than policy-making officers from taking active part in political campaigns.] He said that the Republicans would repeal it if they were in, but they wouldn't help the Democrats to do it and the Democrats didn't have the nerve to do it. It was suggested around the table that there would be plenty of Democratic officeholders ready to be guinea pigs.

I had relatively little to say but when it was suggested that the mood in 1944 would be that the people wanted a change, I suggested that we ought to offer the change with a program which meant a definite change from the status quo, assuring more people of employment and security. Minton and O'Mahoney seemed in agreement on the feeling that throughout the Middle West a lot of the vote against the Administration was actually a vote against the war. They both had the feeling that there were a great many people who didn't want to speak out loud but who actually are opposed to the war in all its aspects, though all agreed that even without this the irritation of the people at having to fill out nonsensically elaborate questionnaires created enough feeling against the Administration.

*   *   *

Washington wartime note: Major Murphy told us about going with Vincent Sheean [the author then serving with the Army Air Force] to the house of Mrs. Robert Low Bacon, where open house was kept for officers in Washington. Murphy reported that he had the feeling it was only for the high-ranking and very social officers. [Mrs. Bacon's house at 1801 F Street, NW, was much frequented in World War II by anti-Roosevelt civilian and uniformed officials.]

*   *   *

Friday, December 18. At the White House, while McIntyre was phoning, I picked up a pamphlet on photography and discovered that it was, in the guise of a book on the technique of lighting and photography, in fact a book of luscious nudes sent to McIntyre by a man who signed himself as J.A.M. Afterwards Rudolph Forster came in and McIntyre told us about his adventures in Hollywood, where he was almost, but not quite, overwhelmed by beauty. Both he and old man Forster were very much interested in this recital.

*   *   *

Saturday, December 19. McIntyre says, "The President thinks up all these bright ideas, but you know as well as I do that he is as impractical as the devil."

Sunday, December 20. New York: Breakfast with ex-Congressman Joseph E. Casey at the St. Regis Hotel. [I find it interesting today that in 1942 the White House arranged for my association with two very similar-appearing young men from widely separated geographical places in American politics, Texas and Massachusetts. Both were similarly interested in the destinies of the Democratic party and themselves. Lyndon Johnson and Joseph E. Casey would not have been deliberately chosen to show better the diverse directions toward which the political roads of destiny may lead.]

Casey, good-looking intelligent-seeming Irishman, indicated, without directly saying so, that he is very anxious to be Democratic national chairman and in defense of himself questioned the validity of the prejudice against another Irish Catholic from the East. He pointed out that he differed from both Flynn and Farley in that he could not be associated with the political boss type of Irish Catholic. This conversation, however, was by the way. We met at the President's suggestion to discuss an idea the President had that something ought to be done to improve the public relations of the government. Casey and I both feel that the President is 100 per cent right about that, but neither of us felt that he had thought through his plan for doing something about it. Neither of us felt that two people like ourselves, well known for our support of the New Deal, could be set up without arousing more criticism than ever. Also we felt that unless the President plans to reorganize the public relations agencies he now has, it would be difficult to fit us in where we could be effective without antagonizing the existing officials or creating more criticism. We plan to see the President around the end of the week.

In his conversation Casey spoke of David Niles. I asked Casey what Niles' influence in Massachusetts had been and he said he had very little position there. He added that they have something on him up there, some sort of police court record, and I gathered that Casey was not very fond of Niles, though he said that there is something "selfless about David Niles, but his brother, Eliot Niles, is a 'brassy kike.'" He is now a captain in the Army and when Justice Frank Murphy came to Massachusetts before the election, his influence with the Irish was immediately destroyed by the fact that Murphy was met on his arrival by Captain Eliot Niles and another Jewish Army officer. When the pictures were published without comment in Massachusetts, he said, all the effect of Murphy's visit was destroyed. He spoke of the dangerous anti-Semitism among the Irish Catholics and said that, so far as the Jew is concerned, it would be a simple matter to organize them into the Ku Klux Klan. Casey said that in his recent senatorial campaign he had gotten a good vote in the supposedly reactionary Republican strongholds, where the well-to-do have an intellectual affection for organized world peace, but he lost in the industrial towns, where he was supposed to get the biggest vote. The President, he says, has been rather insistent that he stay in Washington but that he doesn't want "just a job"; that he thinks he could be more useful back home and that in his law practice he can make all the Treasury will let him have.

[Joe Casey at this time was confident-appearing in his mid-forties. Irishmen had been coming up fast in Massachusetts. Joseph P. Kennedy, son-in-law of John Francis (Honey Fitz) Fitzgerald, mayor of Boston and congressman from Massachusetts, had advanced from banking, shipbuilding, films and liquor to become U. S. Ambassador at the Court of St. James's. Not quite so propelled, Joe Casey had started early in politics. He entered national politics as a delegate to the Democratic National Convention of 1924 in New York and there must have heard FDR's Happy Warrior speech in nomination of Al Smith. Almost regularly he attended national political conventions after that. Also in 1934, in the surge of the New Deal, he was elected to Congress, serving until 1942. Then he assumed the Democratic duty of trying to beat Henry Cabot Lodge, Jr., for the Senate. He lost but still seemed entitled to reward.

[He did not go "back home," as he suggested he might, but remained in Washington as an attorney with important connections. There, later, he attracted attention when under the Truman administration he arranged for Aristotle Onassis, described then as an "international mystery man of shipping and finance," to acquire surplus wartime tankers which were not supposed to be sold to foreign interests. Associated with Casey in this deal was Robert W. Dudley, whom I had known in OWI. Dudley's beautiful sister, Constance, married Casey. Their appearance on the Potomac was pleasing. The ship deal, however, was investigated with much moral indignation by Senator Richard M. Nixon. He charged that Casey had run a half-million-dollar investment into a three-and-a-half-million-dollar profit, taxable only as capital gains. Though charged with "influence peddling," Casey emerged from the incident unscathed.]

Tuesday, December 22. In conversation with McIntyre this morning, discussing a business in which he did not think he would be effective, he used the phrase: "I would be as useless as a second navel."

Thursday, December 24. Christmas Eve at the White House. Women clerks all chattering outside of McIntyre's office and inside Dave Niles, Lock Currie, McReynolds, and myself listening to McIntyre's adventures with the beautiful ladies, all of which go right up to the point and end on McIntyre's insistence on his Methodist chastity. Dave Niles sitting over in the corner looking at the book of nude photographs. German propaganda could use this picture.

Wednesday, December 30. McIntyre talking with young Lieutenant Colonel Frank McCarthy about pilots utilizing training flights to visit mothers, girls, deliver parcels for friends, etc., with resultant kicks from public not able to buy gasoline. McIntyre says he doesn't "even approve of the President going off for weekends to Hyde Park. It means one locomotive and seven cars which have to wait there until he comes back and some little disturbance of railroad schedules."

But if it is a recreation for the President's health it means more than the movement of divisions, says McCarthy. Ten divisions, says McIntyre, and I wouldn't say a word if he was going to Florida—but Hyde Park is where he got this last cold. The house isn't heated but twenty-four hours before he gets there. I don't think he can justify using all that equipment and sometime I'm going to stick my neck out and tell him so.

* * *

On occasion the "inner cabinet," McIntyre, Early, and others, meet in McIntyre's office at 12:30 P.M. for a drink.

* * *

Lunch at the Washington Hotel with Comptroller General Lindsay Warren. Thick man, graying, but really looks tough. [Actually, within an armor of brusqueness, he was a gentle, proud, humorous man, capable of indignation. I had known him for many years as a fellow North Carolinian. He had served in Congress from 1925 to 1941, when Roosevelt named him Comptroller General of the United States.] He told me about scandalous situations in contracts. One shipyard charged government around $25,000 for special train, dinners, all kinds of liquor, etc., to take guests to a launching in Mobile. Army Engineers approved bonus in a contract for $40,000 job to be completed in 60 days with bonus of $100 a day for every day under 60. Contractor completed the job in one day and Engineers wanted to pay him $5,900 bonus.

Army urged him to approve as part of government contract cost of cables from workers in Iceland to wives and sweethearts in United States.

* * *

Joe Casey: knowing he cannot be national chairman of the Democratic party, Casey would like to have full-time executive directorship under chairman such as Jouett Shouse once had in the Republican party. Again spoke of David Niles' lack of influence in Massachusetts and of feeling against the

Jews which comes against Niles as aide to President to injury of Democrats. He spoke of one Jewish friend of Niles in New England as truly a member of the Communist party. Says Niles makes too many promises and has no practical knowledge of politics, which results in more political damage than good. Says Niles started out as a worker for labor, arrested in some strike at Lowell—"he was probably in the right"—ran Ford Hall Forum, liberal institution which brought him close to such Boston luminaries as Lincoln Filene, great merchant, and Supreme Court Justice Felix Frankfurter. Frankfurter thinks Niles is a wonderful man. And, he says, Frankfurter controls all the legal and judicial patronage from Massachusetts, which does not please the people. In Massachusetts stories of murders of Jews in Europe does not arouse the revulsion of feeling it should. People even laugh and say, "Christ, if they would just stop at Blue Hill (Jewish section) it would be all right here." Casey also spoke of the increase in the number of Jews in the federal government, particularly in legal divisions.

Dinner with the Aubrey Williamses at their place in Virginia—old Victorian house approached by muddy road lined by scraggly cedars which Mark McCloskey properly said looked like the ideal setting for a murder story—Mrs. Williams in black velvet pants, youngish-looking but gray—her youngest boy in a bright red shirt. Federal Circuit Judge Wiley Rutledge—obviously very liberal—and wife, who had gone from Illinois to teach Greek in Maryville (Tenn.) College when Williams a student. She is a sickening sentimental type remembering the boys who courted her in Maryville—hair curled on sides but head practically bald on the top. I developed against much protest my thesis that South is really a radical region—Farmers' Alliance—Populism—even lynchings a revolutionary procedure—Tom Watson—Huey Long.

[Despite their lapses in demagogery, Long of Louisiana and Watson of Georgia had brought brilliance to freeing the mass of the people in their states from the long domination of entrenched oligarchies. Huey Long abolished the poll tax in Louisiana even if he also ran roughshod over opponents as he treated the state as his own property. Before Long was assassinated and while he was truculently trying to push Roosevelt further to the left, FDR in an odd coupling spoke of Long and General Douglas MacArthur as "the two most dangerous men in the United States."]

Diary

1943

Saturday, January 2. Joe Casey and I spent an hour and five minutes with the President this morning. Went in, the President looking very well, greeted me, "Jonathan, I haven't taken you into my club yet." I asked, "What club is that, Mr. President?" and he said, "the B Club"—"The Bastard Club." I said, "I suppose that is like the old son-of-a-bitch book." He said, "It's the same idea"—then he went into a discussion of his feeling that the government was not reaching the people through four-minute speakers and the like.

I told him that the program had been organized last July but had fallen flat on its face, and I outlined, without pressing, my ideas. He agreed with them. He said that Jim Landis is a sweet fellow but agreed that he was not at all suited to do this job. Perhaps, he said, somebody ought to be put in OCD entirely independent of Landis to work out this business. He also talked about some ideas he had about the government purchase of a radio station in Cincinnati with broadcasts for the whole country, giving government information without opinion. Perhaps later to correct false statements. He doubted that he could get from Congress, or take from the emergency fund, the money for such a station, or for his other plan for buying time from radio stations. He discussed with approval the idea that Elmer Davis might speak on the radio and that he might be supplemented by such a voice as that of Raymond Gram Swing speaking for the government. He spoke with some contempt of the radio commentator who is "always with us," syrupy voice and with considerable irritation—Fulton Lewis, Jr. [Product of Hearst's International News Service, Lewis, as a commentator for the Mutual Broadcasting System, followed in general the anti-Administration *Chicago Tribune* line.]

He mentioned an article in the *Washington Star* by Constantine Brown which he said was wrong, but added that he liked Constantine Brown. He spoke of Wallace's speech and said where Wallace went wrong was in discussing the mechanism of world peace at this time. [The President was probably referring to the speech made by the Vice-President on the anniversary of Woodrow Wilson's birth, December 28, 1942, in which he spoke of peace and postwar problems. It drew criticism from some quarters, as had one he made at the American Soviet Friendship Congress in November. Congresswoman Clare Luce described Wallace's views as "globoloney."]

Then the President said, and I wondered if it indicated some plan of his own, that maybe all we would need after the war would be one man with his seat in the Azores as a sort of police judge of the world and I wondered if he thought of himself as that one man ruling the world from the Azores.

He talked at some length about a tax program in which each family would be allotted the right to buy certain amounts of food, clothing, and other necessities and that all purchases in excess of those amounts would be taxed. He told Casey and myself to see Elmer Davis and others and draw him up a plan for the organization of the home front, which he wanted presented to him next week.

General Watson came in after the first fifteen minutes and kept standing around. I told the President that the home-front organization in OCD was now under the direction of Reginald Foster of Boston. The President asked, "Could that be the Reginald Foster who's about sixty-four years old?" I told him no, that I thought this was a younger man. General Watson said, "I know him, Mr. President, he married a Hoar." "Why, General Watson!" exclaimed the President. "Yes," said General Watson, "Senator Hoar's daughter." "Oh," said the President, "you mean one without a 'w' on it."

Among other things that the President discussed was the fighting he anticipates in the next Congress against the trade treaties and he told us a long story supporting the use of subsidies, about the growers of olives on the West Coast. Because of the tariff against olives, olives cost America a hundred million dollars a year, while the ten-million-dollar subsidy to the olive growers would reduce the cost to the consumers to sixty million dollars. McIntyre came quietly in the room and seemed to be a very old man against the wall. Altogether this seemed like a very rambling conversation but both Casey and I got in a good deal of talk in spite of the fact that the President as usual did most of the talking. I think I got his full agreement that Landis is not the man to handle the home-front aspects of OCD.

To lunch with Casey at the Mayflower, after which we went to see, on an engagement made by McIntyre, Elmer Davis at OWI. He was very cagey about the whole thing, but agreed that some home-front organization was necessary and basic to revitalize OCD. Both Casey and I got the general impression that OWI has been rather muddling along and not coming to grips with a number of important questions involved. Before Casey and I went out to lunch we went into McIntyre's office and had a drink out of the "inner cabinet," which is a redwood cellaret in which McIntyre says he keeps the liquor for the newspapermen at the White House. I am to see Casey on Monday and we hope to draw up a plan to present to the President as soon as possible next week.

When William S. Knudsen, president of General Motors, first came here as director of the Office of Production Management, the President told him, "Now, Bill, you go ahead and get your men to run this show." Knudsen brought in the list and the President glanced over it and noticed that every member of the list, twenty names, was Republican. He called

Knudsen and said, "Now I am not trying to get political on this thing, but it struck me as a little odd that all twenty of these men are Republicans." Knudsen answered, "Mr. President, in the field of big business like we are doing, in the war effort, all the executives are Republicans—like the men we want." The President said, "All right."

Time went along and two or three lists came through, finally a list came in and the President looked at it and on it was a Democrat from Atlanta. The President called Knudsen, "Bill, you made a mistake, there is a Democrat on the list," and Knudsen said, "No, Mr. President, I didn't make no mistake, he is a Democrat but he voted for Villkie."

Tuesday, January 12. Bridge at the Mayflower in the apartment of Charles Harwood, governor of the Virgin Islands; Admiral David M. LeBreton; Noble Cathcart [my brother-in-law, former publisher of the *Saturday Review,* then serving in OWI]; McIntyre and myself and a colonel who is the Washington representative of Andrew Jackson Higgins, the New Orleans shipyard man.

Yesterday when I spoke to McIntyre about a very dramatic thing the President had done, he said, "Yes, you know the fellow has a lot of the actor in him. Maybe if he had gone on the stage he would have amounted to something."

A beautiful sunshiny day—meeting of inner cabinet in McIntyre's office.

Wednesday, January 13. Dinner at the house of Herbert Elliston, editor of the *Washington Post.* Present: Geoffrey Crowther, editor of the London *Economist,* roly-poly man, who knew more about the internal make-up of the United States than any Englishman I have ever met. He and a young Dane, who came in after dinner, supported the thesis that the English and Americans should take over the trusteeship of the world, exclusive, I presume, of Russia and Germany, for sixty years following this present war. I expressed my feeling that if I belonged to any other groups, I would not trust the rule of the English and Americans. The young Dane, who years ago was with Elliston in China, had the feeling that even if the Germans were defeated in Europe, Russia would not let us use bases in Siberia for the attack on Japan. He said that the Axis that Russia would like best would be one with a greatly weakened Tokyo.

Mr. Byrd, kin to Herbert Elliston's wife, Joanna, elderly New Englander. He alone in the company had any kind words for the Russians and thought they were a sincere people, while Crowther and I felt they were not only insincere in leadership but that they had played too close a game with the Nazis.

Mrs. Mary Churchill, young attractive daughter of Judge Learned Hand. She is working in the War Department though she has money and is much concerned because her ten-year-old boy, Jonathan, coming home from school at St. Albans, has been terrorized by a gang of young Georgetown toughies.

Crowther and I agreed in not being enthusiastic about the Beveridge plan, both felt that it was excellent, but that the extension of social security is not a basis in our time for a crusade. New goals to really stir the blood of people must go beyond any such plan as this one. [William Henry Beveridge, later Baron Beveridge of Tuggal, British economist and social planner, had recently presented blueprints for a new welfare state. It was greeted with serious attention and some derisive comment. A current joke was that we were advancing from social protections from the cradle to the grave to new ones from the womb to the tomb. The next step would be from the erection to the resurrection.]

Crowther said that the British and Americans were able to estimate German, Italian, and even Japanese production better than they could estimate Russian production. The British and Americans have absolutely no information on Russian production. Estimates about Germany are pretty simple, as there are four million foreigners living within Germany and British Intelligence is able to supplement other known facts. Our information about the Russians is absolutely nil and no American or Englishman has been permitted to see any significant aspects of Russian war production plants.

Thursday, January 14. Lunch at the Cosmos Club. Harry D.

White, of the Treasury, and Pritchard, young, fat, amusing assistant to Byrnes, led the conversation to a discussion of the very, very bad political situation in Africa. Both of these men seemed to feel that Murphy had done a very bad job indeed, that he was not to be trusted and that the United States sits on a powder keg in its relations with French officials in North Africa. [Robert D. Murphy, career foreign service officer, and counselor of the American Embassy at the puppet French government at Vichy, had done preliminary work before the North African invasion, in November 1942, as Roosevelt's political representative. He became counselor to General Eisenhower.]

General Auguste Noguès, governor of Morocco, Pritchard says, is still in contact with Vichy France through Tangier. Paul Appleby, who took a good deal less part in the conversation, said that most of the anti-Vichy refugees to North Africa have been released from prison but the other men said that following the establishment of Vichy all officers in the French African army, of the rank of captain and above, were examined for loyalty to Vichy and an army completely subservient to Pétain created. Most of the private soldiers are native troops but they will follow wherever their French officers lead them. It is a good idea to use French soldiers and so cut down the necessity of transporting men as well as arms, but with armed French, the United Nations might be in a hot spot if English and American reverses in North Africa caused these French officers to believe that the Axis might win. Very few kind words for the State Department were said by anybody. There was some feeling expressed that the British were getting ready to let De Gaulle down. Oscar Cox felt very strongly that his agency (Lend-Lease) can expect sharp attacks in the Congress from the Senator Gerald Nye group and that the food situation will be attacked by the same group on the ground that our food supplies are short because we are feeding the Hottentots.

After lunch I went down to see Dr. Will Alexander, who is as anxious as possible to get out of Manpower. "You can go down this hall," he said of the long hall in the Social

Security Building, "and hardly anybody in any office will know what he is doing or what his work is." Throughout Manpower, he told me, they confer and confer and hope that something will happen next week but never get anything done. He thinks Fowler Harper, deputy director, is an empty person whose sole concern is maintaining the immediate good humor of people and never getting anything done. [Harper had been a law professor under McNutt in Indiana.]

Alexander told me that he had been authorized by the Rosenwald Fund to put Charlotte Carr, former director of Hull House in Chicago, on the payroll for three months or six months at $500 a month, but he hoped she was going to get a more productive job than they would be able to give her. He said she had told him very frankly that she was financially hard-pressed. [Miss Carr at this time was apparently insecure in her position as assistant to the vice-chairman of Manpower.]

At the lunch at the Comos Club, there seemed to be general agreement that the Lehman outfit is getting into greater and greater difficulty. Oscar Cox said to me that they had a grand thing to sell but were losing popular support every day by the way they were acting. He seemed to feel that Lehman is a good man but naive. Pritchard said that General William N. Haskell is not only an old man, but his experience was with Hoover in the last war and that Hoover so worked the feeding job at that time as to disrupt any plans of the Allies. [General Haskell, who had recently been appointed director of field operations for Lehman's office of Foreign Relief and Rehabilitation, was sixty-four years old.]

Present at the Cosmos Club luncheon were Beanie Baldwin; Oscar Chapman; Paul Appleby; Aubrey Williams; Randolph E. Paul, assistant to Secretary Morgenthau; Oscar Cox; Pritchard; Colonel Ed Foley, general counsel of the Treasury; a very quiet man wearing glasses; Dave Niles; and Harry D. White.

Friday, January 15. Had lunch with Louis K. Friedman of Pittsburgh, director and secretary of numerous companies, also consultant for Harold Smith, director of the Budget Bureau. Friedman is working on this hunch: he believes that the theory that we must cut down civilian industry in order to provide more manpower for war industry is wrong. He thinks the only way to get more manpower is to give some meaning to the money war workers are receiving in terms of things they can buy. He thinks there are great sources of manpower yet to be tapped, enough to go around in war industry and civilian industry as well. Of course those things using scarce material must be curtailed; scarce civilian necessities must be rationed but he thinks that the government should encourage the production of civilian supplies.

If people can't buy anything with their money, the pools of potential manpower cannot be tapped. Also he thinks that in terms of supply and demand the flow of supply of civilian goods would help to prevent inflation, black markets, etc. This would have to be accompanied by price controls, but he thinks that the control should not be on ceiling prices as at present, which he thinks would have the effect of putting the lowest-price merchants out of business first. It will also have the effect, he thinks, where manufacturers make several grades of goods, of having them concentrate on the highest grade bringing the highest price. He would substitute a price regulation based on the percentage of mark-up permitted. Stores would be permitted to mark up less than the maximum if they wished. He thinks that the ultimate effect in this day of restricted transportation would be increased buying at neighborhood stores.

Joe Casey came in after lunch. He is getting a little tired of sitting on the seat of uncertainty. He had heard from a constituent who was down here seeking a job that the President was out of town. "I think the President is entitled to a vacation if he wants one," he said. Casey told some amusing stories about ex-governor James Michael Curley. One that he and some of his friends, who share his anti-Semitism, spent the other evening in the bar and dining rooms of the Mayflower Hotel getting bellhops to continually page Colonel Finkelstein, Major Cohen, they even paged an admiral with a Jewish name. Casey said he thought it was amusing, but people in the Mayflower would go back home from Washington and say the whole armed services are Jewish.

He was hoping to see Dave Niles, who is out of town, because, despite the change in OPA, a man named Winthrop is being urged to head OPA in Massachusetts; he is publicized as a sound businessman. Casey said he looked him up and he is a valentine manufacturer who has failed, but that he is a close friend of prominent Republicans in Massachusetts. He spoke of Senator Styles Bridges' attack on Democratic Chairman Ed Flynn in the Senate yesterday and said that before Bridges became governor, the highest earnings he had ever had was $27.50 a week as a clerk. Since then he has made money and even gotten presidential ideas in his head. He opened an office in the Copley Plaza in Boston, where the word was put out that in exchange for campaign contributions he could get Army and Navy contracts. [Actually before he became governor of New Hampshire in 1935, Bridges had been secretary of the New Hampshire Farm Bureau Federation, a magazine editor, director of an investment company, and member of the State Public Service Commission.]

Casey spoke about the Princess Martha story. I told him that Dave Niles had said that it represented the identical pattern of the whispering campaign against Wilson and that when John Cowles, newspaper publisher, now working in Lend-Lease, asked me about it, I asked him about his good friend Willkie and Irita Van Doren, whereupon John assured me solemnly that he thought they were very good friends. [Royalty, even in exile, had a fascination for Roosevelt and his attentions to Princess Martha of Norway had become a subject of gossip in Washington at this time. At the same time it was whispered that Willkie had had an affair with Irita Van Doren, literary editor of the *New York Herald Tribune*. So widespread was this last report that when Mrs. Willkie suddenly appeared with her husband during the 1940 presidential campaign, she was said to have remarked, "Politics makes strange bedfellows."]

Wednesday, January 20. Bill Hassett and Rudolph Forster

referred to Eugene Casey, the "executive assistant," as an unwelcome intruder in the executive corridors. McIntyre concurred.

McIntyre told me, but in great confidence, that Walter White, in writing to Mrs. Roosevelt, has addressed her as "Dear Eleanor."

Tuesday, January 26. Went to the White House this morning. McIntyre is pretty cagey, but he said they better not break the story until the President gets back, he didn't know when he was going to get back, but the story better be big. Then he called up Steve Early and said that he had ordered the car for twelve o'clock and he would stop by for Early on the way. [Two days before this in Casablanca, Roosevelt and Churchill had concluded their historic conference in a joint meeting with the press.]

McIntyre asked me to play bridge Saturday afternoon in the room at the Mayflower of Eric Johnson, president of the U. S. Chamber of Commerce.

*   *   *

Hugh Jackson telling of Lehman's shop—the slowness, the timidity of State Department employees. Hugh is studying French on the side. He seems back in his field and with a real desire to feed people, but wondering over public acceptance. Elmer Davis suggested to Lehman that he change his speech at a dinner given Lehman at the Waldorf to take the stress off humanity in his job and say that relief would shorten the war. Lehman, Hugh thinks, is a very conservative man himself though a humanitarian at heart. Hugh not wearing his new black hat in rain. He pointed out that mine was not blocked in the State Department manner. I agreed that mine was the deputy sheriff's and not the diplomat's version of blocking.

Jackson, remembering differences in OCD as to who should sign directives, grinned and pointed out that in the State Department all communications are signed by Hull. He had just had a letter from Fred Hoehler, who, following William Hodson's death in a plane crash, has taken over top Lehman job in North Africa. Hugh says Hoehler is the sort of fellow who likes to get about and report. He is wondering how he will do the administrative job of setting things up and getting them moving.

Saw Alfred Davidson at Roger Smith Hotel and asked him about report Gardner Jackson had been fired from Agriculture by Wickard. He phoned me later that he had confirmed it —that because Pat had done what he ought to do fighting Wickard on Farm Security's side, Pat had given Wickard cause enough to fire him. But "Pat's got to eat and I've been trying to think where there is a place for him and can't think of it." Said he was sure that Wallace was on the Farm Security side along with Milo Perkins, etc.

Courtenay Dinwiddie, whom I knew as child-labor reformer, came in about the same thing. I know he hoped I could get him and others to the President about the food situation. I had to tell him that he would have to go through General Watson and that I was hoping to see the President myself.

Mrs. Brite said she would like to see in one place all the people in D.C. who are unhappy about their jobs. This is apropos of Newman Jeffry, who told me he was about to resign from OCD since Wayne Coy had declined to let him have any field staff to work with labor.

"Sometimes it looks," I told her, "as if this whole government were going to hell in a hack."

Thursday, January 28. At McIntyre's suggestion I took Russell Marion to see Jack Fleming in OWI. Had been fearful that Marion might be too indefinite in his proposal for an all-out governmental campaign to increase the farmer's sense of his importance in the war effort. But Marion proved to be a good native advocate. Fleming agreed that OWI had not been giving attention to the farmer's part of our job in its general programs and asked Marion if he would stay over until today and make the same statement to others in OWI in charge of radio, news, etc. Marion said he had made the statement, he supposed, to forty different people and he was willing to go on making it forever until he got something done.

Marion is perfect as the typical young farmer. He represents in the real sense the people who prefer to live on the farm even if, in the dairy country, it means working from 4:30 in the morning until 8 o'clock at night. He had to leave the farm because his father was not able to buy him a place and in industrial employment he became a mechanic. He saved enough money to establish a dealership in John Deere farm machinery in Dryden, New York. In that job he went up and down talking to farmers, helping them with their work in selling his machines. Now for four months at his own expense he has been trying to get the government's information and propaganda to the farmers in a way that will make sense to them, keep them on the land and prevent the destructive departure of farmers from the land when the food supply is so important.

Lunch at the Cosmos Club, where another aspect of the farm situation came up. Oscar Cox is urging Beanie Baldwin to resign from the Farm Security now and come over to Lend-Lease, where he says he could be more effective in pushing Wickard and others in this food business than he can in Agriculture, where Wickard would really like to fire him. Baldwin is uncertain as to whether to resign now or to go down fighting in Congress, feeling sure that Wickard, under the influence of Ed O'Neal, American Farm Bureau chief, means to minimize, as far as possible, the part of Farm Security in the food production program.

As we were leaving the Cosmos Club, Beanie offered a ride in an official car to Jim Rowe. "You really don't want to stay," said Rowe, grinning, "do you?" [James H. Rowe, Jr., once legal secretary to Justice Oliver Wendell Holmes, had been assistant to James Roosevelt when he was secretary to his father. Later Rowe had been an administrative assistant to the President. Now he was the top assistant to the Attorney General.]

However, the main discussion at the luncheon was of the situation in North Africa. And the chief figure in this discussion was Colonel Bernard Bernstein, who was in uniform though he is still listed in the *Government Register* as Assistant General Counsel of the Treasury. Apparently, he thought that from the political standpoint, the American invasion was badly botched. The original plan was that the Army was to go in and take over in the fullest sense. However, the feeling of the Army that nothing should delay its drive to Tunisia brought about the quick modification of that plan to the present "guest Army theory" with the colonial French in complete possession of all governmental services. Among the French powers in North Africa, Admiral Jean Darlan was a ready stooge of the U.S.A., but General Henri Giraud has some noisy ideas about sovereignty.

Bernstein made the point that the Americans were absolutely unequipped in terms of personnel to do that job even if the policy had not changed. The British were much better equipped in such personnel terms, he said. The feeling of this whole group was very critical of the handling of the whole North African enterprise from the political point of view. Harry White felt that Bernstein pulled his punches in discussing it. Milo Perkins, executive director of the Board of Economic Warfare, suggested the creation of an occupation authority independent of the State Department, coordinating the State Department and all other departments' responsibilities. Paul Appleby, now special adviser to the Lend-Lease Administration, said little but indicated that before he was, in effect, pushed out of the State Department, he was planning the creation of such personnel. Bernstein said that the graduates of the School of Military Government at Charlottesville just sat around and did nothing and that even the school's graduates were pretty critical of it as a rather theoretical operation. Present at the meeting were: Bernstein, White, Perkins, Jim Rowe, Oscar Chapman, Baldwin, Pritchard, Cox, Niles, and the same silent man I couldn't identify before.

Walked across the snow in Lafayette Square with David Niles and met a most remarkable-looking man, big and in a great gray coat buttoned close about his neck, dark graying hair. Ambassador John Gilbert Winant. Looks older than I expected but is in the best sense a really beautiful man—with a rather disconcerting and at the same time not irritating way of staring at you. He has bad teeth with one gap close to the front on the side. He asked me about my father and said he had some correspondence with him on the subject of censorship, but he wasn't any more in favor of it than Father was. "We need some old fire horses like your father in London," he said. He and Niles seemed on very close terms. Niles called him "Gil." Winant said that he had been in this country and had been ill for some time but was getting along all right now. [A wealthy product of St. Paul's School and Princeton, Winant was a man of great social concern. After serving twice as governor of New Hampshire, he had worked with the International Labor Office in Geneva, then as chairman of the Social Security Board. Roosevelt sent him to Britain in 1941 to take the place of Joseph P. Kennedy, who had little faith that Britain could win and less will to see the United States involved in the war. Winant brought total commitment to the Allies' cause and great ability in unifying the efforts of the many and varied American missions in England.]

Wicky (Mrs. Tex Goldsmith) tells me this story apropos of the death of William Hodson in the plane crash in Dutch Guiana and Fred Hoehler's survival to take his job. Story: Hoehler caught up with Hodson's plane in Miami and there was a possibility he might fly with him but there was one more man than there were places on the plane. The choice got down to Hoehler and a major, whereupon the major said, "I suppose we are both equally important to the war effort and I want to be a sport about it, let's throw dice to see who gets the seat." Hoehler lost. Wicky says she doesn't think the story can be true but it is going all around the town. I told her to tell Hoehler that if he denies the story I am going to deny him.

At Cosmos luncheon Lubin and Bernstein agreed that in North Africa the Nuremberg (anti-Jewish) laws have not been modified very much as yet. Someone asked about report that Jews themselves opposed removal for fear it would arouse the Arabs.

"Must have been a local Sulzberger," someone said. And the same man sharply opined that he never knew of a place where they lied so much as in the Department of Agriculture.

Army in its hurry to Tunisia not so much worried by possibility of delay in French fighting us longer but of disruption of railroads, trucks, etc., if we tried to run them ourselves without French aid.

Bernstein and White spoke of a cable to Africa saying that decree fixing rate of exchange should be signed by Eisenhower and not by French. In Africa this taken as meaning that U.S. in D.C. still thought in terms of invading army theory, which had been supplanted. Actually White said it was meant to say that we were in control. Indication of lack of clear understanding between U.S. government and Murphy.

Saturday, January 30. McIntyre and Jim Rowe carrying on long telephone conversation about what to do about Eugene Casey. (McIntyre resents Casey's suggestion that an old-fashioned palace intrigue among those close to the President is destroying him.) McIntyre: "Casey says his self-respect has gone down to 2 per cent. I've told him I can't OK any more of his travel. Agriculture won't pay it and the Comptroller General won't approve. I think he thinks he could beat Tydings [Senator Millard E. Tydings, Democrat of Maryland, who had often voted with the opposition to Roosevelt]. I told him I'd go to bat for him for any job in the government just to show him I wasn't his enemy. I suppose he would like to have Hopkins' job."

Of the President taking up home-front question McIntyre said later he may stay up on Mount Olympus with the gods for a week after he gets back. "I ought not to say it, even to you, but he's getting to be one of these Olympian gods." Talked of Ernest Lindley—"the conceited son-of-a-bitch"— he was a member of a small group of newspapermen at Albany who were friends of the family, they would come in and look at the letters on the governor's desk as they pleased, friends of the family, etc. When McIntyre came in as part of the governor's pre-presidential campaign he insisted that all newspapermen must be treated alike with no inside track for the old crowd. They didn't like it. Lindley in his first book said that if McIntyre knew what the President's program was all about, he never gave any indication of it. Later told McIntyre that he realized he had done him an injustice and meant to correct it in his next book. "He didn't do a damn thing," McIntyre says.

McIntyre says he almost trusts Jim Rowe. He's getting good sense even if he did come in with the Corcoran crowd. Don't get me wrong, they served a useful purpose, but nobody but the Boss could have handled such a team of wild horses.

Notable in McIntyre's conversation is that when he quotes himself as speaking to the President in the old days he calls him Franklin, which he never does now.

While in McIntyre's office Senator Lister Hill, having called my office first, called us both. Laughingly said that I knew that the Lord loved the patient; "Well, he doesn't love me," I said. "We've got to get this thing rolling," said Hill. "It hasn't even got wheels on it," I told him.

Of FDR McIntyre said, "There are five or six things just burning hot but when he gets off he acts like he hasn't even got a job here. He doesn't leave any instructions. Christ, I've been doing things where I haven't got any authority at all but what in the hell are you going to do?"

And plans for the Saturday bridge game. Among those to be present is Joyce O'Hara of U. S. Chamber of Commerce, who is one of his favorite players.

Coming to the office this morning on the old snow through the new snowing. A dog yelping outside the Parker house, where the Parker dog in heat has had all the dogs of the neighborhood yelping for days.

Monday, February 1. Lunch at the Hay Adams given by Mrs. Henry P. Davison and Mrs. Dwight Morrow. Mrs. Morrow couldn't attend. Herbert Agar and Archie MacLeish ran the meeting. Its purpose, Agar said, was to see if it would be possible or useful at a time when there are so very many committees to set up another committee to try to secure American unity on a few minimum things with regard to the peace which the peoples of the world could depend upon.

These minimums, as he suggested them, seem to be limited to the trade treaties and some sort of postwar, extension of Lend-Lease. He was not very specific, indeed both he and

MacLeish seemed to be pretty remote from reality. It may be, as Agar said, that the United States is the only country in the world which has no certain and continuing foreign policy.

The meeting didn't even get off the ground. Nothing was done, though it was suggested that people who were interested could indicate as much to Agar and that something might follow. Winant made a very effective speech in which he suggested that the men were going to be interested in jobs, etc., when they come home. Raymond Clapper said that he thought people were anxious to see some return of a specific kind in connection with Lend-Lease, such as agreements on postwar international airlines. Altogether, however, both MacLeish and Agar seemed to pitch the meeting in the mood of the elegant intellectuals. The two very pictorial men talking big words but without their feet on the ground.

I sat between Tom Eliot and Henry Pringle of OWI. Elmer Davis sat between Agar and Mrs. Davison but he said nothing and left early. Frank Graham [president of the University of North Carolina and member of the War Labor Board] also left early without saying anything. Among others present were Monsignor John A. Ryan; Harry Scherman of the Book-of-the-Month Club; Bill Batt, of the War Production Board; Walter Lippmann; Virginius Dabney, editor of the *Richmond Times-Dispatch;* altogether a company of about thirty. Agar said that they were anxious to take the problem out of the realm of politics because they felt peace ought not to be loaded down with objections of many people to the New Deal, etc.

An amusing incident at the luncheon: Tom Eliot, Henry Pringle, and I decided to have a second cocktail and started toward a tray filled with martinis but a hotel functionary intervened. "Only one to a guest," he said.

[This occasion brought together an interesting cast of characters. The two lady hosts were both wives of partners in J. P. Morgan & Co. Herbert Agar still listed himself as editor of the *Louisville Courier-Journal* but in his ardent Allied speaking efforts had hardly touched ground in Kentucky for months. Raymond Clapper, one of the ablest Washington correspondents, was to die early in the following year in a plane crash while covering the U.S. invasion of the Marshall Islands. Henry Pringle had won the Pulitzer prize for his biography of Theodore Roosevelt. Tom Eliot, congressman, lawyer, reporter, government official with a still greater career before him, was soon to be special assistant to Winant and head of the London office of OWI.]

Tuesday, February 2. Very interesting press conference. Heard the President tell about his trip [to Casablanca]. He was in fine form and began his conference by praising the newspapers for the manner in which they had kept the secret of his trip. I never saw him look so well. All in all it was a very pleasant occasion, in which he said very little that had not already been reported but indicated a great deal, notably his support of General Henri Giraud and his feeling that reports of "politics" and division among French in North Africa were often wrong and generally exaggerated. Afterwards I saw General Watson, who said that he had put Joe Casey and myself down for an engagement a week from Saturday. I told him that while I wanted to go with Mr. Casey, I was very anxious to see the President soon for a few moments myself. McIntyre also said that he was taking my memoranda about public relations to the President today and agreed that it would have to be acted on more rapidly than the engagement General Watson had fixed would permit.

I gathered from McIntyre that on the President's return he, Early, and General Watson all unloaded on Eugene Casey with the insistence that something be done about that situation. After the conference I went across the street with David Niles, who tried to put on an act about the necessity for the Boss's loyal friends to be forever patient. I told him to go to hell—and see what he could do about getting something done.

Lunch with Wilbur Schramm, who is about to resign from the Office of War Information. He thinks he can be either a lieutenant commander in the Navy in charge of one of the Navy schools or dean of journalism at the University of Iowa. Both are attractive jobs and his division in OWI seems to be involved in the same sort of difficulties that so much of OWI is.

Coming downtown this morning I found Massachusetts Avenue lined with a two-foot-high wall of dirty snow . . . the cripple in the wheelchair at the Press Club table . . . Dave Niles says Joe Casey talks too much, that is the reason Frank Walker, new Democratic chairman, opposes him as executive director of the Democratic National Committee . . . "Merry-Go-Round" this morning had dope which must have come from Casey about our job on public relations for President—Herman Kehrli of the Budget Bureau says Landis spends his life in a little world of generals, cabinet officers, etc.—goes to Cabinet—all above and remote from his job. My old Macmillan editor, Jim Putnam, big and hearty, walking down the corridor from my office in State Department on his way by boat to North Africa, showed me his passport . . . The big Negro in the Press Club hat-check room gives no checks but after a careful look at the checker says, "I gotcha." The youthfulness of Walter Lippmann . . . friendliness of Ray Clapper.

Thursday, February 4. David Niles endorses the speculation of Fleet Williams [my long-time editorial associate on *The News and Observer* of Raleigh] that the place where Ed Flynn was really done to death was not in the Senate but the State Department. (1) The case was presented to the Foreign Affairs Committee by a subordinate in the State Department, who did not make out a very good case. (2) Democrats on the Foreign Affairs Committee who voted against Flynn were friends of Hull, particularly Senator George, who is a great friend of Hull. (3) The real crack-up in the case came from Boss Ed Crump in Tennessee, which is Hull's home state. [Whoever was responsible for the outcome, the whole business of the proposed dispatch of the former Democratic national chairman to the Pacific post was a fiasco. Flynn ineptly announced his appointment as Ambassador to Australia before the White House did. Charges of graft and politics were loudly brought against him. Eugene Casey, who himself was regarded as an embarrassment in the White House, was a loud defender of Flynn. Finally, with the bruised Flynn's agreement, Roosevelt withdrew the appointment.]

Monday, February 8. The President is in Hyde Park. He apparently left Friday night and is not expected back in his office until Wednesday. General Watson is away also but Miss Dickinson, in Watson's office, assured me that my name is high on the list of people he wants to see, but that it isn't set down by the day and the hour.

Wednesday, February 17. Had lunch with Dr. Will Alexander. The Rosenwald Fund will have to spend during the next two years about five or six million dollars, which it wants to devote to advancing the people of the South. Its interest is not restricted to the Negro, though, of course, the Negro would be involved. Dr. Alexander asked me if I would try to make some suggestions as to what could be done by the foundation, apart from this, in planning some defenses against the inevitable dislocation, riot, etc., which will probably attend demobilization at the end of the war.

What he wants is something for the long pull beyond these strains. I gathered from Dr. Alexander at the luncheon that he had withdrawn from worry about the Fair Employment Practices Committee, feeling that the matter has become so involved that there is nothing at present that he can do.

He told an amusing story about two Farm Security plantations side by side. One had been cut up into individually owned tracts of sixty acres, the other operated as a cooperative throughout. He talked with one of the individual farmers who knew what he wanted and what he was doing. He also talked with one of the little farmers who was a member of the management committee of the cooperative, who knew all the words of cooperative farming and used them correctly. Afterwards, Dr. Alexander took him aside and asked him to tell him confidentially how he was getting on. Better than ever before in his life, he said. "You know, I believe a man could stick around here for five or six years and save enough money to go off and buy himself a little hill farm."

Dr. Alexander said that Edward O'Neal worked hand in glove with the packers, International Harvester Company,

130

and the Chamber of Commerce of the United States. He said that George Googe, of the AFL, told him that at Muscle Shoals before TVA, a labor man sold out his union and that O'Neal was the man who did the bribing.

Saturday, February 20. Joe Casey and I went to see the President at twelve o'clock. He was very pleasant but I got the distinct impression that he had rather lost interest in the home-front program he had asked us to report on. When we went in the room he was reading something on his desk and asked us to wait a minute while he read. We sat in silence and Joe came over and asked me for a cigarette.

The President said abruptly that he was worried about Gandhi, who looked like he was going to die; the President said he was disturbed about the reaction. He called up the Secretary of State and told him to get in touch immediately with Halifax, the British ambassador, and "make it strong." He said, "The sentiment in this country is with us and we ought to be with it in the event he dies and it won't hurt us if he doesn't." He said something in answer to a question that he didn't know anything about forcible feeding or anything but wanted something done. [Gandhi was in prison, blaming the British for "leonine violence." On February 10 he had begun an announced twenty-one-day fast or hunger strike. Gandhi survived five years, dying in 1948 at the hands of a Hindu assassin, after Roosevelt was dead.]

I couldn't be sure from his half of the conversation (to which he indicated that he welcomed our listening by winks) exactly what program he proposed. Toward the end of the conversation he said, "I doubt if he has got enough experience." Then, turning away from the phone, he asked us what we thought of Clyde Herring, former senator from Iowa, as Ambassador to China. I recalled Willkie's statement about somebody able to speak Chinese and also spoke of Herring's age. I got the impression that Senator Herring hasn't got much chance. [One of the casualties of the 1942 elections, Senator Herring had been elected governor of Iowa in the Rooseveltian triumph of 1932 and senator in the Democratic landslide of 1936. His experience before he came into public office was as an automobile dealer. He did not get the assignment to China but shortly after this he was made senior assistant administrator of the Office of Price Administration. At this time a vacancy in the Chinese post appeared likely due to the illness of Ambassador Clarence E. Gauss, a foreign service officer. On his resignation more than a year later, Roosevelt named Patrick J. Hurley in his place.]

We never got through our memoranda. We discussed the proposed committee to clear differences between department heads. The President said that such a committee already exists, composed of himself, Rosenman, Hopkins, Admiral Leahy, and Byrnes. But he thought it might be a good idea to make a statement about it and perhaps use Baruch. With regard to our suggestion that he see more congressmen, he said that he was seeing all the new congressmen on, I think, the 10th of March.

However, he said, rather significantly I thought, that he wasn't disturbed by opposition in Congress, that he had been governor of New York with a Republican House and Senate but that they had organized an informed, speaking Democratic opposition. He thought such an opposition was needed in this Congress. With regard to patronage, he stressed the fact that very often it was difficult to get the right man or sufficient agreement between the senators and congressmen concerned. He seemed surprised when Casey said that since Senator Prentiss M. Brown took over OPA, Republicans were still being appointed in Massachusetts. [Leon Henderson had resigned from his much beleaguered post in December 1942.]

Casey spoke of the appointment of Charles B. Rugg, lawyer of Boston, to handle the AP case, although Rugg is a violent anti-New Deal Republican. The President made no comment. I got a very definite impression that he feels that his strength is not bound up with successful opposition in Congress, that he expects Congress to pass some unconstitutional legislation. He said he was glad the situation existed in the spring of '43 instead of the spring of '44, which made me wonder whether he had already made up his mind on the fourth term.

He spoke at considerable length about manpower, particularly as it relates to the farm. He said that there is no real manpower shortage in industry though there may be situations in crowded cities which create a condition similar to a shortage. He is beginning to work on a speech to the farmers, and said he planned to urge the farmers to plant everything they could with a guarantee from him that whatever is planted will be harvested. He said draft boards had not shown much intelligence in drafting farm boys but that in some places, he mentioned Georgia specifically, where thirty-six farm boys could have been deferred if they had requested deferment, only four were willing to sign. He suggested that the government might induct the farm boys and then return them to farms with a badge to be worn showing that they had been sent back for essential work. I passed on to him some of Russell Marion's suggestions. He seemed interested. Also he is very much interested in the use of all local labor, the banker and the school child, in crop harvesting.

He told us how Samuel Zemurray, for whom he said he had the greatest admiration, had taken the United Fruit Company away from stuffed-shirt Brahmin Boston businessmen. Also he repeated himself on one funny story, telling us again the joke about Knudsen and the Republicans. In connection with Zemurray, he told a story about Felix Frankfurter. He said Frankfurter asked where Zemurray came from and the President said he was an immigrant boy from Bessarabia and that Frankfurter said he didn't know there were any Jews in Arabia.

I had the general impression throughout the hour and more we were with him that he was talking because he wasn't interested in what we might have to say. At the end of the conference I was planning to stand up and say, "Mr. President, I would be glad if you would give me another assignment," in spite of the fact that Harry Hopkins and some dark little man were standing at the back of the room waiting for us to get out—then he said, "Jonathan, I want to see you very soon." I came back to my office and told this to Lucy, Elizabeth Brite, and Noble Cathcart and they all burst out laughing.

David Niles feels that it would be a good idea if it would be possible to get the impression across that the President is not going to run for a fourth term. Such an impression would mean, he thinks, that the senators and others now fighting Roosevelt would begin to fight among themselves and also that the contestants would vie for the blessing of Roosevelt. "I would like to see an article suggesting the President will not run again." Another article he would like to see is one called "The Great Conspiracy," which would suggest that Willkie has never broken with the conservative wing of the Republican party but that it is by agreement with it that he seems to have done so. This makes it possible for him to hold the conservative support while seeking the support of labor and minority groups. He spoke of Willkie's friendship with David Dubinsky, of the International Ladies Garment Workers Union. Also pointed out that Willkie did not fight Dewey or any other Republican, though he talked a great deal privately in opposition to Republican reactionaries.

As we went into the President's office, Anna Rosenberg, wearing another pert hat, came out, after a big gust of presidential laughter.

Also, in the President's anteroom, General Watson on the telephone ascertained from Norman Davis, chairman of the Red Cross, that Davis has 100 cases of good liquor on hand and he thinks it will last as long as he lasts. [It should have. Davis, financier and diplomat from Tennessee, died seventeen months later, in July 1944.]

Monday, February 22. Molly Flynn tells an interesting story apropos of officials' use of cars. She got from Mrs. Julius Amberg, wife of special assistant to the Secretary of War, the suggestion that James V. Forrestal, in order to avoid criticism, has purchased a taxicab and the driver of the cab is the chauffeur. She said Mrs. Amberg was with the Forrestals and that several cabs came up but Mrs. Forrestal looked at them carefully and said, "This is not the one," until the fifth one had appeared. This story is, I think, based on that circumstance alone and may be entirely untrue. [This story was told perhaps maliciously about several prominent persons during strict wartime gasoline rationing. The rich Mrs. Forrestal was perhaps a natural target. As Josephine Ogden, she had been a handsome member of the staff of *Vogue* magazine when she married Forrestal in 1926. He was with the investment banking firm of Dillon, Read and Company, of which he was president when he came into government. Perhaps emulating Mrs. Roosevelt, Mrs. Forrestal made several trips "on government business" to London, one in 1943 to study the experience of the WRENS (Women's Royal Naval Service) in connection with our WAVES (Women Accepted for Volunteer Emergency Service in the Navy). Arnold A. Rogow, a Forrestal biographer, wrote very gently that her trips "made little contribution to the war effort."]

Wednesday, February 24. Apropos of McIntyre's suggestion to the President that I be made administrative assistant working on liaison with the war agencies, the President sent back a note to McIntyre: "No, not Daniels. I have on another hen." McIntyre said he thought he had another hen on for me, but he had no idea what the hen was going to hatch.

*   *   *

McIntyre made a cryptic statement with regard to Eugene Casey and mentioned the fact that David Niles was looking for a job for him. He grinned and said, "What is Dave doing for himself?"

*   *   *

Also McIntyre regaled Miss Jackson and myself with a story of a spat he had had with General Watson. "Pa" had phoned that he would be late but when he arrived, instead of looking up McIntyre and Hassett (who was going over in Early's place), he went on up to see the President without them. "What are you trying to do, be teacher's pet?" McIntyre asked him. I gathered that the exchange was not angry but good-natured, but that irritation lay beneath it.

*　　*　　*

Dick Neuberger [the writer and later senator from Oregon], who has been invalided out of Alaska as the result of a stomach condition and rheumatism caused by cold, came in to see me. He is disturbed by the lack of war unity in the Army and among civilians. He finds in the Army a growing anti-Semitism and anti-Roosevelt feeling. He reported the incident of a Texas sergeant in Alaska making fun of Roosevelt and all his family to the delight of his mates. On the other hand, Neuberger is very much impressed by the toughness of the Americans, including Southern Negroes, who stood for a half hour in the glacial streams along the Alaska Highway to sink piles for bridges. The morale of the men, however, is very low, he thinks. He hoped there could be some sort of system by which men in outposts could be brought back home for duty after a year's service. He said that at White Horse the temperature often was sixty degrees below zero and that until well into the cold weather even officers slept in tents. He said the equipment of the men was good so far as clothing was concerned, except for shoes, but that the head of the Canadian Mounted Police had asked General James J. O'Connor whether the shoes had been designed by the Army or by the enemy. Neuberger is glad that he took my advice and went into the Army. He wants to go back to Alaska but he has found the going much tougher, I think, than he expected.

Thursday, February 25. "Very confidentially," said McIntyre, "the President is sick. I went up this morning with Bill Hassett and as we were going in the room I said to Harry Hopkins, 'Come in here, I have got a brainstorm.' Hopkins said, 'It won't do you any good.' I said, 'Wait a minute, why can't we use a little psychological warfare?' "

"Now this is deep as a well," he said again. "Last week we said the President was canceling his engagements so he could write his speech. The President said just to notify the public that he is canceling his engagements. Why don't we tell them he is sick? Why don't we exaggerate it a little? Why don't we make this one degree of fever and this toxic condition sound like something? It would do some of these senators good to think of the idea that they might have Henry Wallace President for the next year and a half. I remember people telling me about the cold chills they had when they were told that the President flew to Africa. There will be letters coming in here from women telling Congress to leave the President alone."

"What did the President say?" I asked McIntyre. "I am going to announce it today at twelve o'clock!" he answered.

I asked him about McNutt. He said, "They are out to get him but they won't without a fight and I say more power to him." On the other hand, McIntyre said a little later that it doesn't make any difference whether McNutt is doing a good job, if the Congress and the people are against him, you can't keep him. He said the same thing to the President the other day about Rex Tugwell. He said that as regards this business about Winant as head of War Manpower coming out now, he had suggested Winant to the President back at the time when the President was full of the talk about Harold Ickes for the place. The President had refused to consider it, saying that next to Churchill, Winant was the most important man in England now, popular and influential with the people. McIntyre said, "Ickes wasn't the man for that job and I called him up and congratulated him for having sense enough not to take it."

The White House is going forward with its plans for the smoker for the new congressmen on the 16th of March. The President has not signed all the invitations but McIntyre hoped that he would be able to sign them today. He called up Lyndon Johnson and asked Lyndon to drop down and look it over to see that it was correct. "I am trying to get Lyndon back in here," he said. "He is still a little resentful of the way General Watson treated you and him that day but I know he is just as loyal to the Boss as ever."

McIntyre was having a day with his secretaries, who, he said, were getting so sloppy and careless that he couldn't put up with it any longer, that old man Rudolph Forster was the sweetest guy in the world but he didn't see any sense in enforcing any discipline. So McIntyre is having him a day Simon-Legreeing his girls.

*   *   *

Francis Bradshaw [former dean at the University of North Carolina] came in to see me with the suggestion that if anything was going to be done about McNutt, Frank Graham would be a good man to succeed him in Manpower. I told him I didn't know what was going to be done but that I would see if I could find out. I went upstairs to see Dave Niles, who, while quite cagey, said that he didn't think anything could be done about McNutt at this time. Also he suggested that Frank Graham was too much of the academician. He said he was glad I had come, however, as he wanted to see me.

He said that William J. Donovan, director of the Office of Strategic Services, wanted to get me to head up Psychological Warfare, which he said was the program of directing the underground psychological attack on the Axis. I was not sure at first whether this was something he was doing for the President, but he said not. We also discussed the fact that there is a row between Major General George V. Strong, chief of Military Intelligence, who thinks he should control the OSS, and Donovan. Strong had been to see the President with the idea that Donovan be made a general under him but Donovan was insisting on his own independence. Also there is a fight between Donovan and OWI and between Donovan and Nelson Rockefeller, Coordinator of Inter-American Affairs. Niles said that some time ago Anna Rosenberg had called him and protested against Donovan's activities in South America. I told Niles I didn't feel free to consider the job until I had seen the President, as he said he wished to see me.

In the same conversation I gathered that Aubrey Williams had repeated to Niles an amusing crack made by Joe Casey. Niles thinks Casey is anti-Semitic. He has been opposed for appointment by John McCormack and Sam Rayburn and also, I suspect, by Niles. Jim Rowe, on the other hand, has been strong in the support of Casey. I told Niles that the best man I knew to run the Democratic campaign in the next two years would be Lindsay Warren, who is bored as Comptroller General of the United States and would like nothing better than to get back into politics, if the opportunity should be offered. Afterwards, I said, he might be appointed federal judge for the Eastern District of North Carolina, where Judge Isaac Meekins is reaching the retirement age. Niles, in connection with the Donovan matter, mentioned a man whose name I remember as Goldman in the labor section, but later Moe Beckelman [who worked in OSS] told me he knew of no one in OSS named Goldman. Actually this was Arthur Goldberg, who is acting chief of the labor section of OSS. [Goldberg later became Secretary of Labor and associate justice of the U. S. Supreme Court by appointment of President Kennedy.]

*   *   *

Aubrey Williams tells me in great confidence that he is expecting to leave the government, whether or not he wins his fight over NYA with Congress, on July 1st. That he expects to get a stake and devote himself to the political support of the Administration. He said he hoped Dave Niles was going with him. Apparently neither he nor Niles is very much pleased with the new set-up in the National Committee. Williams felt that the job of the National Committee would be to work with the conventional Democrats while he and Dave would devote themselves to labor and minority groups. I asked him what sort of organization they would have and he said that they didn't need any organization if he had about $300,-000. When he told me this I wondered if there was any connection between it and McIntyre's recent statement as to "what was Niles going to do for himself." I don't quite understand the situation but I begin to realize that a situation does exist.

*   *   *

At today's meeting in the Cosmos Club, Oscar Cox discussed provision of a plan for maintaining the prosperity of the country after the war. Basically it provided for a government guarantee to purchase at a fair price all farm production for several years after the war for the availability of materials to all employers, and for some qualifications on the power of companies to buy war plants. In order, for instance, that Kaiser might be able to make his new car, which he says he could sell for $400 in the Chrysler tank plant if he wanted to do it and Chrysler wasn't going to use it, [he would set up rules] so that Chrysler could not "dog in the manger" the plant in order to eliminate the competition. Milo Perkins has an idea to give each soldier who wishes it a year's training in any type of employment he would like with his base pay continuing. Cox used the figure for plants built at government expense as twenty billion dollars.

I was pretty much alone at the meeting in suggesting that it seemed to me what was needed was not any financial pump-priming plan along old New Deal lines, but some more profound change in terms of full use of our productive capacity built up during the war.

Friday, February 26. Joe Casey spent the afternoon rambling in talk of Massachusetts politics, including a joke about Cardinal O'Connell as the "Papal bull" and Curley's referring to him as the "old SOB." He is talking about going back to Clinton to practice law and also have a sort of branch office here. He says that the George Washington dinner in Massachusetts practically amounted to a tender to him of the Democratic nomination for governor next time. All his rambling indicated, however, that he had very little to do and is not very happy doing it. [Though in January *The New York Times* had reported that Casey was expected to become, as he wished, executive director of the Democratic National Committee, by this time that report or expectation had expired.]

Saturday, February 27. Newman Jeffry, labor man in OCD, tells me about a major in Army public relations working with labor groups. He went to Toronto to attend an American Federation of Labor conference and has since worn the Army ribbon denoting foreign service. Jeffry says the Public Relations Division of Army Services of Supply contains few real labor men but that it is the real hideout spot for young men dodging service at the front.

He told me of another character, a former labor reporter on a Hearst Newspaper, who, he says, at an Atlanta labor meeting made a date with a WAAC, who brought a bottle of whiskey, which he drank; he got her drunk and into a poker game, won ten dollars from her, took her to bed, and then kicked her out next morning.

Newman also says that there is a serious scandal involved in the failure of the OCD to get stirrup pumps to the people. That they are now trying to get them distributed at a profit price through Sears, Roebuck. He says the whole story of the stirrup-pump business has been a mess from beginning to end.

He plans to get out of OCD sometime soon.

Wednesday, March 3. Lunch with Dave Lilienthal, who was talking about the contrast in Willkie's life between his association with David Dubinsky of the United Garment Workers Union, whose members recently cheered him when he spoke to them about Russia, and his association with Edgar Monsanto Queeny, president of the Monsanto Chemical Company, whose place in Arkansas Willkie recently visited. Lilienthal described Queeny as "a leader of the young Turks," who are opposed to the increase of war plants for fear of surplus capacity after the war. A bitter reactionary, Queeny, aged forty-five, is a Cornell graduate, a director and past vice-president of the National Association of Manufacturers, and director of the National Industrial Conference Board. He married Ethel Schneider and has his home in St. Louis. The secretary of the Monsanto Chemical Company is William W. Schneider.

Lilienthal feels that Willkie is working hard at the "all things for all men" job. He knows of no instance in which he was concerned about the Negroes before he ran for President and says that there were numerous bad labor situations in Commonwealth and Southern under his leadership. He does feel, however, that in the matter of civil liberties Willkie has always been sound. Lilienthal feels very strongly that a lot of the New Dealers don't realize that they are the members of a governmental phase that is of the past.

Monday, March 8. The President is still off in Hyde Park and won't be back until Wednesday. [From the beginning of 1942 until his death FDR made 41 separate trips to Hyde Park—an average of a visit a month.]

Lunch with Lowell Mellett, who is cussing Frank Capra, director of Columbia Studios, who under the guise of Army training films is trying to release as a regular feature film the story about Pearl Harbor. Mellett feels that the government should not get into the movie business except in a restricted field and he feels that he now has the movie industry adopting the themes the Administration would like to see it stress. He regards this as important, as the newspapers will be against us and the radio neutral in the next campaign. Also he feels that Capra's Army program would set a precedent for the National Association of Manufacturers to pump the people full of the government's own movies.

It seemed to me that Mellett rather talked too slick about what he has done. His feeling that Louis B. Mayer has come to him and in a sense is eating out of his hand. His pet hate in Hollywood is Walter Wanger, who, he said, tried to keep him from making the principal address at the Academy Awards dinner. Obviously Mellett is impressed like a child by the glamor of Hollywood. He made fun of Louie Mayer for practically saying at the Awards dinner that his son-in-law William Goetz, now a young movie man, might grow up to be as great a man as he is. However, Mellett rather dropped the idea that it was absurd not to have him speak, as he, Mellett, was the movie man of the year. He impresses me as a strange case, almost approximating the pathological.

David Niles said that he still thought I would probably go to Australia but that he and McIntyre had some other ideas if that didn't come off. I told him "nuts," that the whole situation seems to me to be getting increasingly silly. Niles agreed.

The White House impresses me as a well-dressed Georgia

courthouse scene. Everything so unhurried. McIntyre's secretary, Miss Jackson, doesn't come in until after 10:30. McIntyre refers to Miss Grace Tully as "the lady abbess." There seems to be a good deal of feeling among the older attachés there that she is trying to push in. [Marguerite (Missy) LeHand, the President's long-time private secretary, was still alive at this time, though she would never be able to return to work. She died in the summer of 1944.] McIntyre said the President wrote a silly letter to Willkie which he foolishly let Forster read and OK. Miss Tully said she didn't think they ought to pull it back after the President had signed it and McIntyre said, "I am here to tell him when he makes a mistake and not to keep telling him everything he does is perfect."

Tuesday, March 9. Lunch with Newman Jeffry. Afterwards we walked down along Lafayette Square towards the State Department since he was going to the CIO headquarters on Jackson Place. Newman is feeling pretty low. He says he is in a funny position in that Landis only responds to fear and is more afraid of him than anybody else in the organization. He has another budget hearing coming up on the field staff of labor. His labor advisory committee, he thinks, will support him and Newman thinks it is very important to get labor men into the regional offices. OCD, he thinks, could be very dangerous unless something is done but that with nine labor men he believes he could be effective in securing support for the Administration. The AFL, he says, has already gone over to the Republican party.

As we were coming towards the CIO headquarters he said that a strange situation had taken place there also. In the fight against the "Commies" the Catholics had now moved in. Philip Murray is a Catholic and young Jim Carey, of the Electrical Workers Union, and now the Catholic content of the organization has come down even to the stenographers, which made a difference in what the Pope might say.

Newman feels that Murray definitely is not a strong man and that now he is in a constant state over the fear that John L. Lewis will have him killed. He says that when Murray was supposed to have had a nervous breakdown some time ago it was because they caught some Lewis men putting dynamite under his house. Murray all his life was a Lewis subordinate and by silence at least agreed with all Lewis' methods. Now in separation there is a real psychological situation created. Incidentally he said that the Catholic Church in the United States is by and large the working man's church and most of the workers in industrial centers are Catholics.

He said that Gardner Jackson is feeling very low and bitter. Jackson doesn't say so, but he feels that he has devoted all his life to causes close to the New Deal and is now being thrown out. Jackson feels that McIntyre double-crossed him, that he urged Jackson to take the steps he was taking in the Department of Agriculture and then told Wickard about them. I told Newman that I doubted this very much. He also brought up the fact that when McIntyre talked to Jackson on the phone he asked him what his office extension was now, although Jackson has no office, having been fired. I told him I was there when that happened and I was sure it was carelessness. Newman feels that the Administration is collapsing on the home front and he would rather get out of OCD now if that part of it is going to fall to pieces. Speaking of Clare Boothe Luce, he used the phrase "a Vanity Fair Huey Long."

*   *   *

Note: The number of colored messengers in the State Department who wear zoot suits vastly exceeds the number of diplomats in spats and striped pants.

*   *   *

Lieutenant Richard Neuberger said he was on his way back to Vancouver for a check-up before going back to Alaska. He thinks he will be all right this summer but if he has a relapse next winter he will have to come down here. He said he had just been talking to a friend of his in the

Indian Service, the office of which was moved from Washington to Chicago. The man said they hated like the devil to go but they were getting about twice as much work done being removed from all the tug and pull and intrigue in Washington. Neuberger said it occurred to him that it would be a good idea for OWI's Domestic Branch, which is having so much trouble and intrigue with business and advertising men, to pull up stakes and move to Denver or some such place.

* * *

Incidentally, Roy Stryker called me up last night and apparently there had been a lot of hard feelings and hard talk in the Domestic Branch of OWI, particularly the publications division under John R. Fleming, to which Roy has been attached. He says that William B. Lewis and James E. Allen, deputy directors of the Domestic Branch of OWI, have been doing the real organizing for Mike Cowles. They brought a man over from the Navy named Price Gilbert, a former advertising man for Coca-Cola, to take Fleming's place, or at least a large part of his job, and that the first Fleming knew about it, the man was over there.

Henry Pringle's group of writers are very angry at the suggestion that they be placed under Jimmy Allen. Apparently there was an indignation meeting with Davis at which the present staff took down its hair and let fly. Later Davis called in Cowles and said that he hoped they would talk as frankly to Cowles as they had talked to him. Stryker said they really told Cowles. Either Davis or Cowles said that they had felt that Allen was a very reasonable and pleasant person, whereupon somebody in the group said that they suspected that he was pleasant to his superiors but that he showed no respect for anybody inferior to him. Stryker was excited and ultra-confidential. He said he was seeing Cowles today and I gathered that the fighting is still in progress. [Allen (born Moskowitz), then thirty-six, had been director of information for the Securities and Exchange Commission while Landis was its chairman. Afterwards he was engaged in movie production before he joined OWI, stopping briefly on his way to help Landis in OCD.]

Wednesday, March 10. Talked with McIntyre about my situation and he agreed with me and said he had talked to Judge Rosenman, who, he said, had a very high regard for me, and Judge Rosenman agreed that the President ought to act now in my case. At first McIntyre said he and Judge Rosenman thought I ought to prod the President about resigning but I said I didn't see how I could do that when he had said he wanted to see me very soon. I said, "I can't say to the President, 'What the hell, kick me out of here or assign me,'" and McIntyre said, "Of course you can't, but we will do it for you." They agreed they ought to talk to him about it today.

Also McIntyre told me that Dave Niles had suggested that Adlai E. Stevenson was resigning as special assistant to the Secretary of the Navy and that Niles suggested that I be appointed to take his place. McIntyre said, "I would stay out of that mess over there." I told him that I wondered if Stevenson wasn't there because of a personal relationship with Secretary Knox.

During the conversation I also said to McIntyre that what worried me was that my case was really a small example of a big case on the home front and that I was afraid we were going to get a worse licking in 1944 than Hoover got in '32. He said that what worried him was not the election, but things that needed to be done in the next twelve months, and "I don't mean party politics either." He said the President is really interested. "Yes," he said, "the President is beginning to get very interested."

"You told me that after the election in November," I reminded him.

"Yes," he said, "but lots of things have happened to interrupt, things that we don't even know about as well as the big things that we do know about, but he is getting interested now."

As I was leaving, James Noe of Louisiana came in to see

McIntyre. He is so fat he looks like he would pop if you stuck a pin in him.

McIntyre phoned me that Noe knew a lot about the piece that Governor Jones had written and suggested that I talk to Noe. Noe is coming at 3:30.

In *Louisiana Hayride* Harnett Kane describes James A. Noe as "gas and oil man, a smiling entrepreneur, whom Huey had drawn into politics and treated as a favorite son."

* * *

Jimmie Noe came in, all in tones of brown and wearing a watch which he showed me, inscribed "Jimmie Noe, co-liberator of Louisiana." He says that what Pearson reported in the "Merry-Go-Round" about the unpleasant conference between the President and the national committeemen was pretty nearly true. Later, from other remarks which he made, I gathered pretty clearly that he ought to think they were true because obviously he was the informant.

He says that he elected Sam H. Jones governor of Louisiana, that Jones no longer has any strength in Louisiana while he has gone back and joined the Long organization again, after helping elect Jones. He says he is going to be the next governor of Louisiana and invited me to come to his inauguration. Apparently he is pretty close to McIntyre, despite his making most of the fuss as he said at the meeting with the President, having been in to see him this morning and also having a call from McIntyre while he was in my office. McIntyre had suggested that he come to see me about the Jones article in the *Post*. He is a pretty amazing looking creature altogether—and claims he was the man who abolished the poll tax in Louisiana and that he had to persuade Huey to go along.

[Huey P. Long had been seven years dead at this time but the White House, as represented by McIntyre, and perhaps the President himself, was still edgy about the kind of politics he had exercised in Louisiana and in the United States Senate. While some regarded Long as only a clownish demagogue, FDR had recognized him as a menace. Now Long's ghost still marched. His brother, Earl K. Long, had been governor of the state in the late 1930s and would later serve twice again as governor. Sam Houston Jones, an anti-Long man, had defeated Earl Long in 1940, but in this March of 1943 Jones had been sharply critical of the Roosevelt administration in an article in *The Saturday Evening Post*. He warned that the South was ready for revolt against the New Deal.

[Noe who had been an original Huey Long man both in politics and in oil deals, took credit for Jones's election in 1940. Noe had been third man in a three-cornered race, trailing Earl Long and Jones. Then in the second primary Noe, for a political price, threw his votes to Jones. Jones has said that the price he paid was only making Noe Democratic national committeeman. Others said the price also included letting Noe name the man the Jones administration would support for congressman from the First Congressional District. The man Noe named, F. Edwards Hébert, was still serving in 1974 and holding the chairmanship of the House Armed Services Committee.

[As far as I can remember, all there was for me to do with and for Noe at this time was to listen to his truculent boasting. The President, however, was evidently irritated with his remarks about Southern discontent with the Administration at a meeting which he had with him and some other members of the National Committee a few days before and his leaking of the story about it to Drew Pearson for his "Merry-Go-Round." When questioned about this meeting two days later, on March 12, at his press conference the President replied: "I don't think there is any news in that. Let's get ahead with the war." That was that. Fortunately, for him it was. The South stayed solid for him as long as he lived. Noe's inauguration as governor never occurred.]

Monday, March 15. Engagement with the President. In the anteroom while I was waiting was Ed Flynn, youngish-looking man with the type of bald head in which a narrow fringe of hair in the front of his skull is allowed to grow long so it can be combed back in a pompadour of strings pasted to the scalp. He had a snappy brown suit, a florid tie and socks, and a dark-red carnation in his buttonhole. He said he wasn't mad at anybody. While he had been in Mexico a month he had not seen a newspaper or heard a radio and he was at peace with the world.

Before I began to talk to the President, McIntyre took up with him the fact that Eugene Casey, on his own, was preparing to go West and make a speech to a group of farm leaders, who had wired him. With some irritation, the President said, "Tell him not to go and I don't want anybody connected with the White House making any speeches to farm leaders while this thing is going on."

He immediately said to me, "Jonathan, I want you to go somewhere for me, I want you to go to New Zealand." Then he talked about the social program of New Zealand in which he had been interested, though he had never been there. He said he wanted to get it into the heads of the people that they mustn't go too hard on the idea that the only important war is in the Pacific. He spoke rather irritably of some official who is constantly blowing off after the Pacific War Council meetings. Also he remarked that he wanted me to keep New Zealand from trying to become an American state. "I want to get close to them and make arrangements for tariffs, etc., but I want them to stay part of the British Empire." New Zealanders and Australians, he said, are people who are not easy to get to, but are hospitable people after the first meeting has passed.

I said, "Mr. President, it seems a long way from the war, particularly the big fight [the war election of 1944] we are going to have here next year."

"Yes," he said, "it may seem so but actually we have thousands of soldiers in New Zealand. We are going to make a great base for our war wounded and it is an important center."

I told him I was honored to have him ask me to go but I couldn't bear to be out of the country in the big election fight. He said, "I don't want you to stay there very long. I will pull you back so you can be in the midst of things."

I reiterated the fact that I wanted to be in that fight and he promised to get me back in time for the primaries. I told him that I was having some dental work done and asked him how soon he wanted me to go. He said there was no hurry and he wanted to see me again. He remarked that someone ought to see Senator Bailey and didn't know how it would be with Bob Reynolds and I told him Max Gardner could probably fix it up for me. He asked, "Is Max going to run?" I said, "Yes, and he is going to be elected."

[I was too confident. As it turned out, Max did not run for the Senate. Instead his brother-in-law, Clyde Hoey, ran in 1944 for the seat vacated by Bob Reynolds and was elected. My prophecy that Max could "fix it up for me" turned out to be a greater mistake. Senator Bailey balked at my confirmation even before my name was submitted. So I was as out as Ed Flynn though I had more hair. I wore no carnation.]

Friday, March 26. Victor Weybright, with OWI in London, says that Frances Morley, daughter of Christopher, representing the International Student Service, and Daniel Poling, representing the *Christian Herald,* both flew into London on White House priorities. I asked if this was hearsay and he said no, he had seen cables to the Ministry of Information.

Weybright also feels that the difficulty in the OWI, so far as London is concerned, is the stupidity of direction from home rather than failure in the field. He says there are no contentions among the various American groups representing various agencies in London, that, without knocking heads together, Winant has succeeded in becoming an effective coordinator of all, but that in almost all agencies there are contentions between men in the field and officers in Washington.

Saturday, March 27. Talked to Colonel R. W. Ireland in regard to the system of granting priorities on airlines. All flying priorities are now granted by the Army under Colonel Ireland in the Washington office and eighteen offices in the country. The priority is granted on the basis of the necessity of the trip and not necessarily on the basis of the necessity of the traveler. A technical sergeant, for instance, might be more entitled to a priority than a colonel. There is no such thing as a White House priority or a WPB priority. Decisions are all made by Colonel Ireland's staff, though, of course, when the White House or the offices of the Secretary of War or Navy ask for priorities, Colonel Ireland's staff must accept decisions made by them.

Colonel Ireland thinks the situation is working pretty well. They are subjected to pressures. He spoke of Mrs. Claude Pepper, wife of the Florida senator, calling up and asking for a priority from the West Coast for José Iturbi, the pianist, who was going to give a concert at a canteen. However, Colonel Ireland's office discovered that he could get to the concert by train in time and also that while he was giving this free concert, he had two commercial concerts immediately following. He got no priority. A lieutenant colonel in Colonel Ireland's office said he had just been talking to a lieutenant who said, "Well, I guess I will be a private soon, I just turned down a Roosevelt's request for a priority." It turned out not to be the President's immediate family but some relative.

Welch Pogue, chairman of the Civil Aeronautics Board, thinks the priority system is working pretty well now. It was terrible before Colonel Ireland took over. There remains, he thinks, a question as to whether or not his power should be vested in the Army, perhaps it should be with the board, perhaps with Joseph B. Eastman of the Office of Defense Transportation. Eastman seems the best, but Pogue said he was not going to fool with it as long as the Army handled it well.

In conversation Pogue spoke of Senator Bailey, who is chairman of the Commerce Committee and whom Pogue likes. He was talking about Juan Trippe, president of Pan American Airways. Trippe's idea is that Pan American should, in the postwar world, have a monopoly, with some government relationship, on American overseas service. He said that Bailey was very strong for Trippe because of the fact that Bailey is a good friend of Max Gardner and Tom Morgan, both of whom are very close to Trippe. [All three whom Pogue mentioned were North Carolinians. Thomas A. Morgan, president of the Sperry Corporation, was a director and chairman of the executive committee of Trippe's Pan American Airways. Former Governor O. Max Gardner was one of Trippe's Washington lawyers. Bailey was as strong for Trippe as he had been against me. Oddly, I came into the picture as a fourth North Carolinian. Under the law while Pogue's board allotted domestic air routes on its own authority, all foreign routes suggested by the board had to be approved by the President. Somebody at the White House had to handle the presentation of each case for the President's decision. I was given that job.]

Quite off the record Pogue told me that the Army is now building a plane 190 feet long with a 210-foot wingspread which will be capable of carrying the contents of the Twentieth Century Limited.

* * *

Sworn in this morning by Max Gardner's secretary, Mrs. Murphy. [So my White House position was formalized as administrative assistant. Gardner was an old friend. Indeed, he made it his business to be everybody's friend. Courtly and punctilious as a lawyer with influence in Washington, he carefully avoided the plumage and the pitfalls of the influence peddler. He had been chairman of the North Carolina delegation at the Democratic National Convention which nominated Roosevelt in 1932. His term as governor expired as Roosevelt entered the White House. Undoubtedly his move to Washington was related to his position as Democratic leader but as he began practice there he resigned as member of the Democratic National Committee. He never asked me for any favor at the White House save once, when he suggested executive clemency for a little offender who didn't have a dime.]

Max spoke enthusiastically about Tom Morgan. I asked him about Morgan's new wife. He said that his former wife was interested only in painting and art—that they were not congenial and she fell in love with a major in the Army. Morgan allowed her to get a divorce and settled $250,000 on her. Then he married a girl named Celeste Page, who had been a reporter for an aviation magazine and whose father was a professor at the University of Virginia.

[Morgan was a charming and remarkable man. A country boy with only a high school education, he had joined the Navy when he was twenty-one and was serving as "Elec. Engr. U. S. Navy" on the U.S.S. *Delaware* when Elmer A. Sperry installed his gyrocompass, a major step in the electrification of the Navy. Joining the inventor, Morgan showed financial as well as electrical skill which made him Sperry's first aide and successor.]

Monday, March 29. David Niles is deeply disturbed by the evidences of anti-Semitism and says that not long ago Nelson went over to see General Brehon Somervell and that Somervell said to Nelson, "The trouble with you over at WPB is all those Jews you have over there." Niles said that he knew that Somervell felt that way when Somervell worked for him in WPA. He also showed me a letter which had been sent to him by a friend reporting that an Army officer spoke loudly in a café in the presence of Jews and said, "Hitler is 100 per cent right about the way he treats the Jews."

[General Somervell, Arkansas-born West Pointer and World War I veteran, had served as Southeastern regional engineer of the WPA in the relief program of the 1930s.]

Tuesday, March 30. Tom Blaisdell, Jr., New Deal economist now with the War Production Board, came in to see me to tell me the story of Robert R. Nathan and WPB. He began back at the beginning with the old National Defense Advisory Council, which he described as a pretty ineffectual group of people, most of whom thought there was plenty of time before America and that only a few people realized the real imperativeness of the war situation. Leon Henderson, in particular; Lock Currie did, he said, and Nathan. Nathan's conflict with the military grew from the fact that instead of having a really effective Army and Navy, we really have a lot of old men. The fact that we were not adequately prepared was the most important military secret.

Nathan and others kept pushing for greater preparation and Nathan irritated the Army because he was able, despite the military secrecy, to get the facts on our lack of preparation. Finally they had to be sold through pressure. Then when the brass hats were sold they were sold in a tremendous way, so big, indeed, that they neglected the fact that you had to have food and housing for workers and had to consider the possibilities in the American situation. At one time they had the situation fixed so that we could produce terrific quantities of tanks, but actually, due to the manner in which the planning was done, none of the tanks would run for lack of essentials that had been neglected.

There was a fight then over bringing order out of the bigness. This bigness without order was actually served by the President when, as Tom described it, he pulled his production goals out of the hat. Nathan has been the man who has been in front fighting. That brought him into contact with Somervell, who Blaisdell thinks is a really very able man but who resented the fact that Nathan is even more able. This recalls his remarks to Nelson which Niles told me—that there were too many Jews in WPB. However, the present fight, as Blaisdell reports it, takes the form of a struggle between big industrialists in effect headed by Baruch and his man Ferdinand Eberstadt, vice-chairman of WPB, to let the big industries run the show in a process which would result in the cartelization of American industries. This would move, Blaisdell thinks, towards communism or fascism. But he thinks these men are not aware of the philosophical aspects of the things they do. [Eberstadt was particularly close to the Navy's James Forrestal in this fight. They had been at Princeton together and at one time both were partners in Dillon, Read and Company.]

The struggle got to the point of one between big cartels in the formative stage and the American system of free enterprise. Blaisdell was pleased and surprised to find John Lord O'Brian, Republican general counsel of WPB, fighting on his and Nathan's side for free enterprise and going to see Secretary Stimson, his old friend, about it. Finally the thing got to such a stage that Nathan, who had been sick, got Nelson to come to his apartment, or else he went to Nelson's and pointed out that Baruch and his associates had much closer contact with the White House and that he would have to act if they were not going to win. He said Nelson had to fire Eberstadt quickly. At the same time Wayne Coy told Nelson he would have to fire Eberstadt or lose himself.

Blaisdell's group, including Nelson and Nathan, had come to the conclusion that the best man to handle the production job was Charles E. Wilson of General Electric. Nelson finally agreed and without warning to Eberstadt called him in and read him the news release announcing his dismissal. However, things have not been simple since the victory. In the reorganization of WPB under Wilson, the planning committee headed by Nathan has not been left with Nelson or transferred directly to Wilson but has been placed under Wilson's assistant, Ralph Cordiner, president of Schick Razor and formally with General Electric. Cordiner had never called Nathan in to talk to him but he has been to see Stacy May, head of Statistics, who has long been a friend of Nathan's and an associate in his campaigns, and suggested that the planning committee and the statistics section ought to be consolidated. May, who is no great executive, said that if that were done, Nathan ought to head it. Cordiner did not agree. It was in these circumstances that Nathan asked his draft board to call him up. When he asked for the letter canceling his deferment, no one even went through any motions of objecting. However, when Nathan saw Nelson, Nelson said, "The Army is not going to take you, Bob" (Nathan has been sick since he hurt his back some months ago), "and the place for you is here." Nathan definitely did not agree. Blaisdell is to see Nelson tomorrow or the next day and seems to have a feeling that Nathan's usefulness, because of his fights with the Army, is past. Perhaps the fact that he is a Jew enters here also. At any rate, they seem to be determined to get him out of the picture and I gathered that both Nathan and Blaisdell, who have thought that they could provide the guts for Nelson, have now come to the feeling that they made a mistake in tying to a man who never possessed guts.

*   *   *

Talked with McIntyre and Jim Barnes and Dave Niles about the possibility of my serving as a sort of coordinator of existing staff in government to see to it that speeches on pertinent aspects of the Administration's program are made available to members of Congress and others. Barnes also has some idea about giving the congressmen a column on what is going on in Washington for distribution to their local papers. At any rate, I want to find out what staff is available in Washington in the business of writing speeches—how they could be pooled together to make this necessary activity serve the Administration.

Wednesday, March 31. Barney Baruch has a very nondescript-looking suite, ⅜600, at the Carlton. A blond, rather country-looking secretary, with long gums and short teeth, who looks more like a servant or a nurse than a secretary. Barney came in, put in his earphone, and he and I had lunch together. He talked very friendly and affectionately. Told me about the children. Belle is doing some sort of secret work on the coast of South Carolina for the Navy and FBI, Renée, whose married name I forget, is driving an ambulance in New York, and Junior is a lieutenant commander in the Navy. He has developed a system for spotting submarines. Old Barney says young Bernie is very able but also very shy and doesn't like to feel that his father's influence helps him. I told him that I could understand that all right.

As Baruch came in he told me he had just taken on two big jobs, escort vessels and submarines, and added also that plane production was not moving as it ought to be. In fact, he said that if we had produced as we should have produced, we could already have beaten Hitler. We are moving, he said, but like molasses or glue. The Army and the Navy aren't even using the things your father and I learned in the last war, he said. He added that Wayne Coy liked him all right, but thought he was sort of fighting the last war but that the experience of the last war is the only thing we have to go on.

He said it was harder to get good men in this war than in the last because business is now in the hands of managers rather than owners. They work with more lawyers and public relations men about them and have become a business bureaucracy. A notable exception, he thought, were the Du Ponts, who still run their own business—"very dull people to talk to," he said, "but they get things done."

He told me that he and a small group, whose names he did not give me, had made a report to the President which the President was carrying out but in a slightly modified form. "We recommended," he said, and then he drew his finger across his throat, "that they give this to Wickard. That if McNutt did not do better to give it to him, and to give it to Nelson."

He said Nelson had no guts, was unwilling to make decisions; also he told me an interesting supplement to Tom Blaisdell's story of yesterday. He said that before Nelson fired Eberstadt (and incidentally he said he should never have fired him, but should have made him and Wilson work together), the President had asked him (Baruch) to become head of WPB. He was considering it when he went on the train to New York and at Philadelphia was taken with a raging fever which he first feared might be cancer or *anything,* but it turned out to be a swollen gall bladder and liver. In his delirium he kept talking about—they were after Jimmy and he had to get on his hands and knees and go down to Washington and help them. "I wasn't as crazy as they thought I was," he said.

Into his conversation came his faith in two ideas: (1) that there must be a war cabinet and (2) that industry must be made to assume the responsibility for doing its job.

"America," he said, "has the two most dangerous enemies it ever had and our whole industry must be so organized that we can turn its power to either coast. That we can ask for something and it will be coming out. We are not so organized today."

He is a vain old man but a very intelligent old man, with great self-confidence. He thinks that in sixty days he could have so organized production that it would be moving at the rate necessary. He said if he went into WPB he would have carried only one man with him, John Hancock [investment banker in charge of Navy purchasing in World War I].

"He worked with your father in the last war," he said. "I would have called Wilson in and said that I knew of the powers Mr. Nelson had given him—that I was confirming those powers. Now go on and do the job. But they would all know that I knew what was going on and they would also all know that John Hancock was able to take the place of any one of them and do the job better than they were doing it."

His devotion to Woodrow Wilson remains as strong as ever. Also he hates John Maynard Keynes, the economist who fought the Versailles Treaty and is now in a position of dominance in the Bank of England. He said he told Halifax to tell Churchill that if he didn't get away from Keynes, Keynes was going to make an isolationist out of Baruch. Again he said, "I am seventy-two years old and I have noticed this, that if you are right the mob may leave you but it will come back."

He asked me about the Guggenheim fellowships and I expressed my feeling that it was one of the finest types of philanthropies. He said he was thinking about what to do with the millions he had lying around. His children are well taken care of and he was thinking about endowing a school of physiotherapy—that physiotherapy is now in the hands of quacks. He spoke of his admiration for Buck Duke but said that Duke was always just like the rest of us, just a half-grown adult in things other than making money.

"I don't want any job," he said, "and I don't want any money. I have got a dollar more than I will ever need as long as I live."

We talked of Leon Henderson's mistakes and I spoke of his speaking with a cigar in his mouth at Chapel Hill. "He's got the big head," Baruch said, "then he is just a common man. You know what I mean, a worker can be a gentleman, but Henderson is just common and has no manners."

Saturday, April 3. This morning, McIntyre, irritated with Oscar Chapman, who he said begged off from the FEPC job after Ickes had agreed to release him, referred to him in a telephone conversation with Harry Hopkins as the "gutless wonder."

I asked McIntyre how he got along with his "conference" yesterday. He said he was the luckiest man in the world. He got back to the White House just in time to get a phone call from Grace Tully, who apparently was with the President. "I am lucky," he said, "I answered the phone right away and I could hear them say, 'Old Mac stays on the job—others may not but old Mac does.'" He grinned at Rudolph Forster and Miss Jackson.

* * *

Yesterday he gave me a letter which the President is sending to the Secretaries of War and Navy and said, "I wish you would glance over that"—so very naturally I began to read the letter and its attachments. He turned to Miss Jackson and said, "He is a thorough bastard, isn't he?" It didn't seem to me to be evidence of thoroughness but that is the way he talks.

Thursday, April 8. Quite casually Mrs. Ruth Shipley [head of the State Department's Passport Division] told me that the Secret Service at the White House is working on permits to send two White House cars to Mexico. [The White House Secret Service detail was headed by Michael F. Reilly, a charming, debonaire Irishman who gave FDR not only vigilance but devotion to the last hour.]

* * *

Mrs. Shipley went to Sumner Welles's office and talked to him about the project to investigate the foreign staffs of government agencies. Welles told me of a rather stormy session with Elmer Davis over a man named Hausman whom Davis' office wanted to send to North Africa, although he had only been a naturalized citizen for ten days. Davis insisted that his office had properly investigated the man but when he called from Welles's office to his own investigating section they told him that they had made no investigation but had accepted the investigation made in Office of Facts and Figures days. General George V. Strong of Army Intelligence came over and Davis agreed to leave the decision in his hands. Strong interviewed Hausman and later told Welles that under no circumstances would he be willing to have Hausman go to North Africa. Welles said that Robert Sherwood [the playwright, then head of the Overseas Operations Branch of OWI] was an able sort of man but that he had been surrounded by people who he felt were too close to the Communist party.

Welles called in Mrs. Shipley, who, despite her "Mrs.," has a distinctly maiden look, gray hair, pince-nez glasses. I went down to her office, where she sat at her desk, which was heavily laden with all sorts of papers. On a table beside it were a variety of new books and magazines. In a red steel safe in the corner of her room she had the records of people against whom she had protested when passports were issued. Maxwell Anderson, the playwright, was in the safe and Joseph Barnes [writer who had accompanied Willkie on his world trip]. A passport was refused Barnes some time ago but Willkie personally chose him to go abroad with him and the State Department didn't feel they could refuse him. Mrs. Shipley wrote the memorandum which Welles forwarded to the White House. Mrs. Shipley said that they didn't prevent liberals from going to countries even though they knew that when they began to think about the living conditions in these primitive countries their liberalism might be dynamite. There is no mistaking, however, her feeling that such liberals on the face of the earth are dangerous.

Friday, April 9. Eugene Casey said to Jim Barnes and myself, "We have got to get together and work on the President to get this hate of the farmers out of his heart." I expostulated very vehemently and he modified it, but I am afraid he is saying it to other people too.

Monday, April 12. As the President prepares to depart [on

a tour of war plants and training camps and a visit to President Camacho in Mexico], the White House is in something of a swivet over the case of Eugene Casey. Jim Barnes, into whose work field he enters most completely, is particularly active in urging the President to get rid of him. It looks like another case of White House inertia in a difficult spot. Everybody wants to get rid of him and neither McIntyre nor Barnes nor the President nor anybody else wants to take the onus of doing the ruthless job. The present plan is for the President to call him and say that since he has appointed Chester Davis War Food Administrator, there is no longer any reason for his original job, which was connected with liaison with the Department of Agriculture. My only interest in the matter is that Casey is the unauthorized occupant of one of the set-ups provided for the administrative assistants. McReynolds says he took this without any authority when Jim Rowe moved out. That he, McReynolds, has given him notice in writing to vacate but that the White House didn't stand behind it.

* * *

I am wondering how the relationship between McIntyre and Barnes is going to work. The other day McIntyre was talking about appointing some man who is not a Democrat as a personnel director in the little business set-up of WPB.

"I don't want any more of these personnel directors who are not Democrats," Barnes said a little vigorously, and McIntyre looked at him with a sick grin and said, "Hello, Franklin."

Afterwards, McIntyre said that Barnes had a swelled head. Barnes does have a way of boasting about himself which is a little obvious. There has been no mention of David Niles in the controversy over who is to handle the political situation and I am wondering what is his present status. I remember that when Barnes was to be appointed, the President said that he couldn't have three men, Barnes, Niles, and Casey, all handling politics on his staff and Harry Hopkins was to talk to Niles.

Today at the White House you could feel that things were piling up on the President's desk before he leaves tomorrow for his trip. McIntyre had piles of papers which he wanted to see the President about and was complaining again because while the President, he says, gives half an hour to people with not very much business, he neglects his old and regular staff while expecting them to get things done. McIntyre says he makes a point of never assuming any authority that the President hasn't given him. That his stock in trade is when he tells people that the President wants something done—he actually does want it done. He says that Louis Howe used to take the responsibility—that the President liked it but occasionally he would blow up and get mad as the devil. Tommy Corcoran used to say the President wanted things on his own motion. But McIntyre says he is not going to be doing things and then have the President give him hell.

Tuesday, April 20. I went to see Milo Perkins of BEW at his office in Temporary T Building. Perkins devoted most of his time to discussing the background of the struggle with Jesse Jones of RFC, who he thinks is an inefficient but a tough old guy. Perkins speaks a profane and earthy vernacular to describe the failure of Jones's outfit to acquire stockpiles as directed by Congress. Also he described a final meeting with Jones and Will Clayton [big Texas cotton dealer who had come into government as a first assistant to Jones] over the relationships of BEW and RFC, in which he said Jones used everything from talking about crucifying an old man to the toughest kind of tactics. Apparently they got to talking to each other and had a raw row.

Perkins has a list compiled showing essential materials, what RFC did with them prior to the order of April 13, 1942, giving BEW authority, and what BEW has done since. He makes it a very damaging story for Jones and a very dramatic one for BEW. It is all confidential material and he doesn't mean to use it against Jones unless Jones keeps on undercutting him on the Hill. He doesn't want to hurt FDR but if Jones keeps undercutting, he is going to send a copy of it marked "secret" to each one of the ninety-six senators.

162

Perkins is an interesting man. He had coffee sent up for us while we talked and I gathered that he drinks a good many cups a day. Also, though it was raining when we left his office he didn't wear a coat on his way over to have lunch with Don Nelson. He never wears one, or a hat.

Apparently BEW has full control, leaving Jones only clerical functions in terms of all commodities except rubber, which Perkins says William M. Jeffers, U. S. Rubber director, slipped to Jones after Jones had been courting him for a while. That he and Vice-President Wallace, chairman of the Board of Economic Warfare, thought they had better take a licking in that, though they still have supervisory functions over Jones. Some sort of settlement is in progress in the row which will keep BEW's over-all powers but will leave to Jones something more than a clerical relationship to the less dramatic, difficult phases of the work and leave the tougher jobs, requiring more imagination, to BEW.

Perkins said that Herman Baruch, brother of Bernard M., is going to Brazil for them—I think to look at the rubber field. Also he said that two men named Southworth and Hunter have gone to Brazil for the Bureau of the Budget to look over the administrative situation.

Monday, April 26. Nelson Rockefeller, Coordinator of Inter-American Affairs, is a very personable and attractive young man—gives the impression of being entirely frank, eager to be useful. He says that he feels that our relations with Latin America are slipping backwards now due to the number and attitude of Americans of various agencies in South America, particularly, I gathered, BEW. He says that in a country like Bolivia, for instance, the representatives of BEW and the State Department actually are, in attitude, almost like members of antagonistic political parties. The State Department working with the government and the companies while BEW is taking the position that the government is not democratic ("which it isn't," Rockefeller says) and is working with the people in a sense against the government.

Rockefeller, like John McCloy [Assistant Secretary of War], pointed out the "delicate subject." He says that Brazil does not permit the entrance of Jews but that BEW has just sent down a staff headed by Herman Baruch, Bernard M.'s brother, including other Jews, which makes a very unfortunate impression on the Brazilians and plays into the hands of Nazi propaganda. He says that there are constantly incidents like the one reported to him by one of his chief assistants on his return from a trip, of Americans who get drunk in cafés and talk big and loud about making more money in a day than a Brazilian makes in a year. This particular man was fired the next day but there are recurrences of such incidents.

I mentioned the Walmsley report to him and he said, "Now there is a case where our people are sore because Walmsley came back and said we had too many people in Brazil without ever having gone to the CIA office." [Walter N. Walmsley, Jr., a foreign service officer, was then attached to the Division of American Republics in the State Department.]

Rockefeller thinks that the confusion in the field stems straight from confusion in Washington—that BEW has a persecution complex about the State Department's attitude towards it while the State Department knows that BEW is trying to take over much of its function—and a similar feeling between BEW and RFC. In this situation it is impossible to get the heads of agencies around a table where in good faith they will try to work out sensible working arrangements. Everybody is always afraid the other man is trying to outsmart him and the result of their feeling here is reflected in the field. Rockefeller said he could get me all the information I want by this afternoon.

[A little later I made another note about Rockefeller as he moved from the Office of the Coordinator of Inter-American Affairs into position as an Assistant Secretary of State. I was riding in the elevator in the old State Department building, opposite the White House. I had known the black woman who operated it when both of us worked in the Office of Civilian Defense. On a Monday morning she greeted me with news.

["Oh, Mr. Daniels," she said, "you should have seen Mr. Rockefeller's dining room furniture."

[Even in the State Department, I was a little surprised. "His dining room furniture?"

["Oh, yes, sir," she said. "They brought it in yesterday and it's beautiful."

[I imagined that Rockefeller dining room furniture could be beautiful, but here it didn't seem to make sense.

["What's he doing with dining room furniture down here?"

["Oh, he's going to have a private dining room."

[That was clear, but there were also, then, five other Assistant Secretaries and Undersecretary of State Joseph C. Grew.

["Are the others going to have private dining rooms, too?"

[She considered that seriously. "I reckon," she decided, "that if they know he is, they will."]

Friday, April 30. After the President's press conference, at which he read his telegram to John L. Lewis [calling the current coal-mine troubles "strikes against the United States Government itself"], and spoke about his trip, McIntyre and I stopped to discuss the situation with regard to the FEPC. I suggested to the President that he let the whole business be centered in McIntyre rather than have several people around town fooling with it. He agreed and at the close of the conversation I also suggested that if possible the matter should be settled before President Edwin Barclay of Liberia comes to the United States. The President spoke about his trip to Liberia [on his way home from the Casablanca conference] and said that while there he was talking to some of the medical officers, who were appalled by the venereal-disease rate among our Negro troops there.

"I suppose it must be ten or twelve per cent," the President said.

"Ten or twelve!" said the officer. "It's 75 per cent." Venereal disease in Liberia, this officer told the President, is 100 per cent.

"I suppose," the President said, "they all get it before they are grown, as I understand there is no such thing as chastity in Liberia after the age of five or six." Elmer Davis, being present, wondered about the condition of President Barclay,

165

who is due to visit at the White House, and suggested to the President that they could wash off the toilet seat with Lysol.

The conversation shifted in content but not in bawdiness. The President made a few cracks and Davis, he said, looked like his head wasn't bloody but he had been reading about his being beaten—and Davis said of the row between himself and Jeffers and the War Department that some complaints had come that due to the lack of elastic, women weren't being able to keep their pants up and OWI had suggested that if the Army would keep the soldiers at home at night it wouldn't make any difference. Such is the conversation in the presidential office on occasion.

The President looks fine but I was interested when Lock Currie also lingered behind the conference to say that he thought it would be a good thing now to insist on the enforcement of OPA price regulations as part of the protest of the miners; the President repeated a story he had told at his press conference, which Currie and I had attended—about a friend of his who used to work in the Navy Yard here, now making good money, who complains that his wife had had to pay $1.50 for a bunch of asparagus. The President made the point to the man and to us that in the past labor hadn't been buying asparagus in February or March and that this man also admitted that his wife had bought strawberries too at the premium price, though they hadn't been accustomed to eating such winter delicacies before.

The President seems to be using this story to convince himself that prices are not much out of line as some insist. I don't think it sounds very convincing to his listeners. It was the second time I had heard the President repeat one of his jokes to the same group to whom he had told it before and each time he tells it with the mimicry and dramatics of a fresh-told story. With his constantly changing audiences he sometimes forgets that the same audiences come back.

Monday, May 3. Stopped in Lafayette Square near two benches occupied by Bernard M. Baruch, Leo Crowley, and Tommy Corcoran. I don't get Tommy Corcoran's place in the picture except as to making the engagement for Mr. Crowley, but they were trying, in the name of the President, to get Baruch to take over the management of chemical companies formerly dominated by Germany in Latin America. Crowley said he had been up to see Carter Glass in the Mayflower and there seemed hardly any of him left in the bed, he was so little.

Corcoran said he had sent me the words to "I Hate the Constitution," that he had even gone to the trouble to get me the unexpurgated version; I said I had never got it and he promised again to send it.

* * *

Went to see James L. Fly, chairman of the Federal Communications Commission, a balding, harassed, angry man who, when I told him what I had come to see him about, said, "Oh, hell, I thought maybe the President was going to take some interest in this fight that is being made on us. He ought to know that they are hitting at him through us and it is a combination of the Farley crowd plus the Republicans who are attacking us." He went into great detail about the extreme measures taken by the Cox Committee now investigating the Commission, said he was seeing Sam Rayburn tomorrow but he knew that Rayburn was fond of Cox and if Rayburn didn't do anything about the methods being used, he was going to see the President. [Representative Eugene Cox of Georgia, a New Deal foe, had wanted to set up a general investigation of the war effort. The Administration was happy that the Truman Committee was given that responsibility instead.]

* * *

Lock Currie says that when Madame Chiang Kai-shek came over here and found out that liberalism, as represented by Currie and Lattimore, was not really in power any more, she went like a homing pigeon to Willkie and Luce, who are really her type. Currie feels very strongly that the present

Chinese government is corrupt and oppressive and that we have to play a very cagey game with them. [Owen Lattimore, with long experience in China, had been political adviser to Chiang Kai-shek in 1941–42, then became deputy director of Pacific Operations in OWI. He was the author of many books on the Far East.]

Saturday, May 22. Lyndon Johnson says that the Cox Committee investigation is a big job which is being ignored as a little thing, that it is headed by E. L. Garey, who has collected a group of former Bennett goons (Harry H. Bennett of the Ford Company) and anti-New Deal lawyers. Johnson says that the lawyer in charge is a member of an anti-New Deal law firm, which, however, at one time included one of the Roosevelt boys, Elliott, I think. The big story they are working on is that one time there was a Jew who owned a radio station in New York who had gotten into trouble for advertising a prophylactic jelly over his radio station, for relationships with Father Coughlin and Mrs. Elizabeth Dilling.

He was called on the carpet by the FCC; soon thereafter William J. Dempsey, who had resigned as general counsel of the FCC to go into private practice, called on him and said that he had better sell his radio station to him quick and if he didn't sell it, it was going to be taken away from him anyway. The Jew is supposed to have gone to Harry Hopkins and asked for his advice about selling and Hopkins supposedly advised him to sell. Also Niles and Noble, who was an Assistant Secretary of Commerce (so Johnson said) gave him the same advice. Also at that time, according to Johnson's story (which he makes clear is not his story but the story the anti-New Dealers are working on), Dempsey and Tom Corcoran had offices together. As I got it from Johnson, the anti-New Deal lawyers who have been put in hope to use this investigation of the FCC as a take-off for smearing the whole Administration or the important people in it. Dempsey's father is now governor of New Mexico and was formerly Undersecretary of Interior.

[In these hearings Donald Flamm charged that the sale of

his station WMCA at a low figure to Edward J. Noble resulted from Administration coercion. He charged that Elliott Roosevelt was involved and that Dempsey had threatened him. Corcoran was called as a witness in the case, and as a possible participant in the matter.

[Noble, chairman of the Life Savers Corporation, had left the candy business long enough to be Undersecretary of Commerce from June 1939 to August 1940. He was also chairman of the Blue Network, Inc., and president of the American Broadcasting System, Inc. Elliott Roosevelt, never a lawyer, was at this time in military service but before the war he had been much involved in the radio business in Texas and elsewhere. Dempsey had left the FCC in May 1940 to go into private practice in Washington. After prolonged hearings, often marked by partisan anger, the Democratic majority of the committee found no evidence of Administration coercion.

[In addition to charges of skulduggery, it was also charged in the hearings that some FCC employees had left-wing affiliations. Mrs. Dilling had earlier made wild charges accusing a large number of prominent persons, including Mrs. Roosevelt, of Communist connections. Fly, the much harassed chairman of the FCC, resigned in November 1944.

[Lyndon Johnson in 1943 certainly had advance knowledge of this scenario. He was alert to radio information. This same year, 1943, Lady Bird Johnson bought radio station KTBC in Austin, Texas, for $17,500. This was the beginning of the Johnson radio and TV acquisitions, which, when Johnson became President in 1963, the *Washington Post* said were worth $7 million with operating profits of half a million a year.]

Wednesday, June 16. Dinner with the Thomas K. Finletters at 3132 O Street, only a half a block from Wisconsin at the point where the fashionable Georgetown houses meet the remaining section of humdrum pure lower middle class. [Finletter, lawyer and legal writer, was a special assistant to the Secretary of State and a member of the Board of Economic Operations. Mrs. Finletter was born Gretchen Blaine Damrosch, the daughter of Walter Damrosch, the conductor, and granddaughter of James G. Blaine, Republican candidate for President in 1884.]

Theirs is a nice house with a pleasant small garden in the rear, walled and with a pool in it. It was one of the hottest nights of the summer. Nobody was supposed to use cars. I came as the only man in a black tuxedo, not owning one of the linen kind. However, Sir Thomas Lee wore street clothes, just having come to the U.S. with minimum baggage. Still it was a formal occasion. After dinner the men sat in the garden for brandy before joining the ladies.

Enjoyed the company of good, jolly Mrs. Bryan, wife of a naval officer, and Mrs. Churchill, young, pretty, reactionary divorcée apparently of Boston and a good deal of money. She is now working with Herbert Elliston on the *Post*. Incidentally, she said that Mrs. Eugene Meyer [wife of the *Post* publisher] in her national study of bad conditions in the United States [*Journey Through Chaos*] might have taken a look at the ladies' room of the *Washington Post*. Others present:

Ambassador Jan Ciechanowski of Poland and his wife. She a very attractive gray-haired woman speaking perfect English —"Oh, good God," her favorite interjection. He bald, Roman-faced, and looking very much like Joe Davies, whose mission to Moscow he definitely does not like. [He had been educated in England. They had lost a son as an RAF pilot in World War II.] I asked about the big estates of eastern Poland. He said that suggestions that they were feudal were "Soviet lies."

Arthur Bliss Lane—our Ambassador to Colombia—a puffy creature of no great intelligence, but what he has is of a very conservative kind.

A dark, fortyish, Virginia-born real estate man who had lived much abroad—with some sense of humor and with an obviously predatory interest in Mrs. Churchill.

Mrs. Charles Bruggmann, wife of the Swiss minister and sister of Henry Wallace—the only liberal on hand and a shy one. She admitted, grinning, that her car, the Swiss legation one, was among those at Mrs. Evalyn Walsh McLean's party

Sunday night when the *Post* took the licenses and put the list in the papers. She left early and they missed hers.

For dinner we had two large beef rib roasts—Mrs. Finletter explaining that she could have them because three RAF men on departure from the U.S. had given her their ration books.

*   *   *

Lunch at the Southern Railroad Building, where apparently every day the top company officials lunch together and lunch very well too. In our party was George Allen, secretary of the Democratic National Committee, fat man interested in insurance and a good many other businesses, also along with Early and Hopkins in horse racing, something of a hypochondriac, nephew of Private John Allen of Mississippi. His story of his talking a lot with General Eisenhower in London before African invasion about what should be done. Eisenhower stopped him, saying, "Yes, George, there are only two fields in which the amateur is superior to the professional —one is military strategy and the other is prostitution." [Private John Allen was a famous congressional wit.]

Ernest Norris, bushy, gray, pompadoured, small, and lively president of the Southern Railway System.

Spencer, elderly president of Fruit Growers Express Company.

Robert Fleming—bald—president of Riggs National Bank. [Fleming was regarded as the first private citizen of Washington.]

For lunch: Canadian salmon sent by a friend of Norris, French-fried potatoes, a grand salad, corn bread, coffee, vanilla ice cream, cigars. All served by excellent Negro waiters.

Friday, July 16. Carroll Kilpatrick was in to talk about the Wallace-Jones case. He insists that Wallace was given permission by the President to make his attack on Jesse Jones before he made it. He claims as evidence that Wallace himself, before the President said at his press conference that he hadn't read the news story yet, had told a representative of *The Wall*

Street Journal that the President had approved his statement. Also, he says that Wallace's secretary told him that the President had approved it and that after the press conference on the day Wallace's statement was released, the President called up and said, "Henry, I was speaking the literal truth when I said I hadn't read your statement, because you know I just glanced at it." I told Carroll that this seemed very doubtful to me. Kilpatrick was in a very low mood with regard to the President and referring to his scolding of the newspapermen at the press conference about a week ago, he said that you could count on it, every time the President wasn't telling the truth he scolded the press. I am afraid that this may represent newspaper resentment.

[Shortly before this date the feuding between the Board of Economic Warfare and the Reconstruction Finance Corporation had climaxed in a blast by Vice-President Wallace and a hot reply by Jesse Jones. Asked about it at his press conference, the President told reporters that the Wallace statement took him by surprise. FDR did follow that questioning with some pretty tough remarks about the press.]

* * *

Talked with Harry Slattery and after letting him tell me about the case, I suggested to him that the President wished him to write a letter saying that on account of his health he was resigning but asking that there be an investigation of the aspects of the Rural Electrification Administration along the lines suggested by the President. Slattery very definitely, though politely, declined to write a letter. He had written a letter to the President, he said, in which he had, in closing, quoted some line about being a good soldier, but since that time the thing had grown so bad and "these rats" had made such charges against him that any resignation now would seem as if he were resigning under fire. He said that the President ought not to throw him to the wolves.

I assured him that the President's feeling toward him was of the very friendliest sort but that the situation had reached such a stage that controversy in the government had to stop, using the Wallace-Jones case as an example. He said nothing is going to stop the Senate investigation now but frankly he did not arrange it but his friends got the senators to pass the resolution calling for an investigation. He mentioned particularly John M. Carmody and Morris L. Cooke, who had preceded him as REA administrators. He said that Senator Bob La Follette had been very critical of the investigation of him made by the Department of Agriculture. At one point he said that if the President forced his resignation he was "going to make a Pinchot out of me." He said, "The cooperatives are back of me and you would be surprised at the reaction if I should be forced out. They know what I have done in this program." He said that there had already been a defalcation in the funds of the National Rural Electric Cooperative Association of $5,000.

In general Slattery's bitterness does not seem to be directed very vigorously at Robert Craig. He is deeply resentful of Clyde Ellis and Tate's attacks but he seems to blame Secretary Wickard more than anyone else for the situation. He says that in January he wrote Wickard requesting that he remove Craig but that Wickard didn't do it and that also in January he wrote Wickard asking that the solicitor of the department make a decision about the insurance. He feels that Wickard has always been against him and said that he tried to remove him some time ago but that Senator Norris and Representative John E. Rankin and others prevented Wickard from making the change. This last checks with the statement of Carl Hamilton that in the fall of 1940 Wickard first tried to get former Senator James Pope of TVA and as alternative Jack Hutson of the AAA, but that the congressional friends of REA prevented this change.

This afternoon Slattery contended that his health was excellent but later said that he had been burning the candle at both ends and had not had a vacation in four years. [Few men in America had been more devotedly active in the causes of public power and conservation than Harry Slattery. As a young man of twenty-two, he became secretary to Gifford

Pinchot about the time Pinchot became a hero of the Progressives when President Taft dismissed him as head of the Forest Service. Long secretary of the National Conservation Association, he had helped FDR as governor with power problems in New York. The New Deal seemed his natural destination. After work in the Interior Department, in 1939 he was made administrator of the Rural Electrification Administration. Electric service was extended to more and more farms. However, in 1943 bitter feuding had developed within the agency and between Slattery and Secretary of Agriculture Wickard, under whose authority the agency had been placed.

[Slattery was exchanging attacks both as to efficiency and malfeasance with Clyde Ellis, former Arkansas congressman who was at this time manager of the National Rural Electric Cooperative Association. Slattery's own deputy in REA, Robert Craig, resigned in dissatisfaction. As Craig's successor Wickard named William J. Neal, a Democratic politician from New Hamphire, giving Neal special authority which interposed him between Slattery and much of the operations of the agency. Not clearly able under the law to fire him, Wickard made no secret of his wish to do so.

[Beset on many sides, in something like a frenzy, Slattery began to make speeches blaming his troubles on unnamed "Fourth Termers" in the Administration. Also he or his friends initiated an investigation by senators, some of whom were definitely not friends of the President. Baffled, Wickard threw the matter into the lap of the President, who never liked to fire anybody, certainly not a man like Slattery, who in the past had served him well. Yet the impression grew that useful as Slattery had been he was now, to use here a phrase used then, "off his rocker." Looking back at the situation, my feeling is that it was no wonder if he was. I felt much that way when the President gave me the job of easing Slattery out with as little publicity and pain as possible. I did not know the extent of the resulting explosion in which I would be involved.]

Saturday, July 17. Jim Barnes told me this morning that he spent yesterday talking with Edgar Hoover about subversive things which have political connotations. He said that the

1944 campaign was going to be one of the dirtiest campaigns that ever was held, that they are already reviving in the Middle West the stories about Sumner Welles. Jim told me an utterly incredible story about him which he declared was true. I doubt very much that it can be true. He also said that the FBI has information that following the Jones controversy, Wallace's secretary had gone to New York and conferred with a group of Communists, saying that they must become active to keep Wallace from being replaced on the Democratic ticket in 1944. This also sounds a little doubtful to me. Jim has a rather naive willingness to believe tall and terrible tales.

Talked with Dave Niles, who in the course of the conversation said that I could bet any money that Henry Wallace would not be the vice-presidential candidate next time. He also said that Ben Cohen has no more influence than I have in Justice Byrnes's set-up and that he is about ready to commit suicide.

Niles spoke of the strange case in which the President suddenly reappointed George H. Payne to the FCC and then pulled it back. He said that the pressure to reappoint Payne [Republican author and politician] had come not only from Senators Wagner and Meade of New York, but through them from David Sarnoff [head of the Radio Corporation of America and the National Broadcasting Company], and that Anna Rosenberg had a hand also in urging the reappointment.

He said that the most important person in the Department of Justice was Tommy Corcoran and that Corcoran also was going around spreading the story that David Niles and Harry Hopkins were making a fortune for themselves out of the war. Niles is very much perturbed about the appointment of Leo Crowley as head of the Board of Economic Warfare because of his conservative Irish Catholicism. He is very much worried about what is going to happen to Milo Perkins and thinks Crowley will probably move in with his Irish friends very soon to remove everybody of the slightest leftist reputation from BEW, which would mean most of the New Dealers who are left in the Administration.

[In a reorganization related to the feuding between Jones and Wallace, Milo Perkins was on his way out as director, under Wallace. Crowley was given that and other jobs, including most of the foreign economic functions formerly exercised by Jones. Perkins was out of the government before the end of the year.]

I asked Niles why Hopkins didn't do something about these things and he said that very often Hopkins would assure him that something was not going to happen and it would turn out that without Hopkins' knowledge it was happening at that very time. He said that Isador Lubin, the President's statistician (responsibility for whose appointment he claimed) knew absolutely nothing about the BEW order until after it was issued.

Monday, July 19. Saw Harllee Branch, of the Civil Aeronautics Board, who told me that, after receiving the President's letter, they had taken it as a directive to award a certificate for the route to Nassau to Colonial Airlines. They had reconsidered their decision in order to do that and had given National Airlines a certificate to run from Jacksonville to Charleston in order to secure the through service they wanted. The board will suggest that the two companies merge. Branch said they have two tough customers as heads of the two companies and each would probably want to dominate. He said that the board could not defend this decision on economic grounds and that he was afraid it would cause a good deal of criticism in the industry. [The "tough customers" were Sig Janus of Colonial and Ted Baker of National.]

Wednesday, July 21. Conversation with Admiral Leahy in the President's outer office in which Leahy expressed great confidence about the situation in Europe but pointed out that the Pacific thing would be a very tough job, as it meant cleaning the Japs out almost one by one. They had, he said, for fifteen or twenty years prepared themselves for the situation in the Pacific. He seems, nevertheless, very confident about the outcome everywhere.

He also expressed opposition to the proposal to transfer the naval oil reserves to the Department of the Interior and said, without any prompting from me, that the man in charge over at Interior was from the Standard Oil Company of California, that the real man in charge of it at the Navy is Carter, who was a Naval Academy graduate but had left the Navy to work for the Shell Oil Company. I gathered from Leahy's conversation at the White House that he has no relationship or responsibility for the naval oil situation. He said that they had enough oil for the military use, although there was certainly no surplus of it and that the shortage, if it existed, was from civilian uses of oil. Secretary Hull came in looking better than I expected him to look, though older. He sent his regards to Mother and Father and asked particularly about my mother's health. He and Leahy went in together.

[Captain (later Admiral) Andrew F. Carter was an Annapolis graduate who had resigned from the Navy in 1920 to go into the oil business in Texas. Returning to service in World War II, he became executive director of the Army-Navy Petroleum Board. Ralph K. Davies, director and vice-president of the Standard Oil Company of California, was under Secretary Ickes the deputy administrator of the War Petroleum Administration.]

There is something very birdlike about Attorney General Francis Biddle. I am not sure whether it is the shape of his eyes or what. He sits talking without looking at the person he is talking to.

*   *   *

Monday, July 26. Lindsay Warren is very much disturbed for fear the big payments of the Maritime Commission, particularly those involving Henry Kaiser, may result in postwar scandals of the Grant and Harding administration type. Recently, on the 14th of May, he wrote Admiral Emory S. Land pointing out the fact that the price paid by the U.S. government for the Richmond, California, yards from the British Purchasing Commission was based on an audit made for the British by Price, Waterhouse and Company, and that at the time the purchase was made, the head of the Finance Division of the Maritime Commission was a partner in Price, Waterhouse. He showed me a report sent to the Maritime Commission at that time which said that Kaiser had received "unwarranted accrual of early delivery bonuses."

"Kaiser interests appear to be enjoying and exercising undue influence and monopolistic control in the negotiation, securing and prosecution of Maritime Commission ship construction contracts."

On page 122 of the report: "Included in reimbursable costs as legal advice were payments made to George C. Ober, Jr." He gets $20,000 per year from Richmond yards #1 and 2. The report adds: "Mr. Ober is representing West Coast shipbuilding companies as a lobbyist with the Government indirectly financing such activities."

Warren thinks the dominating figure in the Maritime Commission is William Radner, formerly with the Matson Line. [Radner had come from the position of secretary of the Matson Navigation Company in 1942 to be general counsel of the War Shipping Administration.]

Tuesday, July 27. Very fine talk with the President after press conference this afternoon. Barnes, Niles, Casey, and myself. The President is very patient with Gene, who asked him if he could speak at the Minnesota State Fair. The President said no, but suggested some other names. I spoke to the President about the fact which Steve Early mentioned to me at the beginning of the press conference, that Harry Slattery has apparently been talking in St. Louis to the effect that he is going to be kicked out. I asked the President if he wanted me to do anything else about getting Senator George Norris to accept the REA post and he said no, but he hoped the old man would. [One plan to ease Slattery out of his REA position was to persuade ex-Senator Norris to agree to accept the post—a move which his friend Slattery could hardly oppose. This would have also provided a place for the Senator, whose term had expired early in the year. Norris, however, not only declined but spoke of his confidence in Slattery.]

We talked to him about naming a ship after Robert L. Vann, publisher of the *Pittsburgh Courier,* and the President said that he understood he was off the reservation in 1940. Dave said that he told the President that he was and that the reason he was off the reservation was that Vann had written several letters to the President asking for an appointment and he never got an answer to his letter from the White House.

"I can see how that might have happened," the President said.

In the meantime, Dave went on, Joe Pew, of the Sun Oil Company, asked Vann if he, Pew, could come to see him and Pew then went to Pittsburgh and took Vann in his private car and introduced him to Willkie. The personal feeling of Vann accounted for his being off the reservation. Nothing was said about it this afternoon, but I understand that a little item of $40,000 was also involved.

"The big question is," said the President, "if I name a ship after Vann, will the paper support the Administration next time?"

"That is the idea, Mr. President," I said.

[It was announced in August that a ship would be named in honor of Vann as publisher of the leading black newspaper. However, in 1944 the *Courier* came out for Dewey. The best laid plans of mice and men . . .]

Taking advantage of the general talk, I said, "Mr. President, I would like to bring up one other matter while we are here and that is that three of the top jobs are open in OWI and here is a chance to get a friend of the Administration in the job." He said he had talked to Davis but Davis was scared and very anxious to have everything smooth. He said the only friend we have got over there is Bob Sherwood and I said, "Yes, Mr. President, and his first assistant, Joe Barnes, is Willkie's close friend."

"Yes," said the President, "I understand he wrote the book *Around the World in Sixty Days*." The President added, "I spoke to Davis and said suppose I bring Barry Bingham back from London and take him out of the Navy and let him run the Louisville paper and we could get Mark Ethridge up here—or what is the name of the fellow who runs the *Atlanta Constitution?*" I said, "Ralph McGill."

The President went on, "I spoke to Elmer about that but he was afraid to do anything about it. The trouble is that Elmer never has been in charge of anything bigger than one or two people, but I will speak to him again as soon as he gets back."

He seemed to be in grand form and not even General Watson made any real push to end the conversation.

In connection with his talk about OWI, the President said he had suggested to Lowell Mellett that he ought to get somebody to produce a film about the war in which some hero was being presented with the Congressional Medal of Honor by the President, but that where he sat there would be a blank white space in the film and that the sound track would announce that they left out the picture of the President of the United States because it might be construed as political.

Thursday, July 29. Went in to see the President with Welch Pogue. General Watson was very much disturbed by the pressure on his schedule. I told the President it was a grand speech the night before. He said yes, he thought it went over well but that he had just gotten up—that he stayed up two hours after he spoke and drank two bottles of beer. He went immediately into the discussion with Pogue and myself of the airline situation. He said that as long ago as Prime Minister Neville Chamberlain he had discussed the development of the West Indies, British, American, Dutch, and French. That he was anxious to help make those islands produce more than "sugar and niggers." That one of the great ways to do this was through the tourist. He wanted to see hotels on all these islands where the middle-class American family could fly and stay for $5.00 per day per person and not $15 or $20. He described with praise the hotel Bluebeard's Castle (in the Virgin Islands, I think), which is run by Ickes and which even now in the middle of the war is a paying proposition. He spoke of having gone through the West Indies while he was in college and coming up by Miami. He crossed from the islands to Florida on "a tub of a boat." He said he had kicked himself several times because where Miami is today, you could buy all the land you wanted for fifteen or twenty dollars an acre.

He wants a line or lines running through all the West Indies down to the Virgin Islands, Haiti, etc. with a hotel near Henri Christophe's citadel on Haiti. He is planning for conjunction with British lines. He said, incidentally, that he didn't want everybody to have to go to Miami and also—and very definitely—that he did not want Pan American to have all the airlines outside the United States.

He spoke about British plans for postwar aviation and his own idea that all internal aviation in any country should be run without foreigners. That is to say, he would let Pan American go down to Brazil but in its flights within Brazil it would pick up no local traffic. Similarly the British are planning an air line across the United States to Australia. He has no objection to this whatever but with the definite understanding that when the British land in New York they may not pick up any traffic destined for any part of the journey across the United States. While he was talking about the islands and mentioned Trinidad, I asked him if he had ever heard the phonograph record "Everybody Was Glad When Roosevelt Came to Trinidad." He laughed and said he hadn't. I must get a copy of this from Roy Stryker and send him one.

In the midst of our conversation Grace Tully came in and said there was a call coming in for him. He shooed us out of the room while he took it and General Watson looked very happy when he saw us come out so soon. Frances Perkins, Secretary of Labor, was waiting with a delegation. (We talked about Washington weather and she said there were no mosquitoes in Washington.) Hull was due for lunch at one and it was then ten minutes of one.

Welch Pogue did very little talking, although he impressed on the President that on the domestic basis they could not justify the line economically. He also said that it would cost more than three quarters of a million dollars in government money to run the line to Nassau. He never really had a chance, however, to object to the President's plan. The President said that a convention with regard to the development of the West Indies was being worked on now. Pogue spoke briefly about the ownership of the lines but the President said very pointedly that he didn't know anybody in either of the companies.

Tuesday, August 3. "And that is the reason," said Dave Niles, "we can't even think of Wallace for Vice-President again."

Last night at dinner I heard from Beanie Baldwin's wife her feeling that she couldn't quite take the religious relationship between Wallace and Milo Perkins. She didn't elaborate and indicated that Beanie didn't like for her to talk about it. Niles tells me the story. It seems that the big man in the whole business is a rich Texas oil man named Charles Marsh, who some years ago put on the spiritualist play *The Ladder* in New York and let people come without any admission price. Perkins and Wallace are both, Niles says, spiritualists. In the last three weeks of the last campaign some letters which Wallace had written, on Department of Agriculture stationery and on plain stationery bearing the department watermark, got into the hands of the Republicans.

It seems that a medium in the Department of Agriculture, who got fired or something—at any rate he got mad—stole from Wallace's files letters which indicated that Wallace got his directions as to government policies from the spirit world. There were references in the letters to other officials, including Hull, who was called, as Dave said, by some pessimistic name. The letters were first offered to Roy Howard.

"It shows you," said Dave, "that bread cast upon the water will return again. There was a man named Bill Nunn, professor at a Newark college, who had been in charge of white-collar projects for the WPA. I was kind to him. His best friend was Roy Howard's secretary. One day he called me and said it was vital he see me immediately and if possible would I bring Hopkins. Hopkins wouldn't go, but Nunn told me about the letters. They had finally been purchased by Block, the publisher, and he had sent the reporter who uncovered the Ku Klux Klan story about Justice Black to Chicago to confront Wallace with the letters. We were afraid that Wallace, being an honest guy, would say, 'Yes, I wrote them—so what?'

"Morris Ernst," Dave said, "did a good job. He was sent West to meet Wallace, who was coming to Chicago, to see to it that this reporter didn't get to Wallace. Every day the Democrats expected the story to break. I must have lost fifty pounds in three weeks. We went out and dug up some dirty stuff on Willkie, with photographs showing that Willkie's father had been buried in potter's field as a drunkard with whom Willkie would have nothing to do. Only after the presidential campaign began did he have his body moved to a decent part of the cemetery. We let the Republicans know that if they used the Wallace stuff, we were going to use the stuff on Willkie. The Wallace letters were never used, but they are still in the possession of the Republicans."

Charlie Marsh, Niles says, has a big farm in Maryland to which a great many government officials are invited. Marsh owns a lot of papers in Texas and was instrumental, among other things, in electing Lyndon Johnson to Congress. Now Niles says he has sworn to beat Lyndon because Lyndon said that the President was right in getting rid of Wallace.

[In general the facts seem to be as Niles related them to me. Before Wallace came to Washington his friends and neighbors in Iowa had been aware of his interests, as one of them put it, "in oriental religions, and he had a very strong strain of mysticism in him." He and Perkins, who came from Texas in 1935 to be his assistant, were said to share not only very liberal political views but also unorthodox spiritual ones. In this last they were joined by Charles Edward Marsh, who was not a "rich Texas oil man," as Niles put it, but the owner of a chain of profitable newspapers in Texas.

[Wallace had been in correspondence with a group at the Roerich Museum in New York, maintained by Russian-born Nicholas Roerich, artist and author interested in the occult. Roerich had in 1934 headed an expedition for Wallace's Department of Agriculture through China and Mongolia in search of drought-resistant grasses for America. In 1944

Roerich gave his home address as Naggar, Kulu, Punjab, British India, a place noted for art objects related to the worship of Vishnu and Buddha.

[The White House, according to Turner Catledge, famous journalist who was at the time covering Washington for the pro-Roosevelt *Chicago Sun,* first heard of the Roerich letters (called "the Guru letters" in the whispers going around) early in the 1940 campaign. Then it was thought that the Wallace letters were written in their lyrical and mystical fashion to a woman. Some may have been directed to Mrs. Roerich, born Helena Ivanov Shaposhnikov, granddaughter of Field Marshal Golenistcheff Kutuzoff. Roosevelt, Catledge has written, was at first amused and delighted with the supposed letters to a lady as humanizing Henry in a way that could do little political harm. But when the President learned that Wallace's involvement was not physical but metaphysical, Catledge said, he threw up his hands in dismay, saying, "We can handle sex, but we can't handle religion."

[The well-established facts are as Niles told them, though John Cowles, the publisher who was close to Willkie in that campaign, says he never heard of the potter's field story. Morris Ernst, liberal and highly literate New York lawyer, recalled that there was "a panic at the White House when it was learned that many of Henry's letters to a spiritualist lady friend had gotten into the hands of unfriendly persons.

["FDR asked me to fly out to Chicago and I met Henry at the house of Mayor Edward Kelly. He was going to have a news conference and the Boss thought that this story might be crucial in the campaign which was then being conducted against Wendell Willkie. I had some luck and was able to quash the entire story because I had in my possession several incidents in Willkie's life which he would not want to have divulged. As I recall, the entire situation on both sides was put to sleep."

[Cowles's memory is that when Paul Block, publisher of the *Pittsburgh Post-Gazette,* and Roy Howard, chief of the Scripps-Howard newspaper chain, pressed the letters on Willkie, the candidate felt that their use would be politically unwise.]

Monday, September 6. Talked to the President at length this morning with regard to Colonial Airlines. I said, "Mr. President, I don't want to be inquisitive, but I would like to know how strongly you feel about this whole matter." He said, "I don't feel strongly at all about the Colonial line, but I do feel strongly about not having Pan American try to grab everything and I don't like Miami being the only city as an air terminal." He suggested that he didn't think Miami was a very healthy, moral sort of place. He seems to have a rather deep prejudice against it.

I suggested as a way out that he had from me a memo stating that the Civil Aeronautics Board wanted to open for hearing applications for certificates for Caribbean and Latin American lines. That it would be a good idea to say to the board that he felt that this should be done and that the Atlanta coastal lines, which would naturally be feeders to the Latin American and Caribbean lines, ought to be considered with this airline development outside the United States. He said, "That is fine. Tell them to reconsider this whole Atlantic coastal case in terms of reopening the Caribbean and Latin American matter." I pointed out to him, however, that there were certain details of the Atlantic coastal case which had no relationships to lines outside the United States. He agreed that there was no reason why the decision, so far as such items are concerned, should be delayed.

Then he went off again into his dream of the development of the Caribbean or what might be described as the island resort business for ordinary people. He said that he personally would like to have a concession from the government of Portugal for the development of the Azores. He talked lyrically about the beauties of the Azores, of the family of the Portuguese marquis who was exiled some centuries ago and whose family built a castle on one of the islands. He was almost ecstatic about the arboretum that this family has maintained, saying that in front of the house side by side grew a royal palm and a Norway spruce.

In connection with his statement about Pan American and the monopoly, he spoke about the fact that when the New York, New Haven and Hartford, with its subsidiary, the Boston and Maine, held a monopoly of New England railroad business they tried to buy up even the streetcar lines that were feeders to the business and that the process helped make its failure. He spoke about a solider of fortune who had gone to Honduras and had built up an airline system which practically covered the country. Pan American wanted to buy it, he said, "but I wouldn't let them do it." Pan American, he indicated, has got to recognize its position as a great long-distance system and not try to dominate all the little feeders along the route.

While I was at his desk he signed the letter to Aubrey Williams and spoke of him with the greatest affection and asked me what Aubrey was going to do. Then he spoke of Aubrey as a possible successor to Abe Fortas in Interior. I asked him how Ickes would like it and he said he didn't know. [I had prepared a letter of appreciation and fond farewell to Williams for the President's signature as he departed from the National Youth Administration. Later when FDR named him director of the REA, the Senate refused to confirm him on the basis of wild charges of red views.]

Then the President told me he had decided not to transfer REA to Interior and that he thought some job might be worked up for Harry Slattery. I told him that the job was all worked up for Harry Slattery but that Slattery would not take it.

"Well," he said, "you had better get Slattery in here, if he is in town get him in this afternoon at 3:30 and if not, as soon as he comes back." He said that he would be glad if I would work with Welch Pogue in this whole island development proposition.

In connection with the Atlantic coastal airlines the President said there are two things people couldn't touch without getting their hands dirty—one is aviation and the other oil.

Tuesday, September 7. After press conference Elmer Davis deliberately drew up a chair and made it a private conference with the President, while Lock Currie and I waited, each with something to see him about. Davis was talking about some kind of off-the-record conference with the President at which some group would be given background material. I don't know what they were talking about.

When we went up Lock Currie told the President he wanted to make a preliminary report on his new job and to say that he had discovered in a short period of time that the man who was holding up everything was Tom Finletter in the State Department, who he described as a member of a reactionary law-banking firm, Coudert Brothers.

The President said, "You mean Coudert Brothers? Why, they are about to be indicted for trading with Germany through Vichy." Currie said he did mean that firm. The President, with every evidence of deepest interest, pulled over his own memorandum pad and wrote in ink Finletter's name. [Currie, while keeping his place as administrative assistant, had been loaned to the Board of Economic Warfare, now headed by Leo Crowley.

[Coudert Brothers was at this time one of the most distinguished American law firms. The social, intellectual, and legal positions of the two Frederic René Couderts, father and son, were impeccable. Republicans, of course, the elder Coudert had been decorated by foreign governments and his son had recently been given an award for citizen excellence by Columbia University. Like the firm of Sullivan and Cromwell, to which the Dulles brothers belonged, Coudert Brothers was much involved in international law.]

Afterwards I showed my letter to the President providing for the consolidated consideration of new Atlantic coastal airlines and air development in the Caribbean and Latin America. He read the letter carefully and said it was a good letter. I told him that Welch Pogue felt that the position of the board would be greatly simplified if they could make the letter a part of the public record. He agreed to that.

I also said to him that I could not be very much impressed by the complaint of the airlines that this case ought not to be postponed because they had invested large sums over a period in hearings since what they were asking for was permanent enrichment out of the natural resources of the United States. He nodded his head in vigorous agreement. "Of course," he said. Also, I added, "I don't know whether you are aware of the people who are on the board of Pan American." Then I spoke of his cousin Lyman Delano, Norman Davis, and Leo Crowley, who are directors, and I pointed out that Norman Davis was chairman of some sort of security committee in the State Department which had disapproved certain proposals of the postwar aviation committee.

He said, "Why, yes, I know all this and my own law partner, Basil O'Connor, comes to see me and tells me frankly that he represents them but they know that they have a way to come to me with their case through him." He spoke about the fact that Pan American had felt that it had to spend money to corrupt Latin American countries because they said if they didn't do it the Germans, British, and other countries would.

"What worries me, Mr. President, is that if they learn to bribe people in Latin America, they may not forget it when they come home."

He laughed, suggesting that they had by no means forgotten it and that the probability that it didn't exist here was remote. Then he told me, "I would like to see, after the war, four American airlines to Europe, one by way of Glasgow to Scandinavia, one by central England to the Continent, one to France, and one to the Mediterranean." He spoke about the whole competition in the ship lines which brought immigrants to America and said that at one time the cutthroat competition got to the point at which an immigrant could come to the United States for ten dollars. Then there came a shipping pool which constituted an absolute monopoly. I gathered that what he wanted was a controlled competition. I asked him from what points in the United States he would like to see those lines depart and he said because of the distance they would have to be restricted but he thought there might be take-off points at New York and Baltimore.

He was in high good humor after one of the most pleasant conferences with the press that he has had since I have been attending them. Afterwards in conversation with General Watson, the general said, "By the way, the Secret Service has reported Eugene Casey has been going around talking to Pearson and running down Hopkins and others and I told the President about it." I said that I had nothing against Casey and he had never done anything to me but I thought it was dangerous when Frank Walker insisted on his being kept. The general then told me that both Frank and the President liked to settle things without a big row.

Marvin McIntyre looks more fragile than ever. In fact, when he lies on his couch in his office taking a nap, as he very often does now, he looks as much like a corpse as any living thing I have ever seen. Yet when he gets up and talks, he is still as bright as a bird and his old wisecracking self.

Tuesday, September 7. It was interesting recently to walk to lunch at the Army-Navy Club with Adolf Berle and his brother, Major Rudolf Berle, who is in what Berle explained as the black chamber of Military Intelligence. They are both very little men and both walk with amazing rapidity.

Welch Pogue, speaking of the influence in the government of Juan Trippe of Pan American, says that in the Panagra case in which Pan American and Grace Lines have an equal share, Pan American has been able to prevent any program to give Panagra access to the territory of the United States and that when the CAB tried to bring this matter to a hearing the State Department intervened and that the Department of Justice, which at first was on the side of bringing this to a hearing, has somewhat altered its position based, Welch thinks, on a letter which Juan Trippe got Leo Crowley to take to Francis Biddle. Also, a committee on aviation in postwar planning found some of its suggestions which were not along the line of Trippe's thinking had been disapproved by the State Department's security committee, of which Norman Davis, Pan American director, is chairman. He said also that recently when he discussed some aviation matters with Hull and Berle, Norman Davis was present, took full part in the discussions, and constantly voiced the position of Juan

Trippe. He has great admiration for Juan Trippe but regards him as "a buccaneer."

[Trippe in his middle forties was a glamorous figure during wartime in Washington. He was much seen in the Departments, on the Hill, and at the Burning Tree Golf Club, where the biggest politicians and lobbyists played and planned. Nobody doubted his ability or his charm. He was almost the model for the elite American hero. A Yale man who served in naval aviation in World War I before he was twenty-one, he was married to Elizabeth Stettinius, daughter of a House of Morgan partner. He entered the infant aviation business in 1922 as president of Long Island Airways, Inc. That island was not big enough for his dreams. At twenty-eight he became president and general manager of the Pan American Airways System. Even this hemisphere was not enough. Now in a vague proposed partnership with the government, he wanted to operate a monopoly of U.S. overseas aviation under a system which he described as the one "chosen instrument" of American world-wide operations. Deployed in his cause he had lawyers, public relations men, and officials.]

* * *

This morning Walter Brown told me two interesting things:

1. That Marvin Jones has been trying to get William B. Umstead (former North Carolina congressman) to succeed Beanie Baldwin as head of Farm Security Administration. He says that Marvin Jones is devoted to Farm Security and spent his time crying over the cuts Congress made. That he thinks Umstead could get congressional support for FSA, that he would not take it unless he believed in the program and he certainly wouldn't take it to liquidate it.

2. Walter Brown believes that the story about Welles and also the story of General Marshall becoming the commander of the invasion forces for the Allied governments leaked from Admiral Leahy through Constantine Brown. He said he hadn't mentioned this to Justice Byrnes but was going to tell him as soon as he came back. From his office he saw Constan-

tine Brown at least once a week coming in to see Leahy and he thinks there is a substantial leak of information there. Constantine Brown broke both stories.

[Walter Brown, former South Carolina newspaperman, was an aide to James F. Byrnes. Marvin Jones, onetime Texas congressman, had resigned from the U. S. Court of Claims to join Byrnes in the war effort. He had recently been appointed U. S. Food Commissioner. Constantine Brown was a writer for the *Washington Star*.]

Saturday, September 11. In connection with an article on bureaucrats, Lieutenant Colonel L. Corrin Strong, who used to be a Washington businessman or lawyer, told about his famous case of the four dump trucks for Peru. He had received the request for them from the Peruvian military mission in Washington, put in the application, and the War Department wanted to know what the trucks were for, would they take them without tires, how was he going to get them there. He couldn't answer any of the questions but he got the Peruvians again and found that they wanted one truck for each of four airfields, that the American forces used the airfields, that they could get the trucks to Peru. He went back with the exact answers to their questions and got his four dump trucks but the process required several days of work. He also reported the Mexican general whose entire English vocabulary were the words "I want." He told of his experience as a civilian in an ordnance uniform running into General Chiang, who immediately asked him the most technical questions about the muzzle velocity of particular pieces of ordnance, etc., about which he didn't have the foggiest notion.

Lock Currie told another experience as a bureaucrat. The Board of Economic Warfare, he says, handles about 10,000 pieces of paper a day, export licenses, etc. Last week an official came in to him and said that the time had come to fight out the issue with the State Department. That they had refused to forward a letter of the BEW to Bogotá. Currie looked at the letter, it was with regard to a list of American commodities requested from Bogotá and Ex-lax was not listed on the list. This letter, apparently written at the request of the

Ex-lax people, who had considerable investment in good will in Bogotá, demanded that Ex-lax be added to the list of exportable commodities. Lock said he had some difficulty in persuading the indignant BEW official that a letter about Ex-lax didn't seem to him to be one on which to base their fight with the State Department.

Discussion of tapping of telephones. Colonel Strong said that all phones in the War Department are tapped once a month, not so much for security as to check on the use of telephones for personal calls. Randolph Paul said he had all telephone calls to his office recorded by a stenographer, and that Secretary Morgenthau has an instrument on his desk which, by turning a switch, records any call on a disc. [In my time I never heard of any phone taps or other bugging at the White House.]

* * *

The Sumner Welles story which Jim Barnes told me some weeks ago and which then seemed to me incredible, seems now to be undenied. The story, said to be circulated first and chiefly by former Ambassador William Bullitt with the assistance of Alice Longworth and George Earle, former governor of Pennsylvania, is to the effect that Sumner Welles is a sex pervert with predilection for Negro men. Apparently complaint was made to the White House by A. Philip Randolph, the chief of the Brotherhood of Sleeping Car Porters, after it is alleged Welles was caught on a train.

Whether this is true or not, I don't know. I know that Steve Early, when Barnes asked him after press conference about the President's desire for Bullitt to be elected mayor of Philadelphia, said that he "wouldn't do a goddamn thing for that son-of-a-bitch," that he was the first man to start the story about Welles, that he had papers which he tried to get into the newspapers, and that if he, Early, were sitting beside St. Peter when Bullitt and Welles arrived, he would let Welles in and keep Bullitt out. Of the Welles case, McIntyre said, "Thank God I am not pure-minded," and then he said, with some reflection of juvenile obscenity, "Maybe the President is saving him to make him French ambassador." Apparently this story has gone all around, Tom Mabry told me that he heard it in New York from the editor of *Town and Country*. Carroll Kilpatrick told me he had heard it from a number of sources. It is not clear whether the incident had any relationship to recent reports of Welles's resignation or whether those reports revived the stories about him.

[No one will ever know whether the story about Welles was fact or fabrication. It has always seemed incredible to me that a man of such impervious dignity and hauteur could have descended to such bestiality as that with which he was charged. Yet, despite his brilliance and enlightenment, legend made him seem to occupy a sort of Gothic world. In the great Massachusetts Avenue mansion which his wife, Mathilde Townsend, had inherited, she was said every night to turn down the covers on the bed of her long-dead mother. Welles preferred his residence at Oxon Hill Manor in Maryland. Gossip could transform it into a sort of a Jekyll-Hyde house.

[There were certainly those who might have fabricated the story of homosexual acts between the austere, elegant Welles and menial blacks. The very ease of his relations with that other Groton-Harvard man, the President, inspired jealousy in others. And sometimes Welles presumed upon that relation and bypassed the stately but ponderous Cordell Hull. Roosevelt may have encouraged such direct dealing. Historian James MacGregor Burns has quoted the lisping Secretary of State as calling Welles his "all-American thun of a bitch." The lisping of the Secretary of State is certainly accurately reported. FDR liked to quote his cabinet chief as using the exclamation "Jesus Cwhist!"

[Credit or shame for the original circulation of the story, however, definitely belonged to William C. Bullitt, another American of top-drawer Ivy League position. As a young dissatisfied State Department employee, many felt he had betrayed Woodrow Wilson in the fight for the League of Nations. Still he and FDR were congenial old friends and

193

Roosevelt had a high—some thought too high—regard for Bullitt's abilities. Roosevelt sent him as his first Ambassador to the Soviet Union. He was Ambassador to France at the time of its fall to the Germans. Then from November 1941 to April 1942 he held the anomalous position of "ambassador at large." It was during this period that the President unsuccessfully tried to get Pennsylvania Democrats to run Bullitt for governor. Even before that, according to Assistant Secretary of State Breckinridge Long, Bullitt had turned his "vitriolic tongue" on Welles. That tongue spread the story of Welles and the dining-car waiters. Hull got an FBI report and sent it to the White House, where it "disappeared for a time." Welles told Long in the spring of 1942 that the story was "a malicious lie." Finally in September 1943, about the time of this entry in my diary, Welles resigned, by request, but on the grounds of his wife's health. As a private citizen, writing and speaking on foreign affairs, Welles moved with imperturbable dignity.

[Welles was succeeded as undersecretary by Edward R. Stettinius, Jr., Juan Trippe's brother-in-law. With pure-white hair at forty-three, he was spectacularly handsome. Also even with the backing of a Morgan-partner father he had advanced rapidly in business before he entered the government in 1940. He filled a number of defense positions, becoming administrator of the Lend-Lease Administration. Still, when in 1944 Roosevelt named him as successor to the ailing and retiring Hull, some were skeptical. Then in a sweeping reorganization of the State Department, he headed a new undersecretary, Joseph C. Grew, and six assistant secretaries: Dean Acheson, Nelson Rockefeller, Archibald MacLeish, William L. Clayton, James C. Dunn, and General Julius C. Holmes. One of those wits who can always be expected in Washington on serious occasions promptly labeled them "Snow White and the Seven Dwarfs."]

Tuesday, September 14. McIntyre talked yesterday about a leak in the White House to the press, particularly to Pearson. He is convinced that there is one. He formerly thought it was young Pritchard, who is now in the Army, but the leak continues. Spoke about Pearson's story about Madame Chiang Kai-shek and said, "She was a pest to everybody, the Secret Service," etc.

"Did she do too much of this?" Jim Barnes asked, making the motion of drinking.

"No," said McIntyre, "I don't think it was that, but she was queer. Maybe she is going through the change of life. She certainly was a pest to everybody in the White House while she was here."

[The slim, elegant Madame Chiang had come to the United States in November 1942 for a half-year stay, as she said, "on a personal visit for my health." But Roosevelt spoke of her at a joint press conference as a "special envoy." Both were correct. She did come for treatment for a spinal injury but despite some lapses, in seeking aid for China, she moved at an amazing pace to almost universal public acclaim. Yet in the White House, echoing McIntyre, Bill Hassett wrote that "she will be long remembered, along with her retinue, as arrogant and overbearing."]

*　　*　　*

I hear that Harry Hopkins has been in the hospital again but is better and yesterday afternoon was playing bridge with McIntyre, Barnes, and Jesse Jones.

[Hopkins and his wife were planning at this time to leave the White House and take a residence of their own in Georgetown. Mrs. Roosevelt denied that this meant any change in the relations of Hopkins and the President.]

*　　*　　*

I had a long talk with Hugh Jackson, who said that Governor Lehman was about ready to resign unless the President would make it possible, as he feels, for him to do his job. Lehman is terribly anxious to do the job, Hugh feels. He doesn't want to hurt the President but if he does resign, he can't resign because of ill health and will frankly have to say he is resigning because he doesn't feel he can work in view of the interferences of the State Department, which are centered in Dean Acheson's office.

Acheson told me on Saturday all the State Department insisted upon doing was that when the other agencies had discussed and discussed without reaching a decision, the State Department could announce a decision and tell the other agencies what the situation and arrangement would be. Hugh, on the other hand, reports that the State Department is a machinery for delay, and that the set-up for planning and operating has become so complicated as to be practically unworkable. Hugh seemed to me to make out a more convincing case than Acheson, because basically Acheson does insist upon the supreme power in this whole business.

[Acheson, another of Justice Brandeis' brilliant young legal secretaries, had resigned as Undersecretary of the Treasury in 1933 in disagreement with New Deal financial policies. With the approach of war, however, he returned as Assistant Secretary of State in February 1941. In the summer before this diary entry he was also made head of the Office of Foreign Economic Coordination.]

Saturday, September 25. Lunch with Aubrey Williams, who told me that McNutt had just offered him Charlie Taft's job as director of the Office of Community War Services. I told Aubrey that I was delighted he had been offered the place but it put me in a funny position because I hoped Mark McCloskey was going to get it. Aubrey said that he has asked McNutt about that and McNutt had said that even if Aubrey did not take it he would not give it to Mark. Aubrey said it looked as if Mark were having to pay for making a fight which had to be made. While McNutt agreed that that was to some extent true, he also suggested that there were other reasons why he would not appoint McCloskey.

Aubrey is very doubtful about accepting. When I came into the Hay Adams another friend had just advised him that he should accept but Aubrey has a feeling that some of the Congress is out to get him as a man and that there is very little strength in the Community War Services. Also, he has just been offered a position as a full professor in the Teachers College of Columbia University, in which he is supported by even those professors at Columbia who fought NYA on the grounds that the work it was doing ought to be done by the schools. This last sounds to me like vastly the more interesting and important job. I talked to Aubrey Williams about the request to the President that he write a letter to be included among the tributes to Walter White on his twenty-five years with the NAACP. Williams is an advocate of White's and thinks that history will deal more kindly with him than many people in this day. He compared him with Fred Douglass and spoke of Lincoln's generous treatment of Douglass at a White House reception after Douglass had violently attacked Lincoln for Lincoln's belief that the solution of the race problem lay in the separation of the races, perhaps migration to Liberia. He said that when Bilbo said that he stood where Lincoln had stood, he was telling the truth, even if some people did give him hell.

We talked of Harry Hopkins. He said that Hopkins' admiration for people like Baruch and Harriman undoubtedly went back to his days in New York when Hopkins was poor and those were great names. He said that he had seen Harry knock over a couple of desks getting to the phone when Baruch called. He spoke of a pretty mean dialogue between Hopkins and himself when Hopkins was spending all his time out at Joe Kennedy's house here. He said that Harry had once said that if the world was divided between the robbers and the robbed, he would be with the robbers. Also, he said that when he saw Harry recently and spoke of going with the Farmers Union, Harry said, "Aubrey, won't you ever get over being a damn fool?" But at the same meeting he told Williams that he thought Williams was respected by more decent people in Washington than anybody else he knew.

"Harry had to have money," he said, "he lived at the St. Regis and wanted to go to good theaters and have good food." He suggested that maybe Mr. Baruch was helping him along financially.

Wednesday, October 27. Went to see Lindsay Warren, who

told me about the conference with the President on the afternoon before, which I had arranged. Lindsay said that he stayed with the President for over an hour. Several times he had to pull the President's attention back to the question of the final termination of the contracts with the Army, which he thinks should be audited by the General Accounting Office, but that at the end the President had General Watson call Judge John Parker to come to Washington and see what action ought to be taken in the matter. Lindsay told the President he thought the thing had been taken out of his hands and it could only be put back in his hands by legislation. He laughed and said that the President said, "This old dictator has still got a lot of power." Lindsay says that he has been deeply hurt by what he has discovered American business doing in the War Department. He said that he told the President that the people in the Army who are making these contracts and serving the interests involved would not be 10 per cent for him if they had to vote.

Lindsay looked pretty well, though his new upper teeth don't fit. He said that the doctors have found that his heart, kidneys, etc., are in good shape but that he has developed high blood pressure and a sort of muscular tic. He told me that he didn't have a penny in the world, that he couldn't miss one paycheck, but that he felt that he had to get out of the job of Comptroller General. He said that he had been offered a job at a very large salary in Chicago, but that he had told the people it was too far from his fishing ground. He said that he wanted to get away but there wasn't any place to go, that the Navy and Coast Guard have taken over all the places on the beach and while he stayed with the Coast Guard on Ocracoke, it wasn't very comfortable. As much as he would like to get away, he told me, he, of course, would not leave as long as the fight is going on.

I have great confidence in Lindsay but the very atmosphere of the whole General Accounting Office looks sloppy, and the one or two North Carolinians whom I know he has given jobs are not superior people. I ran in to one man as I went out of the building who used to be a circulation solicitor for *The*

News and Observer and who I believe we had to fire. I asked him about what he was doing and he said he had to certify appropriations to the War Department. I think he exaggerated—he is probably a clerk in the division—but his presence is not reassuring.

[I do not recall why Judge Parker of the U. S. Circuit Court of Appeals should have been called in on this matter. He was named circuit judge by President Coolidge. Labor and blacks had prevented his confirmation when President Hoover sent his name to the Senate as proposed justice of the U. S. Supreme Court. His liberal record afterwards proved they were mistaken in their opposition. In his home state, North Carolina, he was regarded with admiration by Democrats as well as Republicans. Roosevelt and Warren both held him in high esteem.]

Tuesday, November 2. Yesterday Gene Casey read to Jim Barnes, Dave Niles, and myself a long memorandum he had written to the President on the farm dissatisfaction with the Administration. It was a pretty effective piece and a very discouraging one. The basic part of which was a Casey denunciation of Wickard. However, when Casey lets his prejudices loose he doesn't stop with effectiveness and twice in this piece he referred to Harry Hopkins by description rather than by name, as a politically inept, personally unpopular, dangerous man in the White House. He read the first reference in the presence of Dave Niles and after he had read it he expounded at some length to Jim Barnes and myself about his hatred of Wallace and his determination to get him.

* * *

Yesterday W. C. Bourne, Jr., representing OWI, came in to see me about the foreign personnel. Billy said he was working in New York under a man by the name of Johnny White, whose name I think is Llewelyn White, formerly of the *Chicago Sun,* whose bitterness against Silliman Evans is unbounded. He said that Evans had completely captured Marshall Field and was preparing by blackmail to hold him—

that he has taken Field to houses in Chicago where Field had been photographed under most compromising circumstances. That Evans has three photographs to use if Field should ever want to break with Evans.

[John Llewelyn (Johnny) White was the first editor of the editorial page of the *Chicago Sun,* coming to the paper from *Newsweek.* He was fired at Evans' direction in mid-1943. Evans had acquired the *Nashville Tennessean* with the aid of Jesse Jones, who also helped him get the Chicago job earlier than he expected. Evans himself was forced out of his lucrative Chicago position. Apparently no blackmail ensued.]

Wednesday, November 3. Lunch with David Lilienthal at the Carlton, on this day when the miners are apparently disregarding the President's demand that they go back to work. John L. Lewis walked out of the Carlton dining room smoking a cigar and with his hat on, looking not at all worried. He sauntered out and then turned like a child playing a game with lines on the floor and marched the whole length of the decoration on one of the rugs. He was quite alone—put his overcoat on and walked out.

David Lilienthal was shocked by Benjamin Sonnenberg. He felt that Sonnenberg was the reason for all the anti-Semitism and his cynicism explained the weakness of his people. He described him as a "well-poisoner." Apparently this all grew out of the fact that Bill Nichols arranged a meeting in order that Sonnenberg might help Dave sell his new book, *TVA—Democracy Marches.*

Apparently Sonnenberg told Lilienthal that he didn't care whether TVA was good or bad, that he wasn't very much interested in it. Dave was shocked at the cynicism and he reported that his eighteen-year-old, who is still an articulate Radcliffe student, was shocked too at his lack of distinction between good and bad. I told him that I found Sonnenberg very amusing. Dave was unconvinced. I told him I thought Sonnenberg approached his book as a doctor might approach a disease, feeling that his job was to tell him how to sell it and that its morals or lack of them were beside his concern.

Dave admitted there might be something to this but still thinks that he is almost the walking figure of dangerous cynicism.

Incidentally, he felt that Bill Nichols' wife had seen so much of what cynicism had done to Europe that she was intuitively wise and good.

Went from lunch with Lilienthal to see Secretary Wickard, who was his normal utterly empty, futile self. Incidentally, Wickard called me early in the morning and let me know that he could see me at any hour of the day except one.

[Benjamin Sonnenberg was—and is—one of the most remarkable and amusing figures in the decades of the middle half of this American century. Short and rotund with a mustache like a line drawn across his round face, he affected a rather Edwardian dress. Somehow he gave the impression of both a plump leprechaun (if there are Jewish leprechauns) and the gamin product of New York City streets. He appeared to make fun of those he courted. But he also showed himself to them as a gourmet ready to share his abundant feasts at the best restaurants, where Mr. Sonnenberg's table was always reserved. He was a devotee of art, literature, and good works. He was, indeed, often as ready to wave the magic wand, which he made it clear he possessed, to promote the book of a writer for free as he was to use it in the service of an aviation tycoon or a movie magnate.

[Sonnenberg's career was completely improbable. Born in Brest-Litovsk, Poland, in 1901, he was educated in the public schools of New York City and, as he added with a beguiling flourish, "by pvt. tutors." He began work as a reporter on the *Flint* (Michigan) *Journal*. From that city of Chevrolets, he went on, more in keeping with his cosmopolitan air, to become a "member of the American Relief Administration, being stationed in Constantinople (Istanbul) supervising relief work in Turkish waters and the Ukraine after World War I." Coincidentally he became foreign correspondent for unnamed American newspapers until 1924. Then after an undescribed gap of four years in 1928 at twenty-seven he set up his public relations bureau in New York, later labeled Publicity Consultants, Inc.

[Primroses seemed to line the path of his progress. He became a Chevalier of the French Legion of Honor. He bought and elaborately refurnished the house on Gramercy Park South which John Barrymore had provided for his wife, Michael Strange. The place glittered with much brass. The lavatories were so elaborate that a copilot seemed necessary to their use. In a private theater he showed the movies of his Hollywood clients. He came to see me as the almost casual acquaintance of Juan Trippe.

[When I asked him recently to refresh my memory about that business he replied in longhand on stationery which bore a sketch of him in his high-buttoned coat and wearing a derby hat:

Dear Jonathan:
It was bracing to hear from you. Alistair and Jane (Cooke) at dinner here the other night & we talked about you.

Having never kept a scrap—no diaries, letters, theater programs, or even dried roses within the cover of a book, I've nothing to send you. In my working, self advancing years, I changed the bath water of my acquaintance secretly, but often—so that I do not possess even a Shriner's Convention hat or an autographed photo of James A. Farley. I never allowed the mascara of my trade to drip into my soup. I was only a cabinet maker who fashioned large pedestals for small statues.

From you I only have the warmest, tenderest memories. You are large of heart with a life enhancing quality rare in the political arenas.

Give my love to Lucy and come and see this autumnal person when you are in New York.

Best
Ben

[I replied that I had never seen the Fifth Amendment taken in so graceful a fashion.]

Thursday, November 4. George Creel told me last night that before the article on Milo Perkins appeared in the *Washington Times-Herald* he had been shown it by Jesse Jones and offered the affidavits in the case, which made up the story. He said the information on Perkins in Texas had been collected by Jones in the fight with BEW.

[Apparently Creel, who earlier had expressed his admiration for Jones to me, had as a frequent contributor to *Collier's* and other publications wanted to have nothing to do with this story. Prepared with the aid of Jones's banking and newspaper mechanisms in Texas, it raked up every possible charge against Perkins, including one that he avoided taxation on his home by listing it as a church of some esoteric sect. Eleanor Medill ("Sissy") Patterson played the story up in her anti-Administration newspaper.]

* * *

Talked with Tony Batchelder, McIntyre's secretary, about him. She thinks McIntyre is worse and I gather is profoundly worried about him. Her diagnosis is that his trouble comes from his very heavy drinking in the past. She said that he was never drunk but that before he went to Asheville, the first thing he would do when he came in in the morning would be to start drinking to hold himself together. I told her that the nervous condition which caused him to need a drink then is causing his stomach condition now. I gathered that all the women on his staff are really disturbed about his condition.

[Fearing a return of the illness which had kept him from the White House before, Mac had gone to Asheville, North Carolina, in late summer. He was not ready to give up again. I kept him informed about what was going on. Also I took on some of his chores. He had returned to Washington, insistently declaring he was much improved, but he died on December 13. No man, unless it was Louis McHenry Howe before him, better loved the President or was readier to speak straight and critically to him.]

* * *

[A lapse of more than a month occurred in my notes at this time, not because less was happening but rather because

I was loaded with more personal as well as official problems. The year had piled up the latter. Early in the year I had without any announcement taken over the handling of all problems relating to the Negro in wartime, so far as the White House should be concerned. A Wisconsin cranberry dealer and Ph.D. in anthropology from the University of Chicago, Philleo Nash, then in OWI, became in effect my assistant in dealing with these matters. He was joined by Theodore Poston, able black newspaperman from the *New York Evening Post*. Both brought concern for the Negro to their work and concern for full black participation in the war effort. Fortunately also both possessed a sense of humor, which at least as much as the fear of the Lord has always seemed to me to be the beginning of wisdom.

[Certainly in the struggle for the advance of his race, Poston was a happy warrior though he was often grimly in earnest. His intensity of purpose, however, never made him blind to the problems among his own people. Wryly, he expressed that in a joke he told me on one occasion when we were baffled in dealing with differences within the black community. He made me promise never to tell his wife that he had told me the story. Then he related it.

[At one of the then strictly segregated beaches on Chesapeake Bay an old black woman was crabbing. She pulled the crabs in and deposited them in a swarming mass in a bucket beside her. A loitering spectator admonished her.

["You better put a lid on that bucket."

[She disregarded him.

["Sho 'nuff," he said, "if you don't put a lid on it, they'll climb out."

["Naw," she said scornfully. "They're just like niggers. If one is 'bout to climb up the others will reach up and pull 'im back."

[We laughed but it was a parable true of more people than blacks alone.

[We dealt, however, with few comic situations. In June in Beaumont, Texas, in Detroit, and in Los Angeles, riots involving blacks and whites exploded. Then early in August

Nelson A. Rockefeller,
attractive young man on his way
up from millions.

General Edwin A. ("Pa") Watson,
gentleman and jester, who under
drawling suavity was steely shrewd.

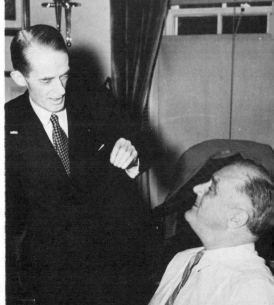

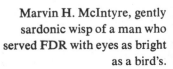

Marvin H. McIntyre, gently
sardonic wisp of a man who
served FDR with eyes as bright
as a bird's.

Photograph taken when
Roosevelt gave Daniels his
commission as press secretary.
Lucy Daniels looks on.
March 24, 1945.

Another picture of
Jonathan Daniels
and Lucy with FDR.
The last formal picture ever
taken of the President.

Jonathan Daniels as press
secretary, 1945. Photo taken by
Karsh of Canada for Time, Inc.

The tragic face from Yalta. From the photographs sent back by
the Signal Corps from Yalta. Daniels had the task of picking
the least haggard ones.

Jonathan Daniels holding press conference, 1945.

Jonathan Daniels with Ellen Hess of *McCall's* magazine, interviewing a family for a story about postwar conditions, 1945.

Funeral of Franklin D. Roosevelt at Hyde Park.

Jonathan Daniels was the top White House staff member
on hand when Harry Truman was sworn in on April 12, 1945.
Daniels' harassed face shows over Truman's shoulder.

Truman's first press conference.
Daniel's head barely shows to the left of Truman.

The changing of the guard: *left to right,* Mathew J.
Connelly, who became Truman's appointments secre-
tary; Stephen Early; President Truman; Charles G.
Ross, who is coming in as press secretary to the
President as Daniels retires.

David K. Niles, presidential
aide and manipulator of
minorities, whose hands tapered
like those of an Assyrian rug
peddler. Shown here in 1947
receiving the Civilian Medal for
Merit from President Truman.

Daniels visits
Truman at the White
House in 1950 to pre-
sent to the Chief
Executive his book
*The Man of Independ-
ence,* which deals
with the life of
Harry S. Truman.

Mark McCloskey, the indestructible Irishman from Hell's Kitchen via Princeton, reads Daniel's book about Truman.

Thirty years later, Jonathan and Lucy look at pictures from the past.

Adlai Stevenson and Jonathan Daniels had come from a social gathering to a convention hall when this picture was taken.

The last survivor of the staff immediately around FDR in World War II, Daniels at seventy-two showing the happy wrinkles of service in the causes of Roosevelt, Truman, Stevenson, and Kennedy.

pandemonium swept Harlem. There was little we could do when such explosions came. We did try to provide some guidance or suggestions when, as in Detroit, the President felt it necessary to send in federal troops. But what we tried to do in the threat of more such occurrences was to watch for the tension spots and try to avoid the development of violence in them. We received regular reports from the FBI and Military Intelligence agencies. We tried to get Agriculture to provide more black farm agents. I discussed with Adlai Stevenson, then special assistant to Secretary of the Navy Knox, the commissioning of more Negro officers. We wanted at least ten or twelve in the Navy. The Coast Guard had commissioned two. The War Department threw into our laps a three-cornered problem of segregation at the center of top-secret activities. At Hanford, Washington, the first big reactors were being built for the production of plutonium. Nuclear detonation seemed threatened by a quarrel as to separate facilities not only for black and white workers but for Mexican workers as well, who were not welcomed in the white dormitories and resented their relegation to the quarters of the blacks. Production, not perfection, was the aim here and my memory is that separate provision was made for all three. Other cases involving prejudice were brought to my desk. Norman Thomas, the perennial Socialist candidate for President, set up a small storm about the case of Private Alton Levy, who had been sentenced to prison for making false and defamatory statements about his commanding officer in private conversations. The President suggested that the verdict might be posted on the bulletin board at the Army and Navy Club to be read by officers not always restrained in their comments on the Commander in Chief. Levy's term was sharply cut.

[As the newspaperman on the presidential staff I also had the job of holding the hands (there was little more that I could do) of representatives of such pro-Administration papers as the *Chicago Sun* and the *Philadelphia Record* who felt that they should have a better shake in newsprint rationing. I remember that David Stern of the *Record* was a par-

205

ticular pain in the neck. There was little I could do but present their pleas to Harold Boeschenstein, charming and fair gentleman who had come from the presidency of the Owens-Corning Fiberglas Corporation to handle this business in the War Production Board. If I didn't get these papers more newsprint I think I at least held back the ferocious Colonel R. R. McCormick of the *Tribune,* who would have denied Marshall Field's *Sun* a single sheet.

[Comic-dramatic incident. A security officer from the Glenn Martin aviation plant near Baltimore telephoned me. He just wanted to check, he said, on a letter from me on White House stationery which had just been presented to him. It asked admittance to the plant of "three foreign military officers and a civilian representative of a friendly nation." I had written no such letter, I told him. A call from me sent the FBI scurrying to the plant. Edgar Hoover told me that Glenn Martin had been instructed to destroy all records of this incident. It turned out, however, that the chief of these foreign representatives was an acquaintance of mine. Moe Berg, the supposedly highly literate baseball player, had forged the letter as a required demonstration that he would make a good operative for our own Office of Strategic Services. This test he flunked.

[In the midst of public duties I was not immune to private problems. For aid in the care of four little girls, my wife had imported from North Carolina a gentle young black woman named Dovey. She came well recommended but one day I got a call from a Negro druggist. A woman who worked for me, he said, had come into his store and asked for a medicine which he knew she hoped would cure her of venereal disease. We rushed her to the offices of Dr. Bernard Leonard, associate of my brother Worth, who was then practicing medicine in the Pacific. The Wassermann test showed that the young woman who had been tending our children, the youngest of whom was four, had a raging case of syphilis. That meant not only sending her back to North Carolina but Wassermanns for all. Benny Leonard came sadly to our house to tell us that the test on our nine-year-old Lucy was positive. But there he found the pediatrician who was tending Lucy for a flaming case of measles.

["Thank God!" said Benny Leonard.

[There were other personal troubles not so humorous in eventuality. I had the flu, as did many others that year. Then while Lucy, Sr., and I were dining with Pa Watson and his wife Frances, we got a call that my absent brother's father-in-law, a gentle, seemingly easygoing elderly man, had drowned in a pond at his place near Chevy Chase. My father wired that my mother had a serious heart attack. She died just before Christmas.

[But business was not interrupted. Ben Sonnenberg dropped by casually to bring books which he thought I might like to read, only casually mentioning the interests of Mr. Trippe. The two sides in the REA fight, pro- and anti-Slattery, made a procession to my door. Nash and Poston came in every day. The President asked me to see what I could do about the disintegrating Office of Civilian Defense, from which Landis had departed or escaped in September to take an assignment in the Middle East. Perhaps gloating a bit, I made a note: "I am a little worried about the Middle Easterners."

[I was working on finding a man to succeed Beanie Baldwin in Farm Security. Henry Morgenthau wanted me to help in publicity for a current bond drive.

[Then before I resumed my diary there came a memo like a prod from an impatient President: "How am I to get Slattery to resign? That is the first thing that has to be done."

[I had tried everything, even to setting up a fancy-sounding job in the State Department, which he declined. Attorney General Biddle and Secretary Wickard were testy with each other about Wickard's legal right to fire the adhesive administrator. Slattery's friends on the Hill were muttering ominously and some there felt that in the Slattery case they had a good chance to hit the Administration.

[My diary began in 1944 with a matter even closer to presidential concern.]

Diary

————————————————————————————————

1944

[The year began with a new spirit of confidence in Allied victory. Evidently weakened Japanese forces were being pushed up the Pacific. Italy had declared war on its old German ally. Mussolini was a sick man in German captivity. At Teheran in November 1943, Roosevelt and Churchill had finally been able to assure the impatient Stalin that they were ready to launch their European landing, creating the second front. The date of the actual landing was fixed for May. As the New Year began, the President in his State of the Union Message cautioned the country against complacency. As he spoke, the White House was involved in a comic mystery melodrama in which the cast of characters included chief figures in the Administration, notably Harry Hopkins, who was still living in the White House when he was out of the hospital. Duty fell to me in its solution.]

Wednesday, January 13. Talked with Steve Early about Harry Hopkins and his adverse publicity. Steve said, "The trouble is to find a clean spot on Harry anywhere." He said that the Beaverbrook jewels can't be explained away because, while they weren't emeralds, they were diamonds.

"I have seen them myself. Fortunately for Harry they were antique diamond clips which had been in Beaverbrook's family for some time. Harry didn't declare them and smuggled them into the country. He sent them over to Gaston [Assistant Secretary of the Treasury Herbert E. Gaston] and said he wanted a statement from them to the effect that they were declared for duty and what about it. They had them appraised and examined (Early didn't mention the value) and established the fact that they were antique and, as such, not subject to duty."

Steve went on. "Harry first married a Jewess and then threw her away to marry his secretary. Apparently that was real love but she died of cancer of the breast and he married this girl Louise Macy. Bernie Baruch knows who she is. Jock Whitney knows who she is."

Steve was confident, however, that Hopkins did not write the famous Sparks letter; it was dated August 17, 1943, and Steve was with Hopkins in Quebec at that time. Also he was sure Hopkins' office wouldn't send out a letter with such a blot on the signature.

[It is necessary to go back in time to set the story in order. A year before this time, in January 1943, the anti-Administration *Washington Times-Herald* had quoted Congressman Clare E. Hoffman, Republican of Michigan, about a bridal gift—valuable emeralds—to Mrs. Hopkins from Lord Beaverbrook, a vastly wealthy Canadian-born British politician. In the multibillion-dollar Lend-Lease program upon which Britain so much depended, Beaverbrook had been as officially concerned on the receiving side as Hopkins had been powerful on the giving side.

[Weight had been given to the Hoffman charges by Representative Joseph Martin, Republican minority leader, and by Republican Senator Hugh Butler of Nebraska. In answer to the charges of a jeweled British payoff to Hopkins, Mrs. Hopkins said, "I don't even own one emerald. It's a lie. I never owned an emerald and don't own one now." Beaverbrook said, "It's all nonsense. The story is all fabrication from first to last, but the Germans will like it." In what seemed a White House denial of the business, Steve Early himself at this time spoke of "the malicious rumors and statements now being published by certain newspapers hostile to the government and to certain officials of the government." In his book *Roosevelt and Hopkins,* Robert E. Sherwood wrote of "the fantastic story of the Beaverbrook emeralds."

[Then in the fall of 1943, C. Nelson Sparks, a former Republican mayor of Akron, where Willkie had begun his legal career, published an anti-Willkie pamphlet called *ONE MAN —Wendell Willkie.* The title was a satiric reference to Willkie's own recent book, entitled *One World.* In it Sparks presented a purported letter from Hopkins to Dr. Umphrey Lee, president of Southern Methodist University in Dallas. In the letter Hopkins supposedly wrote that Willkie would be the Republican nominee in 1944. Sparks presented it to prove that Willkie was a "stooge" for Roosevelt policies, a point which Conservative anti-Willkie Republicans were anxious to make.

[On Christmas Day an aroused Hopkins denounced the letter as a forgery. He called on the FBI to investigate. Then it turned out that the letter, written on authentic White House stationery, had emerged from the Interior Department domain of Harold Ickes, who had little love for Hopkins. George N. Briggs, an assistant to Ickes, had given the letter to Sparks. When I talked to Steve the case had become so amazingly involved that Arthur Krock in *The New York Times* wrote of an investigation of it by a resurrected Sherlock Holmes who appeared on a bench in Lafayette Square disguised as Bernard Baruch.]

*   *   *

Tuesday, January 25. Victor Rotnem told me this morning that there was one thing he knew about that made him distrustful of Ickes. He said that some years ago he had been for a number of years attorney for a trade association of philatelists, and that he later went into business here in Washington dealing in stamps. This was at about the same time that there was some scandal about Jim Farley distributing unperforated sheets of stamps to fellow members of the Cabinet and others.

Some man to whom a sheet of the stamps was given started to sell them and it developed that they brought a very high price on the stamp market, whereupon a scandal developed and the President wanted to make it clear that no member of his Cabinet had sold the stamps.

However, in the meantime Ickes had sent his stamp assistant, a man who is now the President's stamp adviser, to Victor Rotnem's company, where they had swapped some of these stamps for other stamps of equal value. When the President called for his cabinet members to show their stamps, Ickes sent over to try and buy the stamps back or swap them back. The company refused to do so, whereupon Ickes asked them to lend him the stamps if he gave a receipt for them. This was done.

Ickes then took the borrowed stamps over to the White House and showed them to the President, saw to it that a news item got in the papers saying that Honest Harold had shown the President that he still had his stamps, then Ickes returned the stamps to Rotnem's stamp company. Rotnem suggested that a man who would do that might write the Hopkins letter. He also said, "What kind of man always wants to be called 'Honest Harold'? People don't insist on their own honesty."

Rotnem also told me that he had heard that Briggs was introduced to Ed Kelly (who had in turn introduced Briggs to Ickes) by Joseph Wolf, former Democratic national committeeman from Minnesota, who got into some kind of trouble about political patronage in the early days of the Administration. Rotnem said he knew Wolf and called him and asked him and he said he had introduced Briggs to Kelly. Briggs had come back to Minnesota and said he was willing to do anything he could to help kill off Willkie, whereupon Wolf, who thinks Briggs is a good man, introduced him to Kelly.

Last night Rotnem phoned me to say two things had happened during the evening. That they had caught a *Times-Herald* reporter rifling the files in the office of Maynard Smith, that he had been identified and they knew who he was. Also, that Judge Rosenman had called during the evening and

212

said that Harry Hopkins insisted on being named as the injured party in any indictment of Briggs.

This morning the Attorney General and Henry Schweinhaut were both deeply disturbed by this proposal because Hopkins could only be listed on the grounds that Briggs's forgery had injured Hopkins' reputation. Schweinhaut felt strongly that this would mean that Hopkins' reputation, which was allegedly injured, would be opened up for complete examination, and that would make it possible to make the Briggs case a circus for trying all the stories about Hopkins. Schweinhaut called me in great distress about this at twenty past eleven but at eleven thirty he called me back and said, "I ain't mad at anybody, it has just been agreed that we will make Sparks and not Hopkins the injured party."

[Briggs was indicted by a federal grand jury on charges of forgery, mail fraud, and obtaining money under false pretenses. In news reports about the case it was only indicated that he got a $40 loan and $125 for a trip to Texas in seeking the letter for Sparks. He was released on bail but died in the fall before the case could come to trial.

[I worked on the matter with Henry A. Schweinhaut, special assistant to the Attorney General, who was handling the case in the Department of Justice. Hoping then to be appointed to the bench, he was jittery for fear he would make a misstep which would end his chances. As one happy ending to the case he was later named U. S. District Judge of the District of Columbia, a position which he held until his death many years later.

[If there was any such break-in as attributed to a *Times-Herald* reporter, it escaped the news-gathering attention of *The New York Times*.]

Early said that Eugene Casey first came into notice during the purge campaign of 1938, when he went on the *Baltimore Sun* radio station every night for fifteen minutes in the Lewis-Tydings campaign and deflated everything the *Baltimore Sun* papers said. "He did a wonderful job," Early said. It turned out that the pieces were written by Drew Pearson and then broadcast by Farmer Casey. Steve said they were splendid. He said that Casey had made half a million dollars in housing in Washington and then a lot more money on the stock market.

"Everything he touched seemed to turn to gold."

However, he is "a little nuts." After that campaign when Frank Walker and George Allen were trying to raise the money for the Hyde Park museum, they couldn't find anybody to handle Maryland, so Early, on the basis of his speeches in the campaign, recommended Casey. Casey took the job as Maryland chairman and raised three times his quota. He said that Jim Rowe, when he took over Jimmy Roosevelt's job for a while, arranged to have him put on a sort of liaison with the Department of Agriculture. Then Casey began to go around the country and built up his friendship with national committeemen on a very clever basis. He told them they didn't count for much in Washington since their political work was given attention only in campaign years but that he, Casey, could break through the bureaucracy to get them patronage.

["Farmer Casey" did have the right to that title as the owner-operator of a number of dairy farms. Effective as Early may have thought him in the campaign which Roosevelt waged in 1938 to rid the Democratic party of reactionary members of Congress, Millard E. Tydings held on to his Senate seat. He won the Democratic nomination over Roosevelt's candidate, Congressman David J. Lewis, who, in the *Congressional Directory,* described himself as a "self-educated" man who "studied law and Latin" while he worked as a coal miner. For his efforts, however, Casey was made deputy governor of the Farm Credit Administration, then in 1941 appointed to his equivocal position as "executive assistant" to the President.]

Thursday, March 2. Went in to see the President [about Senate committee plans to cite me for contempt for refusing to testify in the REA-Slattery investigation]. I told him that I had joked with General Watson and told him that I had about as much to do with my case as Dred Scott had to do with the Dred Scott case. The President asked me what ever happened in the Dred Scott case—"Did he go back into slavery?" I didn't know. Then he said that his family had owned slaves at Hyde Park and had slave quarters. I asked him how long ago and he said he thought they emancipated them about 1828.

I spoke to him briefly about Negro combat troops and he had the impression that the Negro is inferior in combat. I asked him if he felt that he had any information on which to base such a judgment or was it just a feeling. He said he didn't have any information but that he felt that the Negro was a good soldier in forward movement, such as, for instance, the Russian movement of the last few weeks, but inferior in such an action as that on the Anzio beachhead, where men have had to stay in one place and take it for long periods. He based some of this on the experience of the French with the Senegalese, who were excellent in physical combat.

Then he called Grace Tully and read a long letter written to Justice Byrnes in which he undertook to tell the Senate what had been done in the Slattery case, basing action on Slattery's "health." He said in the letter that he had not known about my testimony before I testified but that he completely approved of the position I had taken and that he felt that this was a matter involving the coordinate position of the executive in government. He said that he would be willing to have a fight with the Senate on such an issue as this one. I told him that the only trouble was that he had said casually at a press conference that he hadn't heard anything about the Slattery matter since last June and that I thought the letter would have to be carefully worded to keep within that record. He agreed, and suggested that I talk to Byrnes about it.

Byrnes doesn't like the President's letter. He doesn't think the President can prove anything about Slattery's health and Byrnes said that very suddenly he began to worry about this case last night. He asked me who was handling the case and I told him I talked to the Attorney General, who said Ugo Carusi was to handle it. He didn't like that very much and spoke of him as just a boy around there and said the Attorney General ought to handle the matter himself. He called up the Attorney General and told him so. He also suggested that I write a letter to Senator Smith asking for a transcript of the testimony.

When I was leaving the President's office, General Watson said he had promised to go to jail with me for six months but he and Jim Barnes agreed that I ought to have a whole year to rest and so I could take both six-month sentences. The President said, "Look out, Pa, they can get you twice, both in civil and military courts."

I went on up from Byrnes's office to lunch with George Fort Milton [who had written much about the confrontation of the President and the Congress in Andrew Johnson's time], who raised the interesting question that if I should be tried at the bar of the Senate the President probably would not have the power to pardon me, as he does not have power to pardon in impeachment cases.

[On February 28, 1944, the Senate Agriculture Subcommittee called me to testify about the Slattery case. Headed by Senator Ellison D. ("Cotton Ed") Smith of South Carolina, whom Roosevelt had tried to "purge" from the Senate two years before, it was hardly a body friendly to the Administration. Indeed, Allen Drury, then covering the Senate for the United Press, said that the case provided "Cotton Ed" with a "concrete means" for forwarding "his vendetta with the White House." Beside him was Senator Guy M. Gillette, whom Roosevelt had also tried to purge from the Senate. The committee counsel was a former Republican congressman from Maine.

[When I had been subpoenaed the President referred me to Attorney General Biddle, who put the matter in the hands of Carusi, his executive assistant. It was agreed that I should decline to testify on the grounds of executive privilege, a position which was to take considerable battering years later in the Nixon administration. As politely as I could, but firmly, I declined to answer any questions about my activities for the President in this matter.

[Then followed the explosion which drew banner headlines in the press. I still keep the original copy of a cartoon by Berryman in the *Washington Star* of Slattery still sitting at the top of a telephone pole which Wickard had chopped in two at the bottom while I looked on. The excitement grew as the committee, according to Mark Stauter of Duke University, who has written the most complete study of the case, "pondered" what to do with or to me. With "Cotton Ed" in the lead, it seemed ready to pounce when it proposed unanimously Senate citation of me for contempt. I don't remember being greatly disturbed by the prospect of jail. As my diary indicates, there was joking about it at the White House, even in the Oval Office of the President.

[As a former senator, now exercising broad powers in the East Wing of the White House, Byrnes seemed most disturbed. Less than a week before, the President's own Democratic leader in the Senate, Alben Barkley of Kentucky, had flared in resentment at sharp words in a presidential veto of a tax measure. Dramatically he had resigned as majority leader. That had been patched up. Barkley had been mollified. But incipient revolt remained. This was no time for "a fight with the Senate on such an issue."

[So back I went to the Senate committee with presidential permission to testify. "Are you the same Jonathan Daniels who was here before?" asked the committee counsel. "Approximately," I said. There were grins all around, all being relieved that the executive-legislative confrontation had been resolved. However, as the *Electrical World* reported, my testimony was "anticlimactic." I had nothing startling to reveal in my narration of my efforts to get Slattery to resign as the President and the Secretary of Agriculture wished. Slattery did resign the following fall with a blast aimed particularly at Wickard.

[I wrote my father: "I had a very interesting time, of course, in this Senatorial committee matter. It all ended up exceptionally well. As a matter of fact, the last time I was before the committee we ended up in a fulsome exchange of compliments, I expressing my appreciation for the courteous manner in which the committee had treated me and the committee counsel making a speech to the effect that the President could have chosen no man who would have represented him with greater dignity, etc., than myself. The compliments got so thick and the orchids were flying around at such a rate that it really became funny. Finally, the counsel suggested that it might be proper for me to sing 'Oh, What a Beautiful Morning,' but I told him that if I did, I was afraid the existing amity would be destroyed. I even had old 'Cotton Ed' Smith smiling. Yesterday at press conference the President said, 'Congratulations, Jonathan.' So I think the incident has really closed with no injury to your trouble-making son."]

Saturday, March 11. Very interesting conference with the President in which he talked with considerable frankness about his relations with England, saying that he and Churchill had been greatly at odds over the question of the continuation of the Italian monarchy and Badoglio. He said that our State Department had been even more earnest in its wish to get rid of the king and Badoglio than he had been and that when he passed a State Department memorandum on to Churchill, Churchill had pretty nearly gone through the roof.

The President was amusingly critical of the British, pointing out that in some cases the British had sold Lend-Lease goods from us to other people for profit. One case was when Ibn Saud of Saudi Arabia wanted to get some pipe to pipe drinking water to the palace; we had had to tell him that we had no such pipe available, whereupon the British furnished the pipe and it turned out to be pipe which the British had received from us through Lend-Lease. The President felt, however, that these incidents were limited in nature. He suggested that Churchill was all-out for a monarchy in Italy while FDR was insistent that the Italian people should have the sort of government they wanted. I gathered that he favored the present government by a committee composed of the six anti-Fascist parties in Italy.

I said that it seemed to me unfortunate that the State Department, with such a view about the situation in Italy, should be forced to accept continual criticism based on the idea that they are for the most reactionary position in Italy. He agreed and I asked whose business it was to see that the public relations of such an agency as the State Department were designed to offset the impression that it is a reactionary, socialite, dull agency. He said that it was OWI's, although it should be done with great diplomacy.

Obviously, the President said, he had to be careful not to let the press say that he had broken with Churchill on any such matter.

"Nevertheless," said Lowell Mellett, "I hope you will have at least one break with him before the election next fall."

The President grinned. "Yes," he said, "I can understand that. Maybe I will have to work out such a break with Churchill."

[Pietro Badoglio, Italian field marshal and duke of Addis Ababa, had been instrumental in the fall of Mussolini. He became Prime Minister in July 1943. He resigned in June 1944, a year before the monarchy came to an end.]

Thursday, April 20. Basil O'Connor struck me as a pretty feeble Irishman who is using to the full his former law connection with the President, while talking about his independence. When I first went in he talked about the slanderous material put out against the Infantile Paralysis Foundation. I asked him if Sister Kenny was involved and he said, "Yes, she is out to make everything she can out of it." He said she had gotten $50,000 from RKO for a movie. She wrote a book and has servants and cars in Minneapolis. He added, "She is just a big bitch who is biting the only hand that ever fed her." He told me that he never made any comment about these matters. "You know they call me 'no comment O'Connor.'"

Then he launched into a long recital of the President's stubbornness in not seeing the inevitability of Juan Trippe's chosen instrument plan for postwar aviation. He said the Boss was about to make a mistake and that although Juan Trippe was the best-equipped man in the whole field his advice was not asked and he was disregarded. He described Adolph Berle with great contempt and then went on to suggest that opposition to Juan Trippe might be based on a campaign contribution in 1940 by American Export. I asked him specifically about that but he said he would tell me later. He talked repeatedly about his loyalty to the President but he made the impression on me that he was out to serve his client first, last, and all the time. He had a suite of rooms at the Carlton with a secretary in attendance although I think he was down here for only a few hours.

[O'Connor, former law partner of the President's, was president of the National Foundation for Infantile Paralysis. It had at first shown interest in the claims of Elizabeth Kenny ("Sister Kenny") that she had a cure for infantile paralysis. An Australian, she had been a nurse in the bush country and with Australian troops in World War I. Having written several books on the disease, she came to the United States in 1940. Acclaimed as something of a saint and a scientist, her autobiography was published and a movie of her life planned. She established the Elizabeth Kenny Institute in Minneapolis, which began to campaign for funds. Then doubts arose as to whether she was saint or quack. O'Connor at this time definitely resented her fund-raising competition.

[American Export Airlines was a prime competitor of Trippe's in his quest for a monopoly of American postwar overseas air service.]

Tuesday, May 16. At press conference on Tuesday, May 16, the President told correspondents—off the record—that he might simply disappear if there were big operations of a military nature, in order that he might devote his full time to them. He mentioned having seen General Mark Clark while he was in South Carolina.

After the press conference I spoke to him about George Fort Milton's books on the Moscow Protocols. He said to me, using a strange phrase, "Here is something you ought to write if I should pop off." Then he went into a discussion of the talks with Stalin with regard to Poland. The President felt very strongly that Stalin had been most generous in his offers, proposing to give the Poles 250 miles of coastline on the Baltic and much richer land in East Prussia than some of the Polish area Russia intends to hold.

The President was disturbed by things I told him, and by

things Dave Niles and Isador Lubin told him, about the activities of the Polish government in Washington, in propaganda in the U.S. Lock Currie said that the Polish government took all of its money in cash from the Treasury (not Lend-Lease funds)—generally in $20 bills. Somebody suggested that the bills ought to be traced.

[Regularly accredited diplomats dealt with our government directly through the State Department. Foreign nationality groups, not always in agreement with the official representatives of their countries, approached the White House deviously sometimes through the administrative assistants, notably Niles. What I referred to as the Polish government in Washington was actually the embassy of the Polish government in exile in London. Its status was increasingly obscure in May 1944, although Ambassador Ciechanowski still presided in his chancellery on 16th Street. He had been chief secretary to Ignacy Paderewski at the Peace Conference in Paris in 1918, when an independent Poland was created.

[A year before, in April 1943, Wladyslaw Sikorski, Prime Minister of Poland in exile in London, had asked the International Red Cross to investigate the murder at Katyn Forest near Smolensk of 14,000 Polish officers who had been prisoners of war in Soviet hands. Stalin thereupon severed Soviet-Polish relations. Those $20 bills could have been going into propaganda against our then ally, Russia.]

The President went into a discussion of the position he holds between the contending British and Russians. He spoke particularly of making a sort of group of free states with free trade in the area—part of Denmark, Bremen, Hamburg, Wilhelmshaven, and the Kiel Canal—somewhat along the lines of the old historical precedent of the Hanseatic League, to be administered so far as foreign affairs are concerned by commissioners appointed by Russia, Britain, and the United States, but with the towns to have complete local government in their own hands—electing their own mayors, etc.

He said he spoke of that to Stalin, who said, "I had not t'ought of it. We will study it." Then he spoke of the business of the British and Russian fears of each other in Persia,

Russia feeling that they have to have a warm-water port. One per cent of the people of Persia rule, the President said, and they are all grafters. The rest live in the worst form of feudalism. Nobody wants to control Persia in such a poverty-ridden condition, so he suggested that they set up a free port to be run by similar commissioners and with free trade with an international railroad, and that both Britain and Russia guarantee the freedom of the remainder of Persia. Stalin said again, "I had not t'ought of it. It is a good idea. I will sign."

The President then gave the impression to me that there had been an agreement signed by him, Stalin, and Churchill for such a set-up in Persia. I did not ask him how binding such an agreement could be on the U.S.

I was impressed by his admiring quotation of Stalin's direct comment in each case, and I asked him, "Mr. President, how does Churchill act in such a case?" He put his hands up defensively and said, "Churchill is acting now as if he is afraid of always getting hit. Ever since Ickes started with the Arabian oil matter, the British have been sending all kinds of telegrams fearful of what we were doing about the business. Finally I had to send them a homely telegram and say that we were not making sheep's eyes at anything of theirs and for them not to make sheep's eyes at anything of ours." He said that "sheep's eyes" had become a regular word among the British since his telegram.

I definitely gathered that the President felt he was in a position where he had to stand between the British and the Russians in their fears of each other, and that as such he could devise plans of adjustment of their various collisions.

Of the Persian thing, he said that if he were twenty years younger, he would like nothing better than to go to such a free city as he proposed and be the American adviser.

All throughout his conversation he indicated an almost boyish interest in geography, and I got the strange impression that in planning the future of the world he was like a boy playing trains with the world, setting up cities, planning free towns.

Incidentally, as the conversation started, General Watson came in and said something about a letter being ready soon. He is talking about Tito, the President said. He made a wry face, indicating Tito was weeping because while he received letters from Churchill and three letters in his own hand-writing from Stalin, he had received no such message from the President. "I don't believe he got one in Stalin's own handwriting," the President said. "He never writes like that."

* * *

Following the press conference held by the President just after his return from his rest on B. Baruch's plantation in S.C., Dave Niles was particularly depressed about the President's condition. I shared his feeling. Niles felt that he looked as if he had been painted up for his appearance. Also Niles had heard from Bill Hassett that the President was going "off the record," that he would not be signing letters to people, etc. General Watson told me that the President was cutting down on his schedule, that he was taking a nap every afternoon. Niles had heard that the President had had a prostate operation. I know that although Niles had not said so directly, earlier he had been worried about the possibility of cancer. Others had heard that the President had had a heart attack.

Certainly at the first press conference it was obvious that the President had not been doing much fishing. He was not in the least sunburned, which was remarkably evident in contrast with the dark suntan of the three reporters who had stayed in Georgetown, South Carolina, while he was visiting at Baruch's place.

[In January the President had seemed to recover from an attack of the flu which he had following the Teheran conference with Churchill and Stalin. However, he remained in a much fatigued condition and an examination in March showed an enlarged heart. In spite of the pressures upon him, he agreed to a long rest at the Hobcaw Barony plantation of Baruch in South Carolina. There he suffered a pain-

223

ful gall-bladder attack but he recovered from it without any cardiac symptoms. Except for a pool of three press service representatives, who accompanied him, he was not seen by correspondents from April 7 to May 9.]

*   *   *

Talking before the press conference to Dave Niles and Bill Hassett, I expressed the opinion that I was not at all sure that the President was going to run again. I was surprised, however, when Bill Hassett spoke up and said, "That would be my hunch also at the present time."

I was to have seen the President with Jim Barnes on Thursday May 11 but I was in Charlotte speaking. Barnes, who saw him, was greatly impressed by his vigor. On May 15 Rosenman was talking as if the President was certainly running for re-election. The President himself speaks about "after November," as if he were running.

Thursday, May 18. Major George Watts Hill and Earl Brennan of OSS came to see me this morning. It seems that the chief of the Southern European Section of OSS abroad arrived in Presque Isle, Maine, this week with "a gentleman." He had no passport except his OSS travel orders. After phoning Washington, Brennan assured the State Department that it would be all right to admit the man. He came to Washington by plane and is at the Statler Hotel under the name of Michele Rossi. He is actually Prof. Guido Pazzi, who was assistant professor at the University of Messina and was never promoted because he was not a member of the Fascist party. He is a native of Bologna. He has had considerable experience in the labor field. He is a socialist and worked with the International Labor Office of the League of Nations, and also before the war he had some relationships with the Russians.

He comes to this country with plenipotentiary powers from Badoglio. Apparently the British are unwilling that there be any Badoglio representative in this country. OSS feels that the State Department's representatives in Italy are dominated by the British. In essence it seems to me that OSS, which says it has the confidence of Badoglio while the British and other Americans have not, has smuggled an ambassador or potential ambassador into the U.S. under the guise that he is coming to give political or economic advice to OSS.

Hill and Brennan asked my advice as to what to do. I told them I did not think it a good idea to bypass the State Department and agreed to discuss the thing with Adolf Berle.

Pazzi is living at the Statler Hotel with a young officer in OSS and it is regarded as very important that nobody know in advance the facts about this matter.

I talked with Berle who is going to see Brennan. While I talked to him Berle picked his nose and rolled the damp results of his picking into little balls, which he disposed of with his fingers. I told Lucy. "Why," she said, "he did it at the dinner table when we were at his house."

* * *

Tuesday, June 6. As we came into the Oval Office to the press conference following D-Day, the President shouted to us to ask what we were all smiling so much about. He was very happy and I said to him that he did not look so downhearted himself. It was one of the biggest conferences I have seen. Inside the circle around the President's desk were Sam Rosenman, Jimmy Byrnes, Elmer Davis, Ed Klauber of OWI, Jim Barnes, Isador Lubin, Steve Early, Tom Blake, Lock Currie, Bill McReynolds, Maurice C. Latta, Captain Wood, a young officer from the map room, Grace Tully—in a dark dress with white flowers on it—her assistant Dorothy Brady—in a yellow suit. Steve Early was smoking a pipe; Fala being petted by Grace Tully and running around the room. The packed ranks of newspapermen and Bill Donaldson called, "All in."

It was one of the President's happiest conferences. For a moment all politics were forgotten by the correspondents. The President himself looked very well in a white shirt, with a dark-blue bow tie with white polka dots, and gray cotton trousers. He smoked with his long cigarette holder. I noticed that again at this conference he put his hand in a cup back of his ear to hear the question of a correspondent. Also at one time he sat back in his chair and tapped the arm with his fingers.

In spite of his obvious elation he said the war is not over by any means. This operation is not over. You don't just land on a beach and walk to Berlin. He said that the approximate date of the landing had been fixed at Teheran as the end of May or the first few days of June. The exact date had only been fixed a short time, and that date had to be postponed twenty-four hours because of the weather. The general date was fixed for the "small-boat weather" which exists in this part of the Channel for only a brief period during the year. He said that Stalin had been informed all about the plan at Teheran and that he was entirely agreeable about it.

Before the mass of the correspondents came in he chatted in great good humor with his assistants and others. I remember particularly that he asked Elmer Davis, referring to a recent statement of the Pope, "Elmer, don't you think the Pope is all wet?"

The President's vanities are sometimes very boyish. I remember at a recent conference he said with a strange sort of pride that he calls both the King of Greece and Peter of Yugoslavia by their first names.

[The President's flip remark to Davis about Pius XII probably related to the concern His Holiness was expressing about the resurgence of Communists who had been suppressed by Mussolini. They had reappeared in force on the Allied side among the partisan fighters in the North after the fall of Rome was assured this month.]

Friday, June 9. Before the press conference this morning Pa Watson said he had been down to the President's map room but that the war news there was not as good as it was in the newspapers. I had lunch today with William (Bill) Douglas Pawley, president and director of the Inter-continent Corporation, connected with the Central Aircraft Manufacturing Company, Inc., USA, Loiwing, China, and also with the Hindustan Aircraft Limited, Bangalore, India.

Pawley is forty-eight years old, was born in Florence, S.C., made money in the Florida boom, kept it and became the manufacturer of airplanes in Florida. He still has interests in Florida, but he has been in the Far East for twelve years. He was the man who hired Claire Lee Chennault to come to China, where he organized the "Flying Tigers." Pawley had taught Chinese and Indians how to make airplanes and is now very much interested in helping India to feed itself by establishing an ammonium nitrate plant in the Indian state at the tip of the Indian peninsula. He is having difficulties with the British getting the plant established because Imperial Chemical Company has slowed things down, wanting the business themselves.

Melvin Hildreth, Washington lawyer and Democratic politician, who had us to lunch (including Pawley's brother and a lawyer named Scott from Florida, who are flying to India in the next few days), told me that Pawley had started out as a milkman in Wilmington, N.C. Pawley himself told me that he met Tom Morgan when as a young fellow he was running a bumboat to the American fleet at Cuban Station and Tom Morgan was a sailor on the *Vermont*.

There is nothing impressive-looking about Pawley. Indeed, he appears like a fairly successful small Florida businessman, but he talks with great enthusiasm about his operations. He has found the Indians highly capable mechanics and engineers—much better indeed than the American engineers who can be secured at this time.

He told a very hair-raising story about being lost in the Himalayas without enough gasoline and everybody getting ready to crash, and then landing in a rice paddy when they had only about one pint of gas left. He is a very interesting person in a day when we are rather inclined to believe that the American soldier of fortune has disappeared. He is about ready to retire, however, and live on his farm out in Maryland while his brother and others carry on his work in the East.

Tuesday, June 13. The President said after press conference today that he had seen "Jesus" Jones this morning and he had said to him, "Jesse, what are we going to do about this Texas situation?" Jones said that he didn't know and the President said, "Well, it seems to me you ought to know." Jones denies any connection with the whole business, of course.

The conversation came up when somebody mentioned Jim Farley. Barnes told the President that Michelson had told him that Farley was planning to make a speech in which he was going to say that the President told him in 1940 that he was not going to run and he told Farley what time to announce. The President said, "Of course that is just not so." We talked politics at great length. The President is obviously more in a political frame of mind than he has been for months. I told him that I thought that if Baruch, Will Clayton, and Jesse Jones wanted to they could clean up the Texas situation within three weeks. The President said that he had told Jones that the same sort of thing had happened about eighty years ago when there were three parties in the field and there was a row among the Democrats and the result was Abraham Lincoln in the Civil War. He said he thought the people in Texas were out to destroy the party system.

At the end of the conference, I said, "Mr. President, you have a great deal more forbearance than I have ever had." Whereupon Gene Casey said, "Mr. President, I wish I had 90 per cent of your patience and you had 10 per cent of my ruthlessness." Grace Tully, who had come in with some papers for the President, burst into gales of laughter, as we all did.

[As early as April of this year there had been anti-Roosevelt mutterings from Texas. Senator W. Lee ("Pass the Biscuits, Pappy") O'Daniel had announced his opposition to a fourth term. Then late in May the State Democratic Convention refused to instruct its delegates for FDR. Whereupon Roosevelt supporters bolted the convention, held their own meeting, and elected delegates instructed for the President. If Jesse Jones had no hand in the anti-FDR business, evidently he did nothing to stop it. In the National Convention both the regular and the rump delegations were seated. Then some of the anti-Roosevelt men walked out. They were not missed in the convention, which was overwhelmingly for the President.]

Before this political discussion, Dave and Jim and I had Jack McCloy, who had been present at the conference, up before the President's desk and brought up the fact that the War Department was planning to announce that all Japanese could return to California. The President smilingly said it could not be done for political reasons—and he went on to suggest that there ought to be some sort of activity for the placement of Japs where they would be acceptable and then he spoke about Dutchess County. He knew they could be placed on many farms there. "I know a fellow there," he said, "who is a good fellow, even if he is a Republican." Whereupon McCloy spoke up in a kind of combination of timidity and boldness and said, "I am a Republican, Mr. President." The President gave no indication that he had heard and went on talking about other things.

He also told me that he had seen the Polish Prime Minister and that he had steered him in the direction of Moscow. He thought what he ought to do was to go to Moscow and talk about the situation. He hoped it was going to work out all right.

The President looked better than I have seen him in months, the difference was not so much in his appearance, color, or his skin, etc., as in his temperament. Today, he is, I would say, obviously a candidate thinking politics. He said one thing in particularly—which it would certainly not do to get around—when I spoke about his forbearance. He said the other day that whatever happens, there is going to be a period between the 7th of November and the 20th of January—indicating that he could cut throats in his own time.

Monday, June 19. Fellow sitting in the back of the taxi cab said he used to be general counsel of the Treasury, complaining bitterly about the fact that he left Internal Revenue to join the Washington office of a big New York law firm. They had all the legal work in New York and all he did was

229

the messenger-boy work in Washington. He was getting a fine salary but he was going to resign. He didn't mind hard work, remembered when they were closing all the banks and he was general counsel of the Treasury—stayed up all night. He was doing a big job of blowing off and after the woman he was talking to got out of the cab, he said, "Isn't it funny to see somebody you know very well and can't remember her name?"

Then he started blowing off to me. He had the cab stop at Casey's across from the State Department so he could get a drink. He had mentioned being idle in the office and waiting for a telephone call and knowing if it came, it wouldn't be anything but a messenger-boy job, he had a terrible inclination to go and get a couple of scotches and sodas, but then he didn't like for the office staff to smell liquor on his breath. The girl in the cab had spoken about being on the *Memphis Commercial Appeal*. In general the whole case sounded like a perfect item of Washington frustration complicated with alcoholism.

Friday, June 23. The President says he doesn't want to do anything on the Sumner Welles–Freedom House–World Freedom Association matter. If he does, they will quote him.

Also, he said, "There would be some people who would have a fit if they thought I suggested it." He said, "All these 'League of Nations–World Peace' organizations don't amount to anything from the standpoint of votes. I remember in 1920 I talked to a lot of them and would get a big response if I said something about the League, but there wasn't a vote in it. I don't see why they don't make Father Divine head of these peace organizations, 'Peace, it's wonderful.' He is the best money raiser in the lot. Any vote they have got we are going to get anyhow."

I thought this would make Clark Eichelberger feel wonderful.

Mrs. Pinchot is calling me from New York about it.

[Eichelberger, a man of the highest aims and motives but an enthusiastic bore, was at this time director of an organization called Commission to Study Organization for Peace. I

230

have forgotten what good cause Mrs. Pinchot was pursuing at this time.]

Tuesday, June 27. Conversation around the President's big desk in which he talked to Niles, Barnes, and myself about the vice-presidency. I told him that the three of us realized that we might be sticking out our necks in asking him, but that we felt we should be more useful in the vice-presidential situation and that we thought a fight at the last minute might be bad. He said, "Of course, everybody knows I am for Henry Wallace." Then he went on to say that he had thought the feeling against Wallace had been largely that of politicians but he was beginning to believe that it went down below. Some people told him that it meant 40 per cent of the vote in their precincts. He said that if you cut that in half and then half again, it still might mean the loss of a million or two votes. He asked when Wallace was coming back. [He was then on a trip to China.] Dave told him that he was arriving on the 9th and was planning to speak on a nation-wide hook-up. The President said, "Well, I told him what to say—it is going to be perfectly banal, pointing out the great trade possibilities for America in China and Siberia after the war." At one point, however, he said, "I think one or two persons ought to go out and meet Wallace and tell him about this feeling about his political liability." Dave said he thought Wallace had said he did not want to run if he was going to be a drag on the ticket. Then the President began to talk over possibilities. Dave asked him about Truman and the President said he didn't know about him, but we all agreed that he had done a magnificent job and had a good press. Then the President mentioned Winant, who, he said, had great ability and made the rottenest speech in the world but when he got through people thought he sounded like Lincoln. Then he said, "There is one we have got up our sleeve and that is Henry Kaiser. He is talking about great plans in employing five million people by building jitney airplanes for everybody. He would make a great appeal." I said, "Do you think you can trust him politically, Mr. President?" and he said, "I don't know."

He said, "You know how the nomination of Wallace came

231

about before. My first choice was Cordell and he sat in my room while I was in bed for three hours and just said he wouldn't be Vice-President. My second choice was Jimmy Byrnes but I talked with Archbishop Spellman and others in the Church and they said that the feeling against a renegade Catholic would be such that any Catholics in doubt would resolve the difference against us—and so at the last minute it was Wallace." The President seemed convinced of the doubts of Wallace's candidacy.

[When I reported the President's remarks about Byrnes and Catholicism in my biography of Truman, *The Man of Independence,* Cardinal Spellman denied that he had given FDR any such advice.]

Wednesday, June 28. Attended a rather futile and depressing dinner given by Bob Hannegan and Paul Porter for what I presume was supposed to be the brain trust of the Administration. I got a feeling of weariness and elderliness rather than of creative enthusiasm from the group. Present were: Lock Currie, Wayne Coy, Dave Niles, myself, Paul Appleby, Tommy Corcoran and Ben Cohen, Isador Lubin and Bob Nathan, Mike Straus and Oscar Chapman, Mordecai Ezekiel, Randolph Paul.

The dinner was held in private dining room 4 on the mezzanine of the Statler, there was a bar set up in the room but nobody seemed to be drinking very much and no gaiety or brilliance ensued from the cocktails. The dinner, including filet mignon, was delicious but no ideas were advanced in general conversation. Hannegan never said anything about why the group was called together and never seemed to pull the group together in interest. Afterwards we waited to hear Herbert Hoover but the radio in the room did not come on. Tommy Corcoran made a wisecrack about "we ought to be eternally grateful to Herbert Hoover, who has been our meal ticket for twelve years."

I had never seen Bob Nathan before. He is a big man and almost the figure of Semitism; "Jewish" nose, thick lips, dark curly hair. He wears a ring and his hands are very big and hairy and also very soft. Randolph Paul seems a depressed sort of vapid type of man but there is a persistence and pressure about him which is obvious. The young team of Corcoran and Cohen is definitely getting older. Cohen looks like a middle-aged rabbi and Corcoran is a bushy-headed and gray-haired Irishman and no longer seems to have very much sparkle in him.

Lock Currie looks very old and last night I think he was a little irritated by the fact that Niles, Barnes, and I waited until he left the President's office to talk, although he very obviously kept hanging around and talking to the President because he knew we had an engagement with him.

Incidentally, Paul Porter told me that in 1942, Edwin W. Pauley, treasurer of the Democratic National Committee, after he had met Henry Kaiser a couple of times socially, called him up and asked him for a contribution. Kaiser said he would think it over, but the next day somebody issued a statement for him, saying in effect that the Democrats were trying to shake down war contractors. Paul said that Pauley said that of course that was what he had been trying to do but he didn't like to see it in print.

Also, Paul said that the statement attributed to Hannegan, publicly announcing that nobody was for Henry Wallace, had not been made by Hannegan, though I gather that is the way Hannegan and Porter both feel.

[Robert E. Hannegan owed his political rise to Harry Truman. Young-looking despite his almost chalk-white face, Hannegan, a policeman's son, had risen to power in the St. Louis Democratic organization in 1934, when Truman first ran for the Senate. At that time the Pendergast power in Kansas City was crumbling and only a last-minute move to Truman by Hannegan in St. Louis assured Truman's victory. Truman carried St. Louis by 8,411 votes. His margin in the state amounted to only 7,976. In 1942, when Truman secured the appointment of Hannegan as Collector of Internal Revenue in St. Louis, the *St. Louis Post-Dispatch* called it a "disgraceful example of plum passing." Truman had replied that Hannegan would be the collector or there would be no collector. With Truman's pushing a year later Hannegan was made United States Commissioner of Internal Revenue. He was well known as a Truman man when early in 1944 he was made Democratic national chairman.

[The Hoover speech which we could not hear was the former President's call for a drive against the New Deal at the Republican convention in Chicago, which was soon to nominate Thomas E. Dewey for the presidency.]

Tuesday, July 11. At the White House press conference this morning there was a long, detailed questioning about the President's agreement with General Charles de Gaulle recognizing the De Gaullists as the *de facto* government of France. It seemed as if the conference was drawing to a close when the President said to Merriman Smith of United Press, "Don't say 'thank you, Mr. President,' I have got something else for you and the doors are locked, so you can't get out. I am interested in preventing accidents," indicating he wanted no rush to the telephone. Steve Early got up and actually did lock the door. Bert Andrews of the *New York Herald Tribune* said, "Are you going to tell us about the fourth term, Mr. President?" The President quipped at him and said, "Well, this time you have guessed right."

Whereupon the President read the letter from Hannegan to him stating that a majority of the delegates were instructed to renominate him at the convention in Chicago. In the midst of the letter and the great suspense in the room the President said, "Wait a minute, I want a cigarette." He lit the cigarette and went on—then he read his own letter of acceptance. At the end of the press conference Admiral Wilson Brown had some military messages in his hand but he said, "I have some messages for the President, but after this it will seem anticlimactic"; and he went out.

Niles, Barnes, Casey, Currie, and I remained after the conference. I spoke to the President about the necessity for a strong minorities plank. He showed me a document drawn by John Steinbeck which in the briefest of terms provided a platform without going into specifics on anything. [I am attaching a copy of it to this diary entry.] I said that I didn't think we ought to limit the statement about minorities to "we intend to protect them," but that rather there ought to be in the sentence the sense of continuity, taking credit for protection in the past. The President rather agreed to this suggestion. He said that he was determined to have a short platform. He had asked Sam Rosenman to draft him one but it had run to 2,500 words. Sam had told him that it was one of the best things he had done but the President said, nevertheless, it is too long. Gene Casey said, "There is one other question, Mr. President. What about the vice-presidency?" The President smiled, "Did you ever know Charlie Murphy?" Casey said he didn't but that Murphy was a great friend of Ed Flynn. [Murphy was the long-time boss of Tammany Hall.]

"Charlie was a wise man," the President said. "When they asked him who was going to be lieutenant governor, he would always say, 'The convention will decide,' and he got away with it for years."

Casey said, "Mr. President, do you mean that the convention will decide *period?* The President laughed and said, "Yes. Of course, there are some people I wouldn't run with."

Earlier in the conference, when he had been asked about his talk with Wallace, he had said, "We talked about China." There was a period there which Casey did not have to ask about.

Anna Boettiger came in after the conference and was present during this talk. She said she had wanted to be at the conference but she only dared peep through the crack in Grace Tully's door because she knew the newspapers would comment upon her facial expression, etc.

[The Steinbeck platform draft could not have been new to me at this time. More than a month earlier I had had lunch with Steinbeck. He was interested in using his talent to help the President. I attached to my diary the scant 300 words which he prepared.]

1. We intend to win the war quickly and decisively.
2. We propose to create and to help direct a militantly peaceful world organization with the strength to prevent wars.

3. We believe that no people can long prosper in isolation, that all must rise together or sink separately.
4. We propose to cooperate with other nations through trade, association and understanding in order that all people may climb to the new peak of security and comfort which technical developments have made possible.
5. We will not permit methods of production or destruction to be used or controlled by men or nations for the exploitation or enslavement of peoples.
6. We believe that a free flow of goods and of ideas are the foundations of world peace and world development.
7. We believe that a thoughtful and controlled economy can support the farmer on his land, the workman in his job and the merchant behind his counter and we know from brutal experience that uncontrolled economy can and will bring us to the edge of destruction.
8. We propose that our returning fighting men shall be secure in their futures—that they shall have jobs in private industry if possible, but we insist that they shall have jobs.
9. We propose to lower taxes when possible but not at the expense of the welfare, security or strength of the nation.
10. We intend to protect our racial, religious and political minorities from those who would deny them the right to live and develop in our democracy.
11. We believe that in the techniques of abundance lie the greatest promise of comfort and security the world has ever seen. We propose to encourage, develop and control those techniques to the end that the greatest good may indeed come to the greatest number and that peace and plenty may live not only in our nation but in the whole world.

[This platform, of course, was too good to be expected to survive. Paul Porter recently wrote me that at the convention he was told by Hannegan that FDR wanted a platform which could be printed on a postcard. The party chairman "handed me a one-page screed written by FDR which was his notion of the platform. I knew this would not fly." So discarding the Steinbeck-Roosevelt "screed," Porter, with "inputs from Ben Cohen, Sam Rosenman and many others," produced a thousand-word document which he told the chairman of the platform committee was "what Roosevelt insisted upon."

["Then the Platform Committee met," Porter wrote. "There surfaced the planks for the Indians, Eskimos, Israelis, Conservationists, Chicanos, and God knows what else."

[Porter added that he worked with my father, chairman of the drafting committee, who had been helping write conventional statements of party purposes, performances, and promises since William Jennings Bryan ran in 1896. "We finally fashioned a platform," Porter said in understatement, "longer than FDR's postal card concept." It was in fact more than four times as long as the Steinbeck-FDR "screed," making more promises but with less music.]

In the long conversation at the President's desk Jim Barnes spoke up for Donald Nelson in the controversy with the military over the control of production and said he was sure I agreed with him. I said I had the feeling that there is a very dangerous situation involved in cutbacks in September and October and that it ought to be in the hands of someone who was politically friendly to the President. The President said, "Oh, yes—every such cutback will have to be approved by the President himself." Lock Currie came in on the other side of the argument, in effect answering Jim Barnes, and said that to go into civilian production now when people are looking for permanent jobs would mean a danger of manpower being scarce in war production. The President spoke of the story in the morning paper about the need for more artillery ammunition. Lock Currie seems to be in most matters in disagreement with the other administrative assistants. He has been the only one who felt that Wallace should be renominated and he is apparently on the side of the military in the struggle over the control of production.

[Donald Nelson was at this point on his way out as chairman of the War Production Board. As early as February of this year the press had reported rumors of rifts and rivalries involving him and Charles E. Wilson. In August Wilson resigned as vice-chairman of the War Production Board, charging false statements about himself by Nelson's personal staff.

In the same month Nelson set off on one of those high-sounding missions on which Roosevelt sent those he wanted gone but did not want to fire, to study economic conditions in China and Russia. Soon Julius Krug, formerly with TVA, was made acting chairman. Nelson's formal resignation came in October. In this July, a few days before this diary entry, Secretary of the Navy Forrestal noted in his diary that he had lunched with Senator Truman in an effort "to persuade him of the unwisdom of permitting resumption of civilian production, which at the moment is the big issue between Charles Wilson and Donald Nelson, Wilson reflecting the views of the services as against any broad scale resumption, whereas Nelson is pressing for it." Forrestal did not think he convinced Truman. But he noted that at this date Truman told him he was being urged to accept the nomination for Vice-President.

[Already at this point some were ironically relating the Nelson trip to China with a similar one Henry Wallace had already made this summer. They noted wryly that Wallace had not only conferred with General and Madame Chiang Kai-shek but had also visited Siberia.]

*   *   *

[Two days after this long, wary talk about his political plans FDR set off, via Hyde Park, on a long trip to the West Coast and the Pacific. In Chicago for the Democratic National Convention, I was not aware of it when his train stopped briefly in the rail yards on July 15 and he gave Hannegan the letter which assured the nomination of Truman and the rejection of Wallace. Members of his Cabinet—notably, I remember, Ickes, Perkins, and Biddle—were more in the dark than I was. In effect, I had already agreed with the President on the necessity to eliminate Wallace. But I was appalled by the ruthlessness with which Hannegan carried out the operation.

[So were many other New Dealers. And Wallace was not the only personage who felt he had a right to feel that he had been done in in the dark. Jimmy Byrnes, believing he had a go sign from the President, definitely felt that way. Sitting behind

Byrnes in the presidential box, I remember how shocked I was when he and Mrs. Byrnes and Ben Cohen alone did not stand in the ovation for the President as he hoarsely spoke to the convention from a cruiser in the harbor of Bremerton, Washington.

[I made no diary notes in those busy days. But going over the records now, it is clear to me that Roosevelt, as always not wanting to seem to hurt anybody, notably Wallace now, was not the only one to arrange for others to play for him a devious game. I come now in my old age to a wry grin about Harry Truman in that connection. He seemed then more than ordinarily the simple, straightforward country citizen. I missed in my 1950 biography of Truman, *The Man of Independence,* what seems to me plain now. It is incredible that he did not know the plan for him which his man Hannegan had long been developing. I feel certain that he played the role of the reluctant candidate with the skill of a maestro. There was nothing in his action which made him seem a man of indecision as Adlai Stevenson seemed in his reluctance eight years later. No man ever played "hard to get" with more conviction than Harry Truman.

[Truman may have truly preferred a place in the Senate, with a vote, to that of a man in that chamber armed only with a gavel. But Truman had confided to Forrestal on July 4, ten days before the convention assembled, that "they" were pressing him to accept the vice-presidential nomination. And this time even those who most vigorously denied the "rumors" about Roosevelt's health recognized that in the choice of a Vice-President they were probably selecting a President. Truman was well aware of that, too.

[Earlier and publicly Truman had proposed the nomination of Sam Rayburn, and then Alben Barkley. Now he had come to Chicago to nominate Byrnes, who had assured him he was the President's choice. For Byrnes, Truman had seen his own old friends, the labor leaders who were supporting Wallace. Of the pressures on himself he had kept Byrnes informed. He finally accepted only under orders from his commander in chief. That historical record is clear but not necessarily complete. Truman so operated that neither the supporters of Wallace nor those of Byrnes could fault him. True or feigned, his reluctance was his armor, as would be his almost abject show of self-deprecation when he came to the presidency nine months later. As one who came greatly to admire Truman, I do not accuse him of conscious hypocrisy. But he was a man who understood the necessity for the well-designed approach to the inevitable. I did not know him well then but I keep a startled recollection of the excessive cordiality he showed me as one of Roosevelt's staff, before the balloting began.]

Tuesday, August 8. Welch Pogue wanted to tell me confidentially that he had altered his position about the future of foreign aviation to the extent that he was inclined now toward government operation, even if this operation involved only as much as 40 per cent government-owned stock, although he had held out at the beginning for the majority of stock. He has a hunch that Juan Trippe, faced with a deteriorating position in his desire to be the chosen instrument of American aviation after the war, will sometime soon make a dramatic offer to sell out to the government, though it will probably turn out to be only a partial sale with Trippe keeping control. Pogue said he was the only member of the board who felt that way.

The CAB is going forward now with hearings on a proposed pattern of United States–foreign routes; the first hearings to begin September 16 and the last hearing to begin in February. The board hopes to get the first case into the President's hands for decision around the middle of February. This, however, is a tight schedule.

Juan Trippe is naturally disturbed by these hearings in which a number of companies are applicants for franchises for foreign lines. On May 12 Senator Bailey wrote Pogue (Pogue believes he is part of Juan Trippe's effort to stop the hearings or to direct them), telling Pogue to inform the Senate Commerce Committee in advance of all actions on the subject, giving the committee a chance to see summaries of all the hearings so that the committee may be heard before decisions. Pogue replied, giving him the picture of the set-up, but Pogue does not feel that the committee should have any right to dictate the decisions or direct them.

Trippe apparently controls the whole Senate Commerce Committee with the exception of Mead of New York and Hattie Caraway of Arkansas. The House committee is rather against the single-instrument theory which Trippe has been pushing. Apparently Trippe has planned to control the matter by the Senate's power to ratify agreements with foreign countries with regard to aviation agreements. In the event that the war in Germany should end quickly and postwar commercial aviation possibilities should be opened in advance of decisions with regard to who is to operate various lines, it has already been agreed that the Air Transport Command will sell tickets to Rome, Cairo, and other points whenever space is available, and thus run interim commercial lines to keep other countries from getting the jump on the United States and protect the United States' position for the future.

Pogue feels that Trippe is the ablest man in the field but that he has absolutely no sense of statesmanship or public interest and that he is absolutely without scruples in these dealings. He said that he tried to get Adolf Berle to get some air agreements with such inoffensive countries as China and Brazil before the Senate in order to begin the Senate processes of ratification before the decisions on the chosen-instrument policy. Before the decision is made in this matter such agreements will be as important to Trippe as to anybody else. Therefore, it is important that the decisions, if possible, be made on these agreements before the decision is made on the chosen-instrument policy. He says that Berle is violently against the chosen-instrument position and that the President seemed at his last meeting with him some weeks ago to still be strongly in favor of the operation of several companies rather than one.

I don't know exactly what Pogue's change of position means. He does not seem to have changed in his feeling toward Trippe, but his new attitude, while not that of Trippe, is in the direction of the chosen-instrument position, though an instrument with some ownership in the government.

Monday, August 21. Jim Barnes was disturbed and active yesterday, Sunday, because of the situation involved in Nelson's assignment to China with General Pat Hurley. The announcement said that Nelson would be gone for several months and that Charles Wilson would be in charge of WPB in his absence. This made it clear that Nelson was being shelved in the reconversion business and that Wilson, representing Byrnes and Baruch, would be in charge of it. [Actually Wilson left WPB four days after this date.] Barnes said that Nelson was ready to resign and that he thought if that happens we have lost the election.

He said that he had talked with Hannegan and Paul Porter and that both of them were disturbed. Hannegan, he said, was trying to get in touch with Truman and ask him to speak to the President about it. I called up Judge Rosenman and told him the situation.

He said it is a pity that Nelson wasn't a stronger man to fight with but he thought we had lost. I said I agreed that Nelson is a weak man who won't fight but he has become a symbol for labor and small business. Judge Rosenman agreed. However, he said that he thought there was no use in doing anything because he thought the assignment of Nelson was made for the very purpose about which I complained. He agreed that he thought that the Byrnes group had prevailed upon the President and that the President had acted to give them full charge of reconversion by this device.

This disturbs me. It is a little bit too much on the clever side. I am afraid the President is being a little bit too clever and I think he made a mistake as well in his denial that he had written to Willkie. Particularly when the correspondents were able to check on the fact that he had written to Willkie.

*　　*　　*

Dave Niles came in this morning and I said, "I am a little sick about this whole Nelson business," and he said, *"You* are sick! I am about to commit suicide about the way this Willkie matter has been handled. I have been working on it for months and I thought I was liaison on the subject, devoting myself to kissing Willkie's ass and this thing was done without my knowing anything about it." He told me, "As I understand it, the letter was written and signed either by Bill Hassett or Grace Tully, saying that the President would like to talk to Willkie about foreign affairs and using some such language as 'when you see that I have returned to this country, will you please get in touch with General Watson for an engagement.'"

Dave said the letter made Willkie mad, giving the impression that Willkie should get in touch with General Watson. Also I gathered that the letter was not signed by the President himself but by either Hassett or Tully. As a result, Dave feels that all his efforts have been pretty much butchered. In view of the way this letter was written, a personal telephone call from Dewey was more effective. However, Dave feels that Willkie still hates Dewey worse then he does the President but that the effort to really benefit from the situation has been badly injured.

Certainly on the Nelson matter and the Willkie matter the President has injured himself with such liberal newspaper people as Carroll Kilpatrick. Carroll called up today to ask if I was still voting for the Democratic ticket and, if so, why? "I think this man is leading us deliberately into the most reactionary position this country has ever taken," he said. There may be some hope in the fact that Judge Rosenman is going up to Hyde Park today to see the President but Niles says he won't fight. Hopkins is also said to be out to get Will Clayton, but I doubt that Hopkins is as effective as he used to be.

[Shortly before this time there had been press reports that Roosevelt had invited Willkie to come to see him. Roosevelt denied this report on August 18. Then on August 25 FDR admitted the invitation and Willkie confirmed it. There was, of course, no outside knowledge at the time about White House bumbling in connection with the matter. Willkie was avoiding taking sides between Roosevelt and Dewey. When Willkie died in October, however, both Republicans and Democrats claimed he would have supported their candidate.]

Tuesday, August 22. Last week I sent to the President a

memorandum from Jim Carey to Philip Murray charging improper conduct on the part of Gerard Reilly and also charging that Bob Hannegan had tried to "fix" a case involving unfair labor practices in a union election in the Famous Barr Department Store in St. Louis. I called up Hannegan and told him the story. He was vociferous and denunciatory but never specifically denied the story. Yesterday Grace Tully called me from Hyde Park and said the President had read the memorandum and asked me to see Jimmy Byrnes and Will Davis. I saw Byrnes and Donald Russell and neither of them was very much impressed—in fact, both said that Reilly had been very cooperative with the Administration and that unless there were more to the charge than was stated, they didn't think anything should be done about it. [Gerard D. Reilly, a Massachusetts Democrat, was a member of the National Labor Relations Board. William H. Davis was chairman of the National War Labor Board. Donald Russell, Byrnes's able young South Carolina aide, was to become governor of his state.]

While I was in the left wing, Harry Hopkins, in shirt and suspenders, came out and greeted me very cordially. He looked pretty well but also a little desiccated, but he had on suspenders which had pictures of a colonial mansion woven into the elastic. He looked very lively but a little spry, like an old man. [After months in and out of hospitals Hopkins had resumed his duties as presidential adviser and actual Lend-Lease chief in July.]

Thursday, August 31. Mary Bingham was telling us last night about Barry's tragic and amusing job in serving as naval escort for a lady VIP to London, "a mink-clad, wild-hatted ambassadress."

According to Barry's version she was a very disturbing lady, often in her cups, throughout the trip. Although Barry was a lieutenant, he had to find ways of suggesting to admirals that they serve her nothing but tea. At one reception he had told the admiral this and he offered her tea, which she declined vociferously. Whereupon, a young officer who didn't know anything about the situation asked her if she would prefer a highball, which she grabbed, and she followed it with

244

several others in quick succession. In fact, she got so high that the admiral became somewhat nervous and suggested that they go to his house—and, still nervous, he said, "I am sorry that due to an accident the water at our house is the color of tea." Whereupon the lady burst into loud laughter and said, "The color of pee, I won't wash in it."

On another occasion Admiral Stark had arranged for a large reception for her, to which Barry was to accompany her, but when he went to get her she said she had to go to another party and would arrive late. She did arrive late in fine fettle. Tony Biddle had gotten all the foreign diplomats of the governments in exile and when they came down the receiving line, Poles, Lithuanians, etc., she would say, "What did you say your name is?" and laughing loudly, "That is the funniest name I ever heard in my life."

Barry came back to London and told Admiral Stark about what a time he had had as lieutenant escorting the lady, that he was about whipped down. Admiral Stark said, "Barry, you have been working mighty hard. I don't see why you don't take a week's leave." They talked about general matters and as Barry started to leave he said, "Barry?" Barry turned around and the Admiral said, "Did she really say, 'the color of pee'?"

Friday, October 25. Information we ought to know now and which should certainly be filed for attention immediately after the election:

Allen Dulles, whose title is Special Assistant to the Minister at Berne, specifically in charge of OSS activities in Switzerland, Portugal, Spain, and France and picked to be the head of OSS political activities in Germany, returned to this country for a few weeks. He conferred on European problems with his brother, John Foster Dulles, who at the time was visiting in the home of Ferdinand L. Mayer, who is political adviser in Washington for OSS. Mr. Allen Dulles' daughter works in the reporting board of OSS in Washington, D.C., where all raw intelligence comes for distribution. In addition to this, Mr. Dulles has very excellent connections with the State Department, where his sister is second in rank among all women employees. This seems to me to be a matter which might be filed for post-election attention.

[Allen Dulles had been a foreign service officer until he resigned in 1926 to go into law practice, joining his brother John Foster Dulles in the powerful and conservative New York law firm of Sullivan and Cromwell. John Foster Dulles was Dewey's adviser on foreign policy in the current campaign. Allen had been treasurer of the New York County Republican Committee. John Foster Dulles was to become Secretary of State under Eisenhower.

[My feeling about this whole Dulles tribe indicates how strong the feeling became in this campaign about foreign as well as domestic affairs. Traveling with Roosevelt, my friend and colleague Bill Hassett spoke of it as "the vilest campaign in living memory." The Dulles brothers were suspect of feeding Dewey foreign policy poison, as when he accused FDR of engaging in secret diplomacy. John Foster Dulles got into the middle of a hot exchange when the Republican campaign manager Herbert Brownell and Hannegan gave their attention to his sore foot, which was his excuse for going by private motor to Washington instead of by train. More seriously Senator Pepper of Florida charged that the Dulles' law firm, Sullivan and Cromwell, represented a banking client which aided Hitler in his move to power in 1933.

*   *   *

[In general I was far away from foreign affairs, however. I had the delicate task in this campaign of trying to prevent explosions injurious to the President's chances from either the leaders of the blacks or the politicians of the South on the increasingly hot issue of Negro employment. From Texas, Louisiana, and Virginia there was vocal if not deeply disturbing talk of Southern revolt. Also in a number of Northern states migration was giving Negroes what might be a balance of power. Senator Richard Russell of Georgia was demanding that the FEPC be disbanded. Negro leaders were demanding that it be given more permanent status. In New York, Channing Tobias and six other members resigned from the State Employment Discrimination Commission, accusing Dewey of shelving a bill to protect Negro employment rights there.

[In September Mrs. Roosevelt sent me a note: "I will gladly speak to any group which you think helpful." I think she knew better than anyone else that depending upon political geography she could be blessing or bane. Nash, Poston, and I, while working for an end to discriminations, were all most eager at this point for the re-election of Roosevelt. Malcolm Ross of the FEPC seemed almost too ready to rock the boat. I remember going to Poston's apartment on election night to drink to the mounting returns for FDR from both white and black areas. Black Congressman William L. Dawson, head of the Negro Division of the Democratic National Committee, thanked me for my help in the campaign but I was much more pleased by a letter from Dr. Will Alexander, expressing his feeling that I was "doing one of the most important jobs in the government."

[I did a draft—not apparent in the final version—of Roosevelt's great speech to the Teamsters Union, which seemed, as we heard his magnificent delivery of it, the turning point in the campaign. I can still hear the laughter about Fala (but at Dewey) in the lines FDR sang out at the Statler banquet: "The Republican leaders have not been content to make personal attacks upon me—or my wife—or my sons—they now include my little dog Fala. Unlike the members of my family, Fala resents this. When he learned that the Republican fiction writers had concocted a story that I had left him behind on an Aleutian Island and had sent a destroyer back to find him—at a cost to the taxpayer of two or three or twenty million dollars—his Scotch soul was furious. He has not been the same dog since. I am accustomed to hearing malicious falsehoods about myself but I think I have a right to object to libelous statements about my dog."

[Looking back now, I am sure that we were not then confident of the 432 to 99 electoral votes by which he defeated Dewey. But already in the pre-election months we were concerned about postwar and not merely post-election matters. As if there would be no question about the future, a week before the election the Foreign Economic Administration was urging me to go to Italy as the successor to William O'Dwyer as U.S. representative on the Allied Control Commission. O'Dwyer, who had only taken the post in June, came to my office to urge me to take the job. He was planning, I think, for his successful campaign for mayor of New York in the following year. However, with the increasing certainty of victory in the war, I was thinking about going back to my typewriter. My agent, Carl Brandt, was pressing me with writing plans. I was hoping that my writing plans might include going to Yalta with Roosevelt.

[In the growing confidence about victory, some startling, some amusing items, are remembered. On my way to Denver in November to speak to the Farmers Union, I stopped off in Chicago, where the national CIO convention was in progress. In what might have been a smoke-filled room but was probably President Philip Murray's suite, a *Life* photographer took a picture of the back of my head and shoulders while I was obviously talking to earnestly listening Murray, Sidney Hillman, Henry Wallace, Beanie Baldwin, and one other person I cannot identify now. *Life* made it its "Picture of the Week" with a caption indicating that I was delivering to them their orders from the Boss. Actually between trains I was just mooching lunch.

[If I deserved no place at the center of that picture Chicago did seem much the center of my America that year. And that Chicago was as varied as the stockyards by the big convention hall; the book-lined apartments of University of Chicago professors who were commuting to war and Washington; the quiet elegance of the lake-shore apartment in which, while the politicians perspired, Adlai Stevenson and his wife gave a party, "Gold Coast"–remote from the angers and austerities of the year. It was, of course, the city of the *Chicago Tribune* but it was also the place of two men I most admired, Carl Sandburg and Lloyd Lewis, who put this war in perspective by their writings of another war long before when Americans were even more divided.]

Wednesday, November 29. Willmott Lewis told a funny story today in two parts. He said that Henry Pringle some years ago had written a profile of Thomas E. Dewey as the young district attorney. They lived in the same section of New York and, as a matter of courtesy, Pringle sent Dewey a carbon copy of the article. Dewey called him up and asked him to come and see him and after a short talk Dewey pointed to one sentence in the article, which said that on Saturday nights sometimes Mr. and Mrs. Dewey played poker. Dewey said, "I wonder if you couldn't change that to bridge?"

Then he told about a man writing for the *Nashville Tennessean* (Hinton, or some such name) who wrote a story about Cordell Hull and was writing about young Cordell Hull going off to free Cuba and remarked in this connection that before long young Cordell Hull at poker had won all the money in his company. He sent the manuscript to Hull and when he got it back the word "company" had been struck out and in Hull's own handwriting the word "regiment" was substituted.

[Sir Willmott Lewis, popular newspaperman who had covered wars all over the world, had been the Washington correspondent of *The Times* of London since 1920. He maintained his club memberships in Washington, London, Shanghai, and Nagasaki.]

*   *   *

Just before the election Jack Houston of the National Labor Relations Board was in my office and told me that Bob Hannegan had called him with regard to the Famous Barr Department Store case, which he wanted dismissed, and in connection with his request he said, "There is only one thing in the world I am more interested in and that is the election of President Roosevelt."

[John M. Houston, a former actor, lumber dealer, and Democratic Kansas congressman, had been appointed to the National Labor Relations Board after his defeat for re-election in 1942.]

*　　*　　*

[Roosevelt's re-election was not reassuring to some who were much concerned in postwar plans of their own. Juan Trippe still clung to his monopolistic chosen-instrument proposal for all American overseas air business. However, that Pan American pattern even for service to Latin America was under attack. Still Pan American was then preparing a brief for the continuation of its monopoly of overseas operations in this hemisphere. I do not recall that during this fall I had been doing any work for the President in connection with his required approval of all overseas route grants by the Civil Aeronautics Board. But I got a startling Christmas present, via Ben Sonnenberg, which must have had Pan Am origins. Lucy and the girls and I went to Raleigh to be with Father on his first Christmas alone following my mother's death. We counted on a fat Christmas even though more stringent meat rationing had just been declared. But we never anticipated the bounty that awaited me.

[There was a Christmas package for me—if you could call it a package—a packing case about the size of a coffin. We opened it with great anticipation and there beside Ben Sonnenberg's card was such a collection of cured and smoked meats as none of us had even dreamed about before. We drooled for a minute or two. Then I said, "Nail it up!" After Ben got it back he in his best gamin fashion assured me that it had been acquired without any evasion of ration rules and it was sent to me only as a small token of his affection. I have often wondered who ate it.

[Still it was a good Christmas, not only in my father's house but in Washington, and for America's concerns in the world. Despite such a period of anxiety as would be created by the Battle of the Bulge, the Allies were converging upon Hitler's German fortress. In the Pacific MacArthur was making his return to the Philippines. And in government agencies as well as in war plants, productive order seemed at last attained out of what had seemed chaos so long. Even old New

Dealers had habituated themselves in the war agencies which
had absorbed them. Sometimes their success seemed almost
comic. I found time in the holiday season to write a Christmas poem to Roy Stryker, who had once seemed the epitome
of frustration in the collapsing Farm Security Administration and was now a chief pictorial propagandist in the Office
of War Information. I attached it to my diary.]

MERRY CHRISTMAS TO STRYKER

or

If you can't be Santa Claus, it's a good
idea to know the route he's traveling.

Roy Stryker struck it rich
But I got the dope on the son-of-a-bitch.
You remember his pictures—the New Deal art,
The dispossessed family in the broken-down cart,
The tenant's children, the dead-end street,
The cotton row under the half-shod feet.
You better remember; we'll not see soon
The hound dog baying to the hungry moon.
This poem is written solely in praise
Of Roy Stryker in a nobler phase.
When the sun went down on the FSA
When McKellar turned the cash away
Our agile Roy didn't mope and cry
He shifted his payroll to OWI.
Now his pictures are pretty; his farmers are fat
His colored folks gleam like grandpapa's high hat.
This is America   so strong   so good!
And Stryker he photographs it as Stryker should.
No labor so hard that our rich will ere welch
And the poor man gets up from his feast with a belch.
Oh Stryker, Oh Stryker, you're the man that we need
In a land all rid of its grief and its greed.
To hell with all the post-war planners, we-must-doers and
    if-we-canners
All we need for the people's world, is Stryker, a camera,
    four men and a girl.

With a click of the shutter, the shy little elf
Will show us a world that won't know itself.
With a Wallace speech and a Stryker print
We can save the world—and also the mint.
So Merry Christmas to Stryker—he's the hope of mankind
And he's neither a dope before nor behind.

[The months ahead were not to be quite that lyrical. The assignment came to me to move over from Death Row to the office of press secretary. A sort of shifting of the guard was in progress. Pa Watson spoke to me about his plan to retire as appointments secretary. He was going to recommend that the President put me in his place when they returned from the approaching Big Three conference. But it was decided otherwise. Early had already made his plans to depart to take a position prepared for him with the Pullman Company by his friend Victor Emanuel, stock broker, director of many big companies, and member of fourteen clubs in the United States and abroad. His interests included steel, aircraft, shipbuilding, utilities. At this time he still maintained his racing stables. Early assured me that in all his days at the White House Emanuel had never asked for a favor. Before he gave up his official position to me, however, Steve wanted to keep the position on a trip abroad.

[It was only announced that I would take his place in dealing with the press. My secretaries and I moved over to the White House to his job with all its perquisites, including a government car and chauffeur. In the face of gasoline rationing Lucy and I had no car, having given up ours to a friend who needed it more. Hassett at about this time said that the pay at the White House ($10,000 a year) was not so good but that the hacking service was the best possible. Also I got increased pressures. I was happy at the chance. So were my friends. I was particularly pleased with one note I received from a friend I had known since we had danced at the same parties during the Wilson administration: "Congratulations—and not slightly," signed "Adlai."]

Diary

1945

January. I have been hearing for some time that Paul McNutt is drinking pretty heavily in the daytime and that when people come out of his office, their associates ask each other if he has been rough on them and whether or not he was drinking. Harold Boeschenstein told me about the tragicomic aspects of McNutt's trip to Europe with representatives of War Manpower and the WPB.

Others thought it was a working commission—apparently McNutt regarded it as a jaunt. He bought himself the most beautiful uniform possible and had on such an array of service ribbons as has not been seen on the Western Front. However, as the trip went on he became bored with going out on inspections and would stay in hotels and drink by himself while the others went out.

Yesterday I learned that Mrs. McNutt had called up Mary Switzer about McNutt's drinking and the family is terribly worried about it. The story is that McNutt has been looking for a job and that he has been considered for some big positions but that as soon as they find out about his drinking the offer disappears.

Incidentally, the European trip, as Boeschenstein described it, was made comic by both McNutt and Maury

Maverick. It nearly killed Maury because the party was everywhere introduced as Governor McNutt's party without any—or hardly any—mention of the other members. Maury Maverick got so he would run ahead of McNutt and introduce himself.

*   *   *

[There was something symbolic about McNutt's reported recourse to the bottle. I suspect now that I wrote of it, at a time when I had been making few diary entries, because it seemed a symptom of the confusions in which I was increasingly involved. Many "for the war only" men were preparing their exits from government as our forces moved forward in Europe and the Pacific. Adlai Stevenson, on his return from a short mission abroad, came by my office in a uniform which he described as "my assimilated military disguise." He was, he said, resuming the practice of law, "a slightly enervating prospect after three and a half years of war and turmoil." I had been doing some private postwar planning myself but when I was offered the press secretary's post, I told my literary agent that, from the point of observation, that was "like moving from the bleachers to the boxes." I was committed for the duration of Roosevelt, a term I did not realize might be so brief.

[As confusion had attended the mobilization for war, so, as victory seemed more certain, there was a sort of frustrating unraveling in agencies and among administrators. Named that year as one of the handsomest men in the United States, McNutt also seemed, as head of the Federal Security Agency and chairman of the War Manpower Commission, one of the most powerful figures in the government. Actually he knew that the skids were under him. At this time when drastic manpower legislation ("Work or Fight") was being sought, it was indicated that he could be spared from that field of battle for an inspection tour of European battlefronts with which he had no direct concern. In the same party Maury Maverick of Texas, chairman of the Smaller War

Plants Corporation, was, as always, both an effective official and a comic character who had little patience with what he named governmental "gobbledygook."

[Others were impatient. As press secretary I encountered a rising restiveness of the correspondents under wartime security rules. They knew, of course, that the White House news provided them in January and February generally constituted a sort of paper front to conceal the absence of the President. The simple fourth-term inauguration, at which he spoke from the South Portico of the White House to a limited audience standing on the snow-glazed lawn, had almost signaled dispersal.

[Not only the President but also his top military and civilian staff moved in strict secrecy to Yalta. With the President, Byrnes left the East Wing of the White House in a state of inanimation. Some felt that FDR took Byrnes along to ease the resentment he could hardly be said to have hidden since the Chicago convention. This gave a top diplomatic status to Byrnes, who felt that Roosevelt, who had denied him the vice-presidency, should make him Secretary of State. The President was not ready to do that. Yet he wished to salve wounds he could not cure. Similarly and almost ridiculously, as the laughing press indicated when they learned it from me, the President carried along the also disappointed Ed Flynn, Boss of the Bronx.

[White House offices were deserted. Pa Watson, already ailing, sailed with the presidential party. Steve Early was off on a sort of farewell junket to press camps in Europe as a special consultant to the Secretary of War. Sam Rosenman was also headed for Europe as chief of a large mission working on supplies for civilians in liberated areas. The gentle, intellectual presidential economist Isador Lubin, oddly coupled with Edwin W. Pauley, oil magnate and political funds collector, was off to Europe as member of the War Reparations Commission. Only Bill Hassett and I remained on duty in the White House. In such interludes as this one Hassett sometimes retired to his books and the bottle.

[When he went to the crucial Yalta conference the President seemed to leave behind an almost disintegrating government at home. New feuds erupted and old grudges were indulged in as war dangers diminished. As he departed he gave me instructions to "try to keep Lilienthal from getting Ickes mad." That was the least of possible—even probable —explosions. Some others seemed like dog fights. One did involve a dog. Since Fala had proven to be useful in the election, just before the President departed, another Roosevelt dog named Blaze served Roosevelt's enemies: he was given a priority place on a plane, taking away the seats of three service men. Blaze was Elliott Roosevelt's dog. Elliott's sister, Anna Boettiger, had thoughtlessly asked for the priority place for the big beast. At that time the confirmation of Elliott's promotion to brigadier general was before the Senate. Oratory broke out there, but it did not resemble the famous oration of Senator Vest of Missouri about the dog as man's best friend. Only pressure based on the fact of Elliott's excellent war record saved him from rejection.

[It seems to me symbolic of the state of affairs that one chore left behind for me was the investigation of military policies and practices with regard to the handling of neuropsychiatric dismissals from service. That was not a pretty situation. I wrote a report for the President about a hundred thousand enlisted men who had been discharged by the Army for disability due to psychoneurosis. Often this was just used as a method of getting rid of poor military material. Of those discharged, 83.3 per cent had never seen service outside the continental limits of the United States.

["Shell shock" seemed far more prevalent at home than in the war theaters. Sometimes that seemed the case in the big wartime Washington bureaucracy, too, often in the highest posts. McNutt was not the only high official to show some sign of psychic damage. As the President departed he seemed to have prepared such shock for tough old Jesse Jones and his stalwart conservative partisans in the Senate. Roosevelt undertook decapitation with a peacock plume. Old Jesse's neck was too tough for that, at least not without some mighty fluttering and blood in the political barnyard.]

* * *

Saturday, January 27. Mrs. Roosevelt stopped by my office, after having her picture taken in connection with the March of Dimes, to talk about a column she had written but didn't think she should publish under her own name. She wanted me to call Walter Winchell and ask him if he might use some of the ideas. I called Winchell at Miami Beach and he agreed. The column was sent to him by telegram signed Joe Jones. However, he used practically none of it in his Sunday-night broadcast but had Ernest Cuneo [newspaperman at that time with OSS] call me on Tuesday to say that he tried to use more but had been prevented because it was said to be too controversial.

While she was in my office, Mrs. Roosevelt talked about the letter which the President wrote to Jesse Jones. She expressed the feeling everybody else has expressed that it was a very unfortunate letter.

She said, "That is just like Franklin, he always hopes to get things settled pleasantly and he won't realize that there are times when you have got to do an unpleasant thing directly, and, perhaps, unpleasantly."

She was conferring with Judge Rosenman and myself with regard to a telegram to the President asking that he try to provide some assistance to Wallace in the confirmation fight. We proposed that he issue an executive order separating Commerce and the loan agencies and announce at the same time that he would sign the George tax bill if passed. The statement to accompany this action would say that it was done with the knowledge and approval of Henry Wallace. This telegram was sent on Sunday, January 28. Judge Rosenman wrote it and it was approved by Mrs. Roosevelt and myself.

While we were discussing it, Judge Rosenman asked me who I thought would be a good man for the loan agencies and suggested both Judge Vinson and Leo Crowley. I told him my own preference would be Vinson. I heard no more of the matter until I turned on the radio at seven o'clock and heard Drew Pearson say that Vinson was being considered for loan administrator.

Incidentally, I find the White House and the newspapermen in the White House to be more concerned about the leaks to Leonard Lyons than to Pearson for the reason that while many of Pearson's alleged leaks are erroneous, Leonard Lyons' stories out of the White House are almost always correct.

[As was customary, at the end of the President's third term all members of his Cabinet submitted their resignations. FDR rejected all but one: that of Jones, who, as Secretary of Commerce, also held the post of Federal Loan Administrator. On inauguration day, apparently without consulting any of his aides, the President wrote a letter to Jones full of fulsome friendship and forthwith dismissal. Henry Wallace deserved what he wanted, he said, and he wanted the Commerce post. As for Jones, the President wrote, he might look around and choose almost any ambassadorship he wanted. Jones was not ready to submit graciously. He and his conservative friends were appalled particularly at giving Wallace the great money power of the federal loan agencies.

[After a bitter fight in the Senate, Wallace was finally confirmed as Secretary of Commerce but only after the big federal lending agencies were separated from the department. The able and popular Fred M. Vinson was nominated as Federal Loan Administrator and head of the Reconstruction Finance Corporation soon after Roosevelt's return from Yalta. That appointment was one thing about which Jones and Wallace could agree in approval.]

Wednesday, January 31. Ickes wrote the President a long letter saying that if Lilienthal jumped on him, he wouldn't be able to stay silent and he wanted the President to know he wanted no controversy. He enclosed an article from *The New York Times Magazine* of January 7. Actually, Ickes has been shooting at Lilienthal before this. However, I went to see Ickes. Ickes told me that he had been talking to McKellar and that some of the things McKellar said about Lilienthal were true and that he had detectives of the Department of the Interior working on the case. It seemed obvious that there is an alliance of antagonism between Ickes and McKellar against Dave.

After I saw Ickes, Mike Straus met me and asked me to come into his office. He outlined Interior plans for a river development set-up. Its chief purpose seemed to me to be to preserve the bureaucracy of Interior and the Army Engineers and to give Ickes over-all authority while making a pretense of preserving the TVA idea.

[As friend of Lilienthal, though emissary from the President, I did not pacify Ickes, the self-described "curmudgeon," though I may momentarily have softened his public utterances. He had long sought to get TVA under his centralized control in the Department of the Interior. Lilienthal opposed the whole policy of centralization in Washington of such basically regional operations as TVA. Now the very title of his article, "Shall We Have More TVAs?" infuriated Ickes with his notoriously low boiling point. He described Lilienthal as the "best and busiest propagandist." That only mildly indicated his private opinion. Dave was not the only one of Ickes' fellow government officials who received the attention of Ickes' detectives. He built a dossier even about Harry Hopkins.

[Power greed undoubtedly motivated the odd alliance of the very liberal Ickes and the rough Tennessee Senator Kenneth McKellar. Ickes wanted domination over everything related to public power. McKellar wanted as political patronage the jobs of TVA employees. Michael W. Straus was First Assistant Secretary of the Interior and a man who put some of the pungency into Ickes' phrases.]

*   *   *

Grace Tully also talked to me about the President's letter to Jesse Jones and expressed regret that it hadn't been submitted to anybody before the President sent it. "But," she said, "sometimes he tells me, 'Don't show that to anybody,'" and in this case nobody saw the letter before it was sent except the President and Grace Tully.

Monday, February 12. [On this day simultaneously with announcements in London and Moscow I gave the press the first communiqué on the Yalta conference. In addition I gave them some background information about the meeting. The correspondents had been hungry for some real news that they could print but even about this serious matter they declined to be entirely solemn. Though most of the correspondents held Early in affection, they were amused about his joining this high-level conclave and they were hilarious about the presence of Ed Flynn, whose confirmation as ambassador had been prevented, among other things, by a report that he had paved some of his own property with city materials, using workers on the public payroll to do the job. A part of the transcript on this historic occasion follows.]

MR. DANIELS: The President's party included Admiral of the Fleet Leahy, James Byrnes—
Q. (interposing) That's in the announcement, isn't it? Is it written down in the announcement?
MR. DANIELS (continuing): Stephen Early—(laughter)—Edward J. Flynn of New York—(more laughter, and many exclamations)—
Q. (aside) Paving the way, evidently.
MR. DANIELS (continuing): Vice Admirals McIntire and Brown; Major General Watson, and Mrs. John Boettiger. (more exclamations) The Prime Minister was accompanied by his daughter.
Q. Which one?
Q. Mary, is it not?
MR. DANIELS: Sarah!—Mrs. Sarah Oliver. And Ambassador Harriman brought *his* daughter—(more laughter)—Miss Kathleen Harriman, with him from Moscow.
Q. (aside) No room for the press.
MR. DANIELS: Mr. Flynn took no part in the conference. (loud laughter)
Q. (aside) Was that trip necessary?
MR. DANIELS (continuing): The President invited him as an old friend, when he learned that he had planned a trip to Moscow.

(more laughter, and exclamations) Mr. Flynn went on from the conference, with Ambassador Harriman and his daughter, to Moscow.

Q. Any race tracks in Moscow? (more laughter)

Q. Paving bricks—

Q. (interposing) A lot of new roads to pave.

Tuesday, February 20. [I issued another communiqué giving a report on the President's travels after Yalta, during which he saw King Farouk of Egypt, Emperor Haile Selassie I of Ethiopia, and King Ibn Saud of Saudi Arabia. The White House press, however, was growing impatient about wartime security regulations. No American reporters had been permitted at Yalta. We had dispatched, however, a trio representing the three wire services to join the President on his way home. They were Merriman Smith of the United Press, Douglas Cornell of the Associated Press, and Robert G. Nixon of the International News Service. The understanding was that they could make no reports until after the President's return to Washington.

[As the *Quincy* steamed homeward FDR met them in two press conferences, one on February 19 and another on February 23, after the death at sea from a cerebral hemorrhage of General Watson. Then he told them that they could only dispatch the news of the death after "we get through the capes," of the Chesapeake. One passage in those conferences would have much interested me.

[One of the trio of correspondents said, "By the way, Mr. President, Jonathan Daniels has handled himself very beautifully."

["Really?" said the President. "I had an idea that at the first conference he got everybody mad."

["No, sir," Smith or Cornell or Dixon replied. "Actually there was a lot of laughter, most everybody was laughing, though the transcript did not show it. Everybody was sort of jocular—friendly, giving."

[And Roosevelt said, "He will do all right when he gets his feet on the ground."

[Sometimes in Washington, sticking to security rules while the British censorship was leaking like a sieve, there seemed little ground under my feet. From England came news of activities there by Americans, Harry Hopkins for instance, whose whereabouts were supposed to be a security secret. That put me on a silly spot. Other leaks in London reached equally silly proportions. One strange source was a minor figure in the government, Walter McLennan Citrine, an electrician who had become a labor politician and later was to become a lord. "Citrine rumors" became a label for some such stories of doubtful origin and credibility based upon the GI term "latrine rumors" for similar circulating reports.

[Two days after the exchange between the President and the press trio at sea, I wrote about political problems in Washington, and about personages in the plan for world order. I worked, however, where restlessness mounted over wartime disciplines among the press as well as the potentates.]

Tuesday, February 20. It looks like Wallace is now going to be easily confirmed, but Aubrey Williams is having tough going before the Senate. Vandenberg has written the President a "gracious" letter, accepting the invitation to serve at the San Francisco conference but pointing out that he would not be bound by any commitments. Also Harold Stassen, here on leave from the Navy, said he would accept though he regarded the appointment as a "political liability" and before he goes to San Francisco he is going to confer with Republican leaders in the House and Senate and with Governor Dewey. I still think the delegation named by the President is practically perfect and I hope he has escaped the mistakes Wilson made in naming his delegation. But the Republicans apparently are being cagey all the same.

[The San Francisco conference was to convene on April 25 to draft the Charter of the United Nations. The American delegation was composed of Secretary of State Stettinius, chairman; Senators Tom Connally (Dem. Texas) and Arthur Vandenberg (Rep. Mich.); Congressmen Sol Bloom (Dem. N.Y.) and Charles A. Eaton (Rep. N.J.). Chosen from outside the Congress were Harold Stassen, former Republican governor of Minnesota, and Virginia Gildersleeve, dean of Barnard College. Miss Gildersleeve did not mention any political affiliation in *Who's Who*.]

This morning Westbrook Pegler wrote himself a column in which he announced that he was going to deliberately break the security code the next time the President went to Hyde Park, after giving him time to arrive at his destination.

I talked to Byron Price, Director of Censorship, who told me that Pegler is the noisiest, but there is a growing resistance against that part of the code which protects the President's trips to Hyde Park and the like. Byron is anxious to talk to the President after he returns and secure some modification of the code along this line, feeling that unless there is such modification, the code may be cracked with the result that important military information will be published.

I understand that Jack Knight, president of the American Society of Newspaper Editors, is one of those who feels that the use of the code to protect the President's movements at home—particularly after he released it during the campaign —is no longer justified.

[The growing questions about news and security had come to a climax with Pa Watson's death. The day after the General died I wired the President: "General Marshall, General Surles, Bill Hassett and I agree in urging you that simple announcement be made of General Watson's death immediately without mention of time or place. We feel that it will be impossible to prevent news from leaking with resulting unfavorable criticism."

[The President vetoed that suggestion. He ordered release of the news be withheld until 5 P.M. on Monday, February 25, when the *Quincy* would have entered American waters. I did the best I could to help Mrs. Watson in the long waiting. I'm not sure how much help I was to her but afterwards she insisted on giving me the watch that Pa always wore when he was impatiently timing presidential visitors.]

Wednesday, February 28. This morning the President returned. I got up early and met Bill Hassett at the White House offices and we went over to the house and waited under the South Portico for the President's car to drive up. He came up in fine spirits from the train which had been parked, after his trip, in the station of the Bureau of Printing and Engraving. Afterwards we went up with him to where he was having breakfast in the west hall room of the White House on the second floor. I remember his bacon and eggs looked mighty good, although I had breakfast before going to the White House.

He spoke, incidentally, of naming Lilienthal head of the Missouri Valley Authority and in such a way avoiding a fight with McKellar over his confirmation. I said that I did not see how he could fail to reappoint Lilienthal even if it meant a fight and that we ought to make that fight. Mrs. Roosevelt joined in that position, but the President made no comment. He looked remarkably well.

[Almost exactly a year before this time I had told the President about a statement which McKellar had made to the press, that Roosevelt had promised to "get Lilienthal out of Tennessee" and "then he didn't do it." The President then authorized me to tell Lilienthal what constituted his supposed promise. When McKellar had come to him fuming FDR told him, "Well, Kenneth, I have been thinking about getting Lilienthal out of Tennessee myself. I would like to see a Columbia Valley Authority set up in the Northwest, and put Lilienthal in charge of it, since he has done such a good job. But I never have been able to get Congress to pass the bill for a CVA. So if you want to get rid of him, you go back on the Hill and get that done." I was also to tell Dave that the President wanted to find some "appropriate circumstance" when he could express his great confidence in him.

[In November 1944, however, while enthusiastically expressing his confidence to Lilienthal and his TVA operation the President tried to get him to take the position of chairman of the Surplus Property Board. When Lilienthal declined the President told him, "Dave, your term expires next May. There is a rule up in that club in the Senate called the rule of personal privilege. They won't confirm you next spring—and McKellar will say you are personally objectionable to him, and that will be that. I want to spare you that indignity. I just don't want you to go through that."

[Evidently in the spring of 1945 he still wanted to avoid such a fight but the MVA was just a dream that was never fulfilled.]

Thursday, February 29. Hassett and I went up to the President's bedroom, where he receives his secretaries in the morning. I remember we waited outside while he talked to Senator Barkley. Anna Boettiger came up and talked with us. There was the sound of the President's laughing in the room when Barkley came out. Anna went in and we asked Barkley what the President had been laughing about.

He said he had been talking to the President about the rumors of his illness and how mistaken they were and had told the President this story—that a drunken man, refused a drink by a bartender, had undertaken to prove that he wasn't drunk.

"Why," he said, "you see that cat there coming in the door? He has got two eyes and if I was drunk I would see four."

The bartender said, "Hell, man, you are drunker than I thought. That cat isn't coming in the door, it is going out."

We went in and met the President sitting up in bed in his pajamas and a bed cape. It is amazing to me how he sits so upright in bed with so little physical structure below his waist to support him. It is perfectly clear that he makes up his own mind about everything without any weakening. I am sure that all of us are probably too deferential to his wishes; even Sam Rosenman and Bill Hassett, who have been working with him longer, seem not to have gotten over the sense of the majesty of the President.

Anna Boettiger had a very bad cold but she stayed with us and it is becoming increasingly clear that she means to be what the papers are suggesting that she is—a sort of special secretary close to the President, handling details for him and serving as intermediary for others who handle details for him. This was even clearer to me later in the day before the

President delivered his speech when Anna and her husband, John Boettiger, were working on revisions in the cabinet room. Anna started to pick up the phone but said, "I am not supposed to be in this part of the house," and John made the call.

[About this time Anna had a long talk with me. She reported that Byrnes had behaved very badly at Yalta, acting in a way which disturbed her father. I gathered that Byrnes had been concerned about his position vis-à-vis Stettinius and others but that, as a onetime court stenographer in South Carolina, he had made good notes of the conference. However, she had been greatly concerned about the strains on her father. She told me that Dr. Howard Bruenn had told her that he must greatly restrict his activities. So she had a plan. The President should see very few people. In so far as possible I was to see those who wished to see him and then pass on the matters presented to me to Anna and her husband for decision without burdening the President with any but the greatest matters.

[I knew then that no such plan could possibly work. It could have amounted only to something like the almost regency which Mrs. Wilson and Dr. Cary Grayson had assumed out of necessity during the former President's illness. All but a month of the four-year term to which the President had been re-elected remained. But what she said made me realize to a greater extent than ever the precariousness of the President's health.]

Saturday, March 3. Sam Rosenman stayed behind after Bill Hassett and I left the President's bedroom and came over to my office about an hour later. He told me he had just been having quite a time with the President. Before we had gone in that morning, Jimmy Byrnes had been in with the President. Sam told me that Byrnes had sold the President the idea of appointing Fred Vinson as Loan Administrator and making him, Sam, Director of Economic Stabilization. Sam told the President that he did not want it and would only take it if he commanded him to. We talked about it and Sam was aware of the fact that John L. Lewis would say a damn

Jew was crucifying the miners. At the same time, Sam told me that he had told the President he did not want to be Solicitor General, that he didn't want to serve with Biddle, whom he does not trust or respect as a lawyer. I said I had always thought the President would appoint Sam as Secretary of Labor. He said he would love that, but of course he would want it only if it was a real Department of Labor.

In the meantime, he was planning to leave Sunday for England, where he will join the group he had left when the President called him from his mission, looking into the civilian supplies of liberated countries, to meet the President at Algiers and help him prepare his message to Congress.

He was anxious that I announce his return to England as soon as he arrived because he was aware that some columnists had said that he had run back with the President because he found the job was too hot.

Incidentally, Sam was terribly distressed and lower than I have ever seen him, after the President finished his message to the Congress on Thursday. He had a feeling that the President's ad-libbing had made a mess of his speech and that some of the things he had put in were going to have a very bad reaction. Bill Hassett and Grace Tully felt the same way about the speech and I must say that I agreed with them, but the public reaction had been all to the good. Rosenman said that nobody could stop the President from ad-libbing now. The ad-libbing made quite a job for us. Eben Ayres and I, with the help of Jack Romagna and the congressional stenographer's report, had to get a version including the ad-libbing ready for the *Congressional Record* by midnight. We did it and I haven't heard any complaints on the revised version— but it was quite a job.

The President left tonight for Hyde Park.

[John L. Lewis was at this time threatening another coal miners' strike.

[Eben Ayres, a Pulitzer prize reporter, was assistant to the press secretary. Romagna was the official White House stenographer.]

Bill Hassett has said for some time that he does not expect

Early to carry out his talk about leaving the government. He said that he had talked that way for years, but always in the end he stayed. Hassett definitely dislikes Early and told me that one time when Early had been nasty to him, he had called him a coward and a son-of-a-bitch and said he could not even talk to a girl on the telephone without berating her. Early cringed and called his staff in and asked if he was the kind of a son-of-a-bitch Hassett had called him. He said Early had not even known when the President appointed him, Hassett, as presidential secretary.

Hassett also told me about Early's favorite woman employee, whom he also dislikes. He says nobody in the White House likes her and that her name is "Stinky." He said that Early had been infatuated with her and when she was about to have her baby he was so considerate of her that it became a joke and that people began to suspect he was the father, but that apparently the child looks so much like his real father that no one can doubt his parentage. He said that Early had gone to the circumcision ceremony and had worn a black hat. He also said that Early had sent her a fur coat in the pouch from Quebec. He said she is not only unpleasant but not very smart. When she was leaving to have her baby Early had asked Roberta Barrows [General Watson's beautiful red-headed secretary] to ask the young woman's friends to come to a party for her, and that Roberta had gone to Bill Hassett in some distress and reported she didn't have any friends.

I think what Bill says is true, but I find that Bill, while one of the sweetest people in the world, also has very strong prejudices, particularly against the Jews. He is a lighthearted Catholic and will make fun of his church, but I believe he is devout. He was particularly amused by Pa's conversion to Catholicism on his deathbed. He said that Pa had not long ago built his house in Virginia and become a Mason, with the particular idea in mind of running for the Senate to succeed Carter Glass. Bill was amazed by his statement last summer that he was going to join the Church as soon as the election was over.

Sunday, March 4. Lucy and I had lunch with the Boettigers, who had quite a group—a combination of Seattle and military government. A fat young colonel who is secretary of General Clark's general staff was there, also Colonel Howe and his Irish-born wife. Colonel Howe is the son of Mark Antony De-Wolfe Howe of Boston. A man named Fussell, who was formerly a reporter on the *Post Intelligencer* and is now working in the Treasury Department. Justice William O. Douglas and his wife. We had a very pleasant luncheon and Lucy felt that they were particularly pleasant to us. Here again we could feel Anna's determination to be something more than the President's daughter in the White House.

[Anna shared her father's antagonisms. Before I took over the presidential press job Harry Luce, who had once been my boss, had been barred by the White House from touring the Pacific theater. This is supposed to have happened in 1943. As told, however, it seems odd that the duty or burden of informing Luce of this affront, and doing it in the President's name, was given to the Republican Assistant Secretary of War, John J. McCloy. I hope that if I had been on duty then I would have sought to have mitigated the order or soften the blow. Clare in Congress and in speeches elsewhere had given the President reason for fury. Luce had backed Willkie in 1940 and was preparing to support Dewey in 1944. Still, politics aside, I had known Luce as a great editor and a good employer. Now Anna asked me to look into the sudden appearance of Clare Luce in England. My formal report to her was written in a somewhat facetious vein.]

March 12, 1945

Dear Anna:

MEMORANDUM FOR MRS. BOETTIGER:

In connection with your inquiry about the travels of the Lady from Connecticut:

1. The first announcement of Clare's present trip came in a press release from her office on March 5th that she had "flown to London on the invitation of the British Embassy to survey the work of British women in the war."

2. This was amended, if not denied, next day in London by "a War Office spokesman" who, according to UP, said that she "was on her way to Italy to visit the Italian front at the personal invitation of Field Marshal Alexander, Allied Commander in the Mediterranean." The spokesman said he did not know the purpose of her visit, and could not confirm New York reports (actually they were Clare's reports) that she planned to stay in the United Kingdom to study women's part in the British war effort.

My spies in TIME, Inc., tell me that the Luces are in process of a developing new devotion—from past criticisms of England to a new reverence for Britain and British institutions as sources of stability in a disturbing (to Luces) world.

My nature is such, however, that I cannot dismiss lightly the fact that Clare as long ago as 1942 and in an unhappy Burma was writing about Alexander: "his keen honest blue eyes blazing faintly."

There may be a gleam in 'em still in Caserta.

[Clare Boothe Luce had been in Burma when Field Marshal Harold Alexander was extricating British and Indian forces there. Alexander, as commander of Allied forces in Italy, had his headquarters in the royal palace in Caserta. The surrender of the German Army in Italy was signed there in this month.]

Tuesday, March 13. The President was telling us the other morning that at the time when they were trying to think of a name for the United Nations, which must have been in December 1941 when Churchill made his first visit to the White House after Pearl Harbor, the President went into Churchill's room one morning to tell him an idea he had for a name.

He sat down in Churchill's room and Churchill came out of his bath without a stitch of clothes on. "He looked like a fat cherub," the President said. He said, "Winston, I have decided I have found a name, 'United Nations.'"

Churchill, standing strip stark naked, nodded in approval and only after he had indicated his approval of the name did he apologize for not having any clothes on. Later Churchill told the King that he was the only Prime Minister England had ever had who had been received by the chief of a state while entirely naked.

The President plans to leave by train for San Francisco about the 20th of April, and to arrive in San Francisco to make his speech at the opening of the session there; then immediately to go back to his train at Oakland and leave, possibly going south to see the members of his family, Elliott's children and Jimmy's wife, who are living in southern California.

He turned down with pleasure the invitations of a number of people in San Francisco to give him a penthouse, an estate, etc., for the duration of the conference. He recalled that back in the Wilson administration, he was made a United States commissioner to the world's fair in San Francisco and that he went out on the train with Vice-President Thomas R. Marshall and the other federal fair commissioners, Franklin K. Lane and Adolph Miller. While they were on the way the Vice-President, without saying anything to any of them, accepted an invitation to a big dinner from William Randolph Hearst. The next day the others of the party all got invitations and promptly turned them down.

The President said, "Hearst has never liked me since—or before."

I remarked, "Vice-Presidents sometimes have a way of accepting strange social invitations."

Anna said, "Don't they, though?"

The President keeps a great many things completely to himself. Yesterday afternoon he made it clear that he had an engagement from four o'clock on, but said nothing to any of us about what sort of engagement it was.

[Only later did I realize that this was one of his precious meetings with Lucy Mercer Rutherfurd.]

Twice within recent weeks we have followed Dr. Bruenn into the President's bedroom.

[Dr. Howard G. Bruenn, a young heart specialist and a commander in the Navy Medical Corps, first examined Roosevelt at the naval hospital in Bethesda in April 1944. Thereafter he was in practically constant attendance on the President. His electrocardiograph machine was a White House fixture.]

Anna is really a remarkable girl and a great help to her father. She obviously has great gifts as both a companion and an assistant. The other day when we were talking about Mackenzie King, the President said, "I would like to have him get some publicity." Bill Hassett quoted a poem made up by newspapermen on another visit of MacKenzie King. It goes like this: "William Lyon Mackenzie King. He never gives us a God damn thing." Incidentally, the other day when they were talking about dinner with Mackenzie King, Anna said that her mother had said that the Morgenthaus were great friends of King.

"Who told her that?" the President asked. "The Morgenthaus?"

This morning the newspapermen were disturbed to see Secretary Stimson come in to see the President when he was not on the engagement list. I went and asked Bill Hassett about it and he said to tell them he had forgotten to tell me. "Incidentally," he said, "the President also forgot to tell me."

Mrs. James Forrestal was in Grace Tully's office today for an off-the-record visit to the President.

[Mrs. Forrestal appears to have been something of a pest. At Hyde Park in July 1943, the President declined to see her. Of the present occasion Hassett, then acting as appointments secretary, wrote, "Mrs. Forrestal got in by the back door and upset everything by staying thirty-five minutes, talking about nothing in particular. Couldn't shoo her out." My understanding was that even in this crowded time the President was trying to work out something to occupy her mind and time, I believe in connection with the preservation of the Decatur House on Lafayette Square.]

*   *   *

Grace Tully came in to talk to me on Saturday afternoon about the filling of the vacancy created by Pa's death. Judge Rosenman had suggested that Pa should be succeeded by either Steve, whom he thought did not want to come back to the news job, or by Frank Walker. Miss Tully felt certain that Steve was not coming back, at least not for any length of time. As successor to Watson, she mentioned the possibility of some Democratic newspaperman and asked me if I had any suggestion. She also mentioned George Allen and Lyndon Johnson. When I mentioned Allen to Hassett, he said, "He is just a buffoon."

[Though something of a court jester, George Allen was far from a buffoon. His clowning served his advance both in government and in private business, in which he was vice-president of the Home Insurance Company of New York. In both he looked out for George. Lyndon Johnson, serving his third term in the House at this time, already had his eye on a Senate seat.]

Joe Davies came in to see me and told me that in 1934 he had arranged, at the request of a client, a job for Early which was to have paid him $50,000 a year salary and $25,000 a year as a drawing account and to give him the privilege of buying at the then market price at any time within five years 15,000 shares of the stock of the company, which was selling at 15 and which Davies said he told Early he was sure would go to 50. However, he said that Early had turned it down and said he would have to stay with the Boss.

* * *

Bill Hassett and I talked with George Fox about General Watson's death. He said that he had had a cardiac condition shortly after the conference which made it impossible for him to pass his urine, that they had given him an injection which had cleared that up promptly (he pissed all over the place), but that he had not been well and while they were in the Mediterranean they first noticed a slight thickness of speech and then a paralysis of the right arm. They had hoped that this seepage in the brain would be absorbed but instead it had progressed and death ensued. I learned in connection with Pa's death that it was the same sort of cerebral hemorrhage which had been the trouble of Missy LeHand, but that in her case she did not die, but lingered for many months.

[Fox had risen from the ranks as physical therapist to several Presidents and was at this time a lieutenant commander.]

*   *   *

Bill Hassett and I were talking about the leaks that Leonard Lyons gets in his column which are remarkably accurate, much more so than those that get into the columns of Pearson and others. The White House hit the ceiling not long before the election when Leonard Lyons published in his column that the President had been given penicillin. The terrible thing about it was that he had been given penicillin.

*   *   *

On Saturday the 3rd, Senator Arthur Vandenberg of Michigan called me. Earlier in the week he had phoned to say he did not feel the President had answered his letter regarding his invitation to be a delegate to the San Francisco conference in which he insisted that he had to be free to express his own views in the delegation and afterwards. I had then told him if he would write another letter to the President, I would present it to the President. He sent the letter and I drafted a reply for the President, in which the President said clearly that he expected the Senator to be free.

Also Saturday Pat Hurley called and said he had just arrived from China and he told the newspapermen he would not talk to them until after he had seen the President. The President said to tell Hurley and General Albert Wedemeyer to take a four-day rest and he would see them on Wednesday or Thursday.

[From March 8, when I announced his return from Hyde Park, until March 24, when he went back there, was the longest period the President spent at the White House during his fourth term. In addition to his administration troubles at home, word was coming to him, too, of disintegration of his hopes in China and Russia, even as good news came from the European and Pacific war fronts. Hurley and Wedemeyer had frustrations to report about their efforts to create unity in China. I remember Charles ("Chip") Bohlen, able career diplomat who had served as Roosevelt's interpreter at Yalta, stopping to talk on the passage by the rose garden between the executive offices and the White House. He told me, "The Russians are acting up."

[Roosevelt was trying to make order in the immediate circle around him. He already knew that Byrnes was departing in pique. Pa Watson was dead. Steve Early was preparing to leave. Sam Rosenman had returned to his mission in Europe. So on the very crowded day before leaving again for his beloved Dutchess County he released a "Statement by the President."]

"I have asked Steve Early to remain as Secretary to the President until I have an opportunity to find someone to fill the vacancy created by the death of General Watson. Steve had hoped to resign when he returned to Washington from his recent assignment in France.

"Jonathan Daniels, who has been acting in Steve's absence, will be appointed Secretary to the President in charge of press relations. Bill Hassett, who has had charge of appointments since the death of General Watson, will take up again the duties of his old office.

"I hope to be able by early June to name a permanent Secretary in charge of appointments. At that time Steve will be free to enter private employment, in accordance with the wishes he has expressed to me."

[The copy of that statement in my files has written across the bottom: "To Jonathan—And may the Lord have mercy upon his soul—Steve Early." I was relieved. Steve had seemed to be standing on one foot and then the other, eager to go and ready to stay. Maurice Latta, the tall, quiet successor to Rudolph Forster as the career clerk at the White House, had resolved the dilemma by preparing my commission and bringing it to the President's desk. That noon in the Oval Office pictures were made of the President handing me the commission with Lucy standing very prettily beside us. At the time I was not aware of the haggardness of the President, which is so evident to me in the picture now. It was the last formal photograph ever made of him.

[Some sort of divine help seemed needed. Just as I was appointed, the Senate, with McKellar riding high with charges of communism, rejected the President's nomination of my friend Aubrey Williams as head of the Rural Electrification Administration. At the same time the President was complaining about the dilatoriness of Congress in giving him legislation he needed. He had to listen to others in trouble, like Governor Lehman, who was suffering under mounting criticism of his United Nations Relief and Rehabilitation Administration. Baruch had to be seen to give an appearance of importance to the mission he was making to England, which in fact was largely a mission for the glorification of Baruch. Already there were suggestions that Roosevelt had given away too much at Yalta. Some sensitiveness attended the idea that Roosevelt was giving anything to anybody. One small matter involved an offer he had made to present a plane as a gift to King Farouk. General Alexander Surles, chief of War Department public relations, and I suggested "that all reference to the President and the gift aspects of the matter be eliminated and it be stated that the plane is being presented by the United States Government to King Farouk. It is also suggested that, if there are any Lend-Lease aspects to this presentation, these aspects be stressed." With a pen showing this time no faltering, FDR okayed the memo with debonaire self-denial of any credit for himself.

[Some were suggesting that he was giving away everything, particularly to Russia. And sometimes, wearily, he did not seem to care to contradict them. In a discussion of his plans to attend the first United Nations Conference in San Francisco, it was suggested that he wait for an opportune moment in its sessions when, difficulties having arisen, he could appear and dispel them with a "wave of the magic wand." Wryly he expressed doubt that he had now such a magic wand to wave. He was preparing for that appearance, however. He talked of going back into Dutchess County history in that speech and the time when men from that county and others were ratifying the Constitution of the United States, not as a perfect instrument but as a brave beginning. Difficulties, however, did not wait for such a time. Already circulating were what he regarded as misleading interpretations of what had happened at Yalta, particularly about the agreement that not only Russia but also two of its appendant republics have places and votes in the United Nations.

[Archie MacLeish and I, who were working with Bob Sherwood on the San Francisco speech, were authorized by the President to draw up a statement on this complicated matter. That assignment led MacLeish and myself to one of the most distressing experiences of our lives. The decision to make this statement had been made at a conference in the President's office at 11:45 A.M. on March 29. He had just gotten in that morning from Hyde Park and was preparing to leave at four o'clock that afternoon for Warm Springs. That left a very brief time to prepare the statement and get the President's approval.

[He was in his upstairs oval study working with Grace Tully when MacLeish and I appeared with the statement. Though the weather outside was magnificent—the wisteria was in full bloom on the South Portico—the room seemed a place of gloom. Tully, obviously protective, was tending papers he was tediously signing. Wearily he was telling her of items he wanted to be sure went along. He looked bone-tired, haggard, almost torpid.

[Apologetically, we presented the paper. His eyes became alert above the words. With seeming precision he made a slight change in the first paragraph and pushed the paper back to me. We departed in haste. Then—when we reached the elevator in the hall we discovered that the change he had made in the first paragraph turned into confusion the rest of the statement. We had to go back into the room of that gaunt man. MacLeish wrote me of that moment later: "I remember particularly the pain of the decision to go back and ask the President to reconsider. You had a great deal more courage

277

than I. If the decision had depended on me, I would have let it go as it was—which would have been very bad indeed." The truth is that it took whatever joint courage we had. We did go back and without any rebuke to either of us, the President corrected the paper. That was the last time I ever saw him.]

Hail and Farewell

Word from Hassett in Warm Springs was more encouraging than the feelings he was committing then to his diary. I remember that as the only active secretary at the White House, I was reassuring people about the President's health and deluding myself at the same time. Even in Warm Springs the Boss had great things and little things to worry him. Byrnes at this time was preparing for his departure from the government. His resignation reached the President at Warm Springs on March 30. Hassett that day was shocked by the President's appearance. He wrote that the Boss only commented wearily that it was "too bad some people are so primadonnaish." About that time the Boss sent me a telegram about one of his most persistent importuners: "Will you get word to Harold Ickes that I did nothing about the REA vacancy and will have to wait till I get back before I do anything about it."

One incident which might have amused the President if it did not irritate him was a cry of pain from Barney Baruch. It came to me in a long message from London marked SECRET. A reporter for the service publication *Stars and Stripes* had interviewed him, he radioed me, with the promise that he would be shown the story before publication. Before this he had declined to see any newspapermen, "explaining I was not free to

279

discuss nature of mission. Before coming here I was told many soldiers gloomy about future and was strongly urged that if I could I should take opportunity to reassure GIs about adventure in prosperity lying ahead which I sincerely believe."

But, declared Baruch in a transatlantic scream, he was never shown the story, which was shared for publication with the Associated Press. Words which he never uttered were put into his mouth. In his message he quoted them with horror: "One reason I am here is to hold the big stick over the big boys to make damn sure they are not going to foul up the peace." He signed the message, "Affectionate regards." Nobody was hurt by the incident except Baruch, who as a wise old man did not like being made to sound like a fool.

I shared the message with Hassett at Warm Springs: "I thought you might be interested in the attached top secret lament from Bernard M. Baruch. I am afraid our innocent visitor to the United Kingdom has been victimized by the bad, bad newspaper boys. Anyhow, he apparently understands as well as the rest of us that in the story as printed he certainly seemed to extend his corporate limits." I do not know whether Hassett showed the message to the President or not. I am sure that if he did, he did so snickering.

This was on April 6. Hassett and the President were joking together at this time about the press. The Boss was declining an invitation to attend the banquet of the Gridiron Club on Saturday night, April 14. Of this august organization of Washington newspapermen Hassett noted that the President "likes the members; hates the club; thinks it takes itself too seriously."

Others beside the Gridiron Club and Mr. Baruch were taking themselves very seriously then. Still it did not seem a solemn time. On the afternoon of April 12 I was talking in my office with Anna Rosenberg, whose perky hats and gay banter, twinkling flattery and subtle persistence had given the President so much pleasure. The April outside my windows matched the hat she wore. Then suddenly Early came in with the word from Mrs. Roosevelt that the President was dead.

I made no diary entry about that tragic and tumultuous time. Instead where such an entry might have been are two sheets of notes:

April 13, 1945

List of people who are coming to the White House.
To be given by Mr. Ayers.

*

Give Mike Reilly the list of 17 newspapermen
who will cover the funeral at Hyde Park.
Names plus White House credential will be sufficient.

*

Reilly will also take care of four movie companies
and four still photographers.

*

Must take care of "Yank" representative, on
deal with Col. Boettiger.

*

Mr. Page, Worden Funeral Home, Hyde Park, Hyde Park 96.
If casket is coming vault, if so, what dimensions of vault?
If not in vault, what size of casket?

*

If not in vault, and vault is desired, what kind?
Conolite (?) concrete composition, vault obtainable in
Poughkeepsie. Understand metal vaults not obtainable,
however, might be for this occasion.

*

Where and what time will train arrive in Hyde Park?

*

Are taxis needed? If so, how many?

*

Flowers?

Mr. Lesene, Patterson Funeral Home, Atlanta.
Casket   28¼ inches wide
         82⅝   "   long
         24¾   "   deep
Not in outside box.

Resting on special bier, built to fit in the car.

Casket is very heavy and must be taken out of the car through the window.

Across the bottom of these notes I scrawled in pencil:
"Later I learned from Anna or John Boettiger that Mrs. R. thought a bad job had been done by the undertaker. Steve Early said, 'He was a chiseling son of a bitch. His bill was $3,100 (?) and he wanted to be giving interviews to the newspapers.'"

[In an interview which Fred W. Patterson of the Atlanta undertaking firm did give in the May 1945 issue of *Southern Funeral Director,* he reported with dignity that he and his associates met a challenge in a manner of which he was proud.]

Shortly after this time, in more formal fashion than in notes for a journal, I described that Thursday afternoon and evening of the President's death day. Automatically as the senior White House aide on the spot I worked with the clamorous press in covering the story of the departed President and the advent of the new one. Yet sometimes I seemed only a figure in a swarm. It was nearly dark when Truman drove into the White House grounds. And behind him swiftly in the deepening twilight of a hot April the personages who constituted the government of the United States began racing through the guarded gate. Then the people came to mass themselves against the great iron fence. In the Executive Offices most of the faces were familiar, though some from the Congress who came now in a hurry had been less than loyal to the man who had been President in the morning. Friends and foes made a combination of grief and expectations.

Truman, who had gone first to the White House residence to express his sympathy to Mrs. Roosevelt and hear her loyal hopes for him, walked slowly along the covered back gallery by the rose garden to meet the crowding company in the offices. In the long cabinet room he looked to me like a very little man as he sat waiting in a huge leather chair. The majesty seemed missing. Then as the clock under the portrait of Woodrow Wilson in the cabinet room passed 7:09, he took the oath which instantly transformed "Harry" into "Mr. President." There were more newspapermen and photographers than officials in the room. They sprawled over the cabinet table. They quarreled almost automatically among themselves for better places of vantage. And at their plea I got the President to take the oath a second time, not for greater certainty, but for more pictures.

The President of the United States, with Mrs. Truman and Margaret, walked down the hall to the big lobby past the wide Philippine-mahogany table there, so often piled with the coats of newsmen. His car turned into a procession which roared out to his Connecticut Avenue apartment, where he ate a roast-beef sandwich in a neighbor's flat. Behind him the tall reception clerk spoke an old day's-end speech above the noises of the lobby.

"The President has left his office."

He spoke transition. And despite the loyal, undisturbed transfer of power, not only grief but a sort of reasonless resentment remained behind the President among those whose work in that night had only just begun. Part of it was directed at some who had crowded in though in his lifetime they had denied Roosevelt support on crucial issues at crucial times. Some had come who were already ready before he died to investigate their cherished illusion that he had deliberately brought on Pearl Harbor to involve his country in the war. Others were even then preparing to question the pattern of the peace he had hoped to make.

Not all the millions listening to the news were moved by grief. We rejoiced in a story which I still hope is true. It concerned Mrs. Tom Finletter, wife of the State Department official and daughter of the conductor Walter Damrosch. She entered an elevator in a New York hotel where a colonel in full uniform was waiting. Just as the operator was about to close the door an excited bellman ran across the lobby to them.

He spoke the shocking news. "Roosevelt is dead."

Out of the stunned silence the colonel muttered aloud, "Good. It's about time."

For a moment Gretchen Finletter stared incredulously at the man. Then with her arm swinging as her father had never swung his baton, she slapped the colonel full in the face.

"Operator," the officer cried, "call a policeman. I want this woman arrested for assault."

"Do," she said. "I want the colonel arrested for treason."

In the executive offices there was little time for grief or resentment. The President could hardly have reached his home when at 8:08 P.M. I tried to get him on the phone. That was not easy. This was long before the day of the bugging of White House phone lines but one of my secretaries made a transcript:

MR. BURNEY (Secret Service Agent): Burney.
MR. DANIELS: Mr. Daniels. It is pretty important, I think, that I speak to the President. There is a very strong desire for a statement to go overseas specifically stating by the President his intention to vigorously prosecute the war. Now, I don't want to bother him, but I feel that this is a matter that he ought to be bothered on.
MR. BURNEY: Well, Mr. Daniels, he gave express orders, and I just haven't the authority to change them. Do you want to come up in person? We will take a message to him.
MR. DANIELS: Mr. Burney, for the time being I am acting as Secretary to President Truman.
MR. BURNEY: That is correct.
MR. DANIELS: And as press Secretary to the President I would appreciate it if you would disturb him and say that I asked that he be disturbed.

(pause here)

MR. BURNEY: All right. We will do that.
MR. DANIELS: Thank you.
PRESIDENT TRUMAN: Yes?

MR. DANIELS: Hello, Mr. President.

PRESIDENT TRUMAN: Yes.

MR. DANIELS: I am very sorry to disturb you, sir, but they are asking very much for a statement for overseas consumption in order to meet enemy propaganda, a quotation from you to the effect that you mean to vigorously prosecute the war against both our enemies.

PRESIDENT TRUMAN: That is perfectly all right.

MR. DANIELS: Could you give me a quotation, or would you like me—for me to write a brief statement to that—

PRESIDENT TRUMAN (interposing): We will prosecute the war with all the vigor we have, to a successful conclusion on both fronts, the east and the west.

MR. DANIELS: All right, sir. I will fix that. Thank you very much, and I am sorry to have disturbed you.

PRESIDENT TRUMAN: That's all right. Thank you.

The offices now were emptied of politicians and/or statesmen. I went over to the residence and met the distaff side of the mansion, left behind by Mrs. Roosevelt when she flew with Early and Admiral Ross McIntire, Navy surgeon general, to Warm Springs. The strong Tommy Thompson, Mrs. Roosevelt's secretary, and the fragile-looking but efficient White House social secretary, Edith Helms, were there. Anna, beautifully self-contained, joined us. They made a scene which might have been duplicated in any house the master of which had died. Back in the offices I chaired a meeting in the Goldfish Room of White House staff, State and War Department technicians of protocol and pomp and ceremony, and railroad representatives. Preliminary plans were made on the basis of word from Early and Hassett with Mrs. Roosevelt.

I was late to bed and to bed with the knowledge that, unlike Roosevelt had been, Truman was an early riser who would expect the old staff to help him in his new duties. I was the first to talk with him in the Oval Office but soon all the executive offices seemed too small to hold the company of well-wishers for him and for themselves who poured into the building. I had no time for a diary that day. But I made some notes, cryptic-seeming now, relating to the essentials of the day. Harry Hopkins came in looking like a ghost. Jimmy Byrnes had been sent a plane by Forrestal so that he might quickly be on hand.

Of course, I wrote no record on April 14, the day of the great funeral ceremony in the White House. While I think that David Lilienthal exaggerated my emotion and fatigue on that occasion, I accept his journal entry about me then. He wrote:

"The most broken person I talked to was Jonathan Daniels. Really looked very bad, red-eyed, evidently had about all he could stand. The last words we had had, after a pleasant luncheon at the Carlton two weeks ago, were about the President's health. As he paused on the curb to cross over to the White House west entrance, I said, 'Well, I'm glad to hear you say those pictures of the President don't really tell the story; that he really is as vigorous as you say. See you don't let anything happen.' 'Don't worry about that; *that* won't happen,' he had said. He tried to refer to that conversation this afternoon, but broke up in the middle of it."

Actually Lilienthal then had more to lose than I, though his grief was less personal. With his term of office coming to an end he feared that his great work and achievement at TVA might be ended. His first reaction at the news of FDR's death was that Throttlebottom in the person of Truman might be President. Others shared that fear.

I know that when I talked to Lilienthal that day I was aware that President Roosevelt with his great peace plans at stake had decided not to make the fight with McKellar and his cohorts which Dave's reappointment would involve. Of course, I did not mention that to him. But I was as aware as he was that the elevation of Truman to the presidency had also advanced the power of McKellar as president pro tem of the Senate.

The formal grandeur of the White House funeral ceremony was followed by the exquisite springtime rites in the hemlock-hedged garden at Hyde Park. The train which had moved at a funereal pace northward moved at an accelerated pace back to Washington. Liveliness in the cars made it a sort of headlong wake across the reaches of New York, Pennsylvania, and

Jersey. In the President's private car Jimmy Byrnes, who had left Roosevelt presumably because of health, talked eloquently and informedly to Truman and others around him with highballs in their hands. It was a smoke-filled lounge.

Then back in the executive offices work went on. The presidency, if not Presidents, was eternal. At Truman's request I continued as press secretary until he could put his own close associates into the positions closest to him. I found him a man pleasant to work for, considerate and direct. It did not take long to see through the mask of his self-deprecation. Still, in Roosevelt's chair he made no image of the great prince which Roosevelt even in his lightest moments was to those around him. Sometimes Truman seemed almost deliberately to shatter such an image by use of a barnyard vocabulary.

Early in May he talked to me about the reappointment of Lilienthal as chairman of the Tennessee Valley Authority. Better than the rest of us he knew what the press was saying at the time—that his elevation "put Senator Kenneth McKellar of Tennessee in one of the most powerful positions any man ever held in the Senate." The Senate was crucial to a President particularly at this time in history. And Lilienthal, though precious as a symbol to many people at home and abroad, was expendable. Yet Truman was sending Lilienthal's name to the Senate nevertheless. He was prepared for the consequences and not fearful of them.

With eyes twinkling behind his thick lenses, he told me, "McKellar will have a shit hemorrhage."

He laughed at his own rough phrase. And in the room beside him, I knew that majesty did not always have to be decorative or decorous. But beyond deft phrases, wisdom, dedication, it required intestinal fortitude. Both the men I served possessed that, the crippled Roosevelt and the myopic Truman. Both brought honor and humor to the great issues of their lives. They are never safely separated.

Truman in Roosevelt's chair was a man fit to fill it. I never doubted that again nor ever had reason to doubt it. It took some pundits and philosophers, also politicians, a long time to discover that. Yet the certainty now is that America and I were blessed by the continuity of two such dissimilar men so similarly devoted to their country and beyond it to the best hopes of mankind. As an old man now I am grateful for the fortune that put me beside them when I was younger and we together believed in the possibility of the best of possible worlds without ever being lost in solemnity about that faith.

Ave atque vale.

That old phrase goes back into antiquity. For those who understand that even the greatest men merely serve the passing scene, it is adequate for eternity.

Index

Baruch, Bernard M., 32, 41, 49, 132, 154, 156–58, 163, 164, 166–67, 197, 210, 223, 228, 242, 276, 279–80
Baruch, Herman, 163, 164
Bastedo, Philip, 80
Batt, William L., 127
Baumgarten, Bernice, 10, 33
Beaverbrook, Lord, 209, 210
Beckelman, Moe, 139
Bell, Jack, 50
Bennett, Harry H., 168
Bennett, John J., Jr., 62, 77, 80, 81
Berg, Moe, 206
Berle, Adolf, 189, 219, 225
Berle, Rudolph, 189
Bernstein, Bernard, 122–23, 124–25
Bethune, Mary McLeod, 94
Beveridge, William Henry (Baron Beveridge of Tuggal), 115
Beveridge plan, 115
Biddle, Eric, 63
Biddle, Francis, 78, 177, 189, 207, 215, 216, 238, 267
Biddle, Anthony J. Drexel, Jr., 245
Big Three Conference. See Yalta conference
Bingham, Barry, 179, 244–45
Bingham, Harry, 179
Bingham, Mary, 244
Black, Hugo, 28, 182
Black, Josephine (Mrs. Hugo), 28
Blaine, James G., 170
Blaisdell, Tom, Jr., 153–55
Blake, Tom, 225
Blandford, John B., Jr., 64
Block, Paul, 182, 184
Bloom, Sol, 262
Board of Economic Warfare (BEW), 21, 100–1, 123, 162–64, 172, 175, 176, 191–92, 203
Boeschenstein, Harold, 206, 253
Boettiger, Anna Roosevelt, 235, 256, 260, 265, 266, 268–70, 272, 282, 285
Boettiger, John, 266
Bohlen, Charles ("Chip"), 275
Bombproof jobs, 35, 50, 52–53, 55
Bourne, W. C., Jr., 199
Bradford, Mary Rose (Mrs. Roark), 26
Bradford, Roark, 26, 27
Bradshaw, Francis, 138
Branch, Harllee, 176
Brandeis, Louis, 38, 39, 196
Brandt, Carl, 10, 247
Brennan, Earl, 224, 225
Bridges, Styles, 119
Briggs, George N., 211, 212, 213
Britain, 52, 67–68, 221, 222, 224
Brite, Elizabeth, 35, 80, 121, 133
British Intelligence, 115
British Ministry of Information, 67
Brown, Constantine, 112, 190–91

Brown, Prentiss M., 132
Brown, Walter, 190, 191
Brown, Wilson, 234
Brownell, Herbert, 246
Brownlow, Louis, 97
Bruenn, Howard, 266, 271–72
Bruggmann, Mrs. Charles, 170
Bryan, William Jennings, 237
Bullitt, William C., 76, 86, 90, 103, 192, 193–94
Bureau of the Budget, 29
Burns, James MacGregor, 193
Butler, Hugh, 210
Byrd, Harry, 23, 24
Byrnes, James F., 14, 41, 42, 48, 51, 79, 81, 132, 175, 190, 191, 215, 217, 225, 232, 238, 239, 240, 242, 244, 254, 260, 266, 275, 279, 286, 287

Cabinet, 258
Camacho, Manuel Avila, 52, 161
Campaign (1944 election), 76, 98, 146, 149–50, 175, 234, 235–37, 246
Capra, Frank, 142
Caraway, Hattie, 240
Carey, Jim, 244
Caribbean, 185, 187. See also West Indies
Carmichael, Albert, 86
Carmody, John M., 173
Carnegie Corporation, 97
Carr, Charlotte, 117
Carson, John, 24
Carter, Andrew F., 177
Carusi, Ugo, 215, 216
Casablanca conference, 120, 128, 165
Casey, Constance Dudley (Mrs. Joseph E.), 107
Casey Eugene, 17, 92, 120, 125, 128, 129, 135, 149, 160, 161, 178, 189, 199, 213–14, 234, 235
Casey, Joseph E., 104–7, 108–9, 111, 112, 113, 118, 128, 129, 131, 138, 140
Cathcart, Jim, 59
Cathcart, John, 59
Cathcart, Noble, 114, 133
Catholics, 80, 102, 105, 106, 143–44, 268
Catledge, Turner, 184
Censorship, 124, 262, 263
Central Intelligence Agency. See CIA
Century Association, 40
Chamberlain, Neville, 180
Chaney, Mayris, 7
Chapman, Oscar, 87, 117, 123, 159, 232
Charlotte Observer, 56
Chennault, Claire Lee, 227
Chiang Kai-shek, 168, 191, 238
Chiang Kai-shek, Madame, 167, 195, 238

291

Dewey, Thomas, 62, 77, 81, 95, 96, 134, 179, 234, 243, 246, 247, 249, 262, 269
DeWitt, John L., 25–26, 84
Dies Committee, 8, 31
Dilling, Elizabeth, 168, 169
Dillon, Read and Company, 135, 154
Dinwiddie, Courtenay, 121
Divine, Father, 230
Donovan, William J., 138, 139, 225
Doolittle, James H., 66
Douglas, Melvyn, 7, 28, 99
Douglas, William O., 99, 269
Draft boards, 43
Drewry, Patrick Henry, 77
Drury, Allen, 216
Dubinsky, David, 134, 141
Dudley, Robert W., 107
Duke, Buck, 158
Dulles, Allen, 187, 245, 246
Dunn, James C., 194
Du Pont family, 157

Earle, George, 192
Early, Stephen, 2, 12–13, 71, 76, 92, 120, 128, 135, 192, 209, 210–11, 213, 214, 225, 234, 252, 255, 260, 268,/273, 275, 280, 282, 285
Eastman, Joseph B., 151
Eaton, Charles A., 262
Eberstadt, Ferdinand, 154, 155
Edison, Charles, 103
Eichelberger, Clark, 230
Eisenhower, Dwight D., 12, 84, 125, 171, 246
Eisenhower, Milton, 66
Eleanor and Franklin (Lash), 7
Eliot, Tom, 127, 128
Ellis, Clyde, 173, 174
Elliston, Herbert, 114, 115, 170
Elliston, Joanna (Mrs. Herbert), 115
Emancipation Proclamation, 30
Emanuel, Victor, 252
Ernst, Morris, 183, 184
Ethridge, Mark, 179
Evans, Silliman, 199, 200
Ezekiel, Mordecai, 42, 43, 87, 232

Fair Employment Practices Committee (FEPC), 19, 94, 95–96, 159, 165, 246, 247
Fala, 92–93, 225, 247
Famous Barr Department Store, 244, 249
Farley, James A., 47, 80–81, 105, 167, 211
Farm Credit Administration, 214
Farm Security Administration, 21, 22, 30, 121, 122, 190, 207, 251
Farouk, King (of Egypt), 261, 276
Fauset, Crystal Bird, 93–95

Federal Bureau of Investigation (FBI), 35, 36, 174–75, 205, 206
Federal Communications Commission (FCC), 167, 168, 169, 175
Federal Deposit Insurance Corporation, 75
Federal Loan Administration, 258
Federal Security Agency, 57, 254
Field, Marshall, 23, 39, 40, 199–200, 206
Filene, Lincoln, 109
Finletter, Gretchen Damrosch (Mrs. Thomas), 169–70, 283–84
Finletter, Thomas, 169–70, 187
Fish, Hamilton, 45, 49
Fitzgerald, John Francis (Honey Fitz), 106
Flamm, Donald, 168–69
Fleming, John R., 121, 145
Fleming, Philip B., 57
Fleming, Robert, 171
Fly, James L., 167, 169
Flying Tigers, 227
Flynn, Ed, 63, 74, 105, 119, 129–30, 148–49, 235, 255, 259–60, 261
Flynn, Molly, 39, 134
Foley, Edward H., Jr., 117
Foreign Economic Commission, 247
Forrestal, James V., 49, 134–35, 154, 238, 239, 286
Forrestal, Mrs. James V., 134–35, 272
Forster, Rudolph, 14, 92, 104, 119, 138, 143, 159, 275
Fortas, Abe, 84, 87
Fortune magazine, 38
Foster, Reginald, 112–13
Foundation funds, 97
Fourth term, 70, 132, 134, 234
Fox, George, 273, 274
France, 52, 234; Vichy government, 14, 116, 187
Frankfurter, Felix, 38, 109, 133
Friedman, Louis K., 117–18
Fry, Charles, 53–54
Fuller, Horace, 81–82

Gandhi, Mahatma, 20, 41, 67, 68, 131
Gardner, O. Max, 150, 151, 152
Garey, E. L., 168
Gauss, Clarence E., 132
General Electric, 155
German army schools, 83, 84
German intelligence, 36
Germany, 51, 52, 67, 114, 209
Gilbert, Price, 145
Gildersleeve, Virginia, 263
Gillette, Guy M., 216
Giraud, Henri, 123, 128
Glass, Carter, 167, 268
Goetz, William, 142
Goldberg, Arthur, 139
Goldsmith, Wicky (Mrs. Tex), 124

North Africa, 82, 83–84, 91, 101, 116, 122–23, 124–25, 128
Nunn, Bill, 182

Ober, George C., 178
O'Brian, John Lord, 154
Occupied area administration, 83–84, 86, 87, 88, 90–91, 123
O'Connell, William Henry, Cardinal, 140
O'Connor, Basil, 188, 219–20
O'Connor, James J., 136
O'Daniel, W. Lee ("Pass the Biscuits, Pappy"), 228
O'Dwyer, William, 247
Office for Emergency Management, 29
Office of Civilian Defense (OCD), 5, 6–7, 8, 10, 14–15, 27, 38–39, 59, 79–80, 99, 111, 112, 113, 120, 121, 140, 141, 143, 144, 146, 207
Office of Community War Services, 196
Office of Defense, Health and Welfare Services, 8, 58
Office of Defense Transportation, 151
Office of Economic Stabilization, 41
Office of Facts and Figures, 22, 23, 71, 160
Office of Foreign Relief and Rehabilitation, 26, 86, 88, 117
Office of Government Reports, 22
Office of Naval Intelligence, 35
Office of Price Administration (OPA), 37, 42, 76, 119, 132, 166
Office of Production Management, 113
Office of Strategic Services (OSS), 138, 139, 206, 224, 225, 245, 257
Office of War Information (OWI), 44, 58, 61, 66, 71, 79, 107, 113, 114, 121, 127, 128, 138, 145–46, 150, 166, 168, 179–80, 199, 204, 251
Oliver, Sarah Churchill, 260
O'Mahoney, Joseph C., 102, 103
Onassis, Aristotle, 106–7
O'Neal, Edward, 122, 130–31
ONE MAN-Wendell Willkie (Sparks), 211
One World (Willkie), 211
Oval Office, 2, 217, 225, 275, 285

Palace Guard, 2, 16
Pan American Airways, 151–52, 185, 186, 187, 188, 189–90, 250
Parker, John, 198
Passport investigations, 159–60
Patronage, 37, 76, 132
Patterson, Eleanor Medill ("Sissy"), 203
Patterson, Frederick, 93
Patterson, Robert P., 42, 43–44
Paul, Randolph E., 117, 232–33

Pauley, Edwin W., 69, 74, 102, 233, 255
Pawley, N. C., 227
Pawley, William Douglas (Bill), 226–27
Payne, George H., 175
Pazzi, Guido, 224, 225
Peace organizations, 230
Pearl Harbor, 5, 6, 10, 283
Pearson, Drew, 36, 81, 82, 147, 148, 189, 194, 195, 213, 257, 258, 274
Pegler, Westbrook, 263
Pell, Robert, 81, 82
Pendergast machine, 233
Pentagon, 64
Pepper, Claude, 246
Pepper, Mrs. Claude, 151
Perkins, Frances, 238
Perkins, Milo, 121, 123, 162–63, 176, 182, 183, 202–3
Persia, 221–22
Pétain, Henri, 116
Pew, Joseph N., Jr., 179
Philadelphia Record, 205
Pickett, Clarence, 63
Pinchot, Gifford, 173–74
Pinchot, Mrs. Gifford, 9–10, 230, 231
Pittsburgh Courier, 178–79
Pittsburgh Post-Gazette, 184
Pius XII, Pope, 226
Playboy officers, 35
Plow That Broke the Plains, The (documentary film), 22
PM newspaper, 23
Pogue, Welch, 151, 152, 180, 181–82, 186, 187, 189, 240–41
Poland, 220–21
Poletti, Charles, 86
Polier, Justine, 28
Poling, Daniel, 150
Pope, James, 64, 173
Porter, Paul, 42, 87, 232, 233, 236, 237, 242
Poston, Theodore, 204, 207, 247
Postwar planning, 63, 90, 112, 114–15, 139–40
Poteat, Douglas, 100
Pratt, Trude (Mrs. Eliot D.), 31, 33
President's Birthday Celebrations, 33
Press conferences, 6, 120, 127, 165, 171, 172, 186, 188, 225, 261
Price, Waterhouse and Company, 177–78
Pringle, Henry, 127, 128, 145, 249
Pritchard, Edward F., Jr., 42, 44, 81, 87, 116, 117, 123, 194
Progress and Poverty, 101
Public Power, 173
Public Works Administration (PWA), 57